FUNDAMENTALS OF SOCIAL WORK

About the Editors

Prof. Sushma Batra, MSW, M.Phil, Ph.D., has more than 35 years of teaching experience in Department of Social Work, University of Delhi. Apart from this, she has been pursuing her special areas of interest to work with older persons and persons with disability over the years. She had guided number of research scholars in pursuing their research work as part of M.Phil, Ph.D. Programme on various issues related to social work discipline. She was the Honorary Director of Women Studies and Development Centre of University of Delhi, Head of the Department of Social Work, University of Delhi, Honorary Director of Utthan, and Extension Project of Centre for Child and Adolescent Well-Being of the Department. She has authored many books on various issues relating to social work and has published many articles in reputed journals.

Dr. Bishnu Mohan Dash, MSW, M.Phil, Ph.D. ICSSR Post-Doctoral Fellow, presently working as Assistant Professor, Department of Social Work, Bhim Rao Ambedkar College, University of Delhi. He is recipient of Academic Excellence Award, 2018, and Best Teacher Award, 2019 (Government of Delhi) authored/co-authored/edited eight books and published articles in reputed journals including Sage, Routledge, Blackwell & Wiley etc. His areas of interest are Rural Development, Child Welfare, Social Work Education and Field Work Practice.

FUNDAMENTALS
OF
SOCIAL WORK

Edited by
Sushma Batra
Bishnu Mohan Dash

CONCEPT PUBLISHING COMPANY PVT. LTD.
NEW DELHI-110059

ISBN-13: 978-93-88937-91-7 (H.B.)
ISBN-13: 978-93-88937-92-4 (P.B.)

First Published 2021

Published and Printed by

Concept Publishing Company Pvt. Ltd.
A/15-16, Commercial Block, Mohan Garden,
New Delhi-110059 (INDIA)
T: 91 11 25351460, 91 11 25351794
E: publishing@conceptpub.com; *W*: www.conceptpub.com

Cataloging in Publication Data--Courtesy: D.K. Agencies (P) Ltd. <docinfo@dkagencies.com>

Fundamentals of social work / edited by Sushma Batra, Bishnu Mohan Dash.
pages cm
Contributed articles.
Includes bibliographical references and index.
ISBN 9789388937917 (HB)
ISBN 9789388937924 (PB)

1. Social service—Vocational guidance—India. 2. Social service—Vocational guidance.
I. Batra, Sushma, 1953- editor. II. Dash, Bishnu Mohan, editor.

LCC HV10.5.F86 2021 | DDC 361.3202354 2323

Preface

The book "Fundamentals of Social Work" provides an overview of various basic aspects of social work profession. The book has been divided in two parts. Part one is comprised of nine chapters and part two also includes eight chapters.

Part One, introduces the reader with the basic concepts in social work, social work education and its relation with other disciplines; theories in social work; methods recognized in social work; roles and functions of a professional social worker, and genesis of social work education as a discipline in India and other parts of the world. It also covers attributes and skills required to be a professional social worker.

Nita Kumari has authored first chapter of this book titled "Introduction to Social Work". The chapter introduces the reader with defining social work profession and its mission. It gives brief introduction on code of ethics—values and principles. The chapter also provides a brief description on the scope of social work profession, roles of a professional worker and methods of working with people and communities.

Puneet Kumar Ojha has contributed a chapter titled "Social Work and Its Relationship to Other Disciplines". The chapter introduces the young readers the basics of social work and its relation with other disciplines such as medicine, psychology, history, sociology, public administration, law and economics. Social work discipline draws its knowledge base from various disciplines of social and biological sciences to understand various aspects of human life and redress complex human problems.

Sayantani Guin traces the evolution of social work practice in India from charity approach to human rights approach in her chapter titled "Social Work in India: From Charity to Human

Rights". She highlights the contribution of British rulers in introducing a new outlook in thinking among the Indian masses. In present times, the trend in social work practice is towards protecting and promoting the rights and dignity of people. She further brings new trends in social work education, highlighting role of IGNOU in imparting Social Work education offered through open and distance learning.

Sheeba Joseph has documented the genesis of social work profession in other parts of the world in her chapter titled "A Glance through the History of Social Work in UK & USA". Social work has developed through centuries like all other disciplines. Long back, social work as a discipline has attained a professional status in USA and UK, but in India the social work profession is still struggling to attain a professional status. This chapter will help the students to understand how social work as a profession evolved and the developmental milestones in the history of social work profession. The first section explains the genesis of Social Work in UK and the later part, highlights the development of the same in USA.

Charu in her chapter "History of Social Work in India" has discussed the history of social work in India, the emergence of professional social work and the gaps and challenges in the professional social work in India.

In her chapter "Theories in Social Work", Beena has highlighted four major theoretical perspectives that form the basis of Social work as a profession. These are the Psychodynamic theory, Conflict theory, Social learning theory and the Systems theory. Social work has its own values, a body of knowledge, specialized skills and methods to do Social work. There are a number of theories that are incorporated in the body of knowledge that help us understand concepts, explain various occurrences.

Lokender Prashad and Kumar Satyam, in their chapter "Methods in Social Work" have highlighted Social Work as a unique profession, having its unique methods of offering solutions *via* problem specific intervention strategies. The writers have documented methods of working with people and its relevance in fast changing globalized India.

Swati Bist in her chapter "Roles and Functions of Professional Social Worker in Selected Field Work Settings" has enumerated the generic roles and functions of a professional social worker.

The social work professionals are interface between various welfare agencies and clients. It further evaluates the functions and roles of a professional worker in selected field setting, specifically in various institutional set up. The chapter also focuses on the possible intervention in the non-institutional community set up.

In the last chapter in this section Prof. Batra has listed down personal attributes of a social worker, such as, genuine, hopeful, trustworthy, creative/innovative, flexible, empathetic, resilient, self-aware etc. It further enumerates skill required to be a successful and efficient worker, such as knowledge about social work profession, listening skills, organizational skills, communication skills, analytical skills and documentation abilities etc.

Part Two: Contemporary issues in social work practice and education have been compiled in this part. The book also features social work profession in international scenario and its relevance.

Ravindra Singh has given arguments as to what makes social work a professional discipline in the chapter titled "Social Work as a Profession". The chapter further documents various professional bodies across India promoting interest of social work profession. The chapter also highlights challenges before social work profession in India. It is still struggling in India to gain recognition as a profession. There is a wide gap between class room teaching and field practice. The author emphasise on setting up of a national level regulatory body to establish credibility of the profession.

Binod Kumar has enumerated essentials in social work profession in Indian scenario in his chapter titled "Prerequisites of Social Work Profession: Contextualizing India". The absence of national level social work council, non-regulation of professionals; hence they are working in vacuum. The need for social work council has been realized and consultation for the same is under process. Like any other established profession social work also has basic ingredient, which requires to be adhered to. The way core competence has been inculcated among Indian social worker has led it to be an urban centric profession. He asserts that there is a dire need to reinvent social work education to suit the current milieu and Indian sensibilities.

Swati Bist in her chapter "Integrated Method in Social Work Practice" gives brief insight into the history of social work profession. It also discusses ecological perspective providing framework to social work profession to deal diverse and complex social situations. The chapter highlights problems of women facing violence, focusing domestic violence, and therein use of integrated practice to address the same. Delhi Police has set up special cells for women (Crime Against Women Cells, and Special Cell for Women and Children) to combat violence against women, particularly violence at home. The chapter evaluates the services being offered by these special cells in NCT of Delhi in the light of integrated social work practice.

Pankaj Gupta & Shresthi Sharma have authored a chapter titled "Generalist *versus* Specialist Social Work". The chapter tries to understand both the specialist and generalist orientation and their importance for the growth of social work profession. The chapter begins with the conundrum, on generalist and specialist, and tries to bring more clarity about both the terms. Since, both the terms are related; we also tried to find the common domain in the two.

In the chapter "Strength-based Practice: An Alternate Approach to Social Work", Kislay Kumar Singh highlights a new approach in social work profession that has shifted the focus from deficits to strengths, known as strengths-based approach to human problems. This approach asserts on discovering and enhancing the capabilities, knowledge, resources of individuals. This involves a systematic understanding of the situation from the client's perspective. A client must be seen in the light of their capacities, competencies, possibilities, and hopes in order to help him/her from any circumstances. It constitutes resources existing within and around the individual, family, or community. The strength-based approach values two things—(a) the power of the self to heal, and (b) strategies to recognize the helping environment.

Dimple Mishra has covered the issue of indigenous literature in social work education in India through her chapter titled "Social Work Education and Review Committees in Social Work : An Indian Perspective". The chapter sheds light on trends in social work education and curriculum across various parts of India. It brings limitations in social work education. The author highlights need for development of indigenous knowledge base in social work education in India. The chapter also sheds light on contribution of Indira Gandhi National Open University (IGNOU) in developing indigenous literature and expansion of social work profession.

Avtar Singh has touched the issue of globalization in his chapter titled "Impact of Globalization on Social Work Education and Practice". He discusses the impact of globalization on Social Work Education and Practice. In his chapter, he examines as to how social work as a profession has responded to the changing climate of the world. He suggests that social work needs to develop a new framework of action, in which the awareness of globalization processes will provide a foundation to establish new and modern social work. Overall, this framework needs to include cultural, economic, social and political features on theory and practice but also to develop openness to new experiences and paradigms, a commitment to lifelong learning and creation of a morally active and responsible profession aware of globalization forces.

In the last chapter, Manju Goel has covered a new dimension in social work in her chapter titled "International Social Work". The chapter provides an introduction to social work practice in an international context. The chapter will help the students to acquire an analytic frame of reference for understanding central problems addressed by cross-cultural and global practice at the micro, meso, and macro levels as a base for international social work practice. After reading international social work course one is able to conceptualize dynamics of power, oppression, and justice in the context of the relationship between the social worker and clients in international practice settings. Global social work deals with problems that are caused between countries, that occur across national boundaries or that are issues that countries work together to collectively solve.

It is hoped that the book shall serve as a guide to young budding social work practitioners, students of social work and social work educators.

Sushma Batra
Bishnu Mohan Dash

Contents

Part Two

Contributors

Avtar Singh, Associate Professor, Department of Social Work, Dr. Bhim Rao Ambedkar College, University of Delhi, Delhi. **E-mail:** *avtar.singh08@vahoo.com*

Binod Kumar, Assistant Professor, Department of Social Work, Dr. Bhim Rao Ambedkar College, University of Delhi, Delhi. **E-mail:** *binod.attorney@gmail.com*

Bishnu Mohan Dash, Assistant Professor, Department of Social Work, Dr. Bhim Rao Ambedkar College, University of Delhi, Delhi. **E-mail:** *bishnudash2006@gmail.com*

Beena Antony Reji, Associate Professor, Aditi Mahavidyalaya, University of Delhi, Delhi. **E-mail:** *beenaareji@gmail.com*

Charu Sethi, Ph.D. Scholar, Department of Social Work, University of Delhi, Delhi.

Dimple Mishra, Research Scholar, School of Social Work, Indira Gandhi National Open University (IGNOU), New Delhi. **E-mail:** *dm747542@gmail.com*

Kislay Kumar Singh, Assistant Professor, Department of Social Work, Dr. Bhim Rao Ambedkar College, University of Delhi, Delhi. **E-mail:** *mailkislaysingh@gmail.com*

Kumar Satyam, Assistant Professor, Department of Social Work, Dr. Bhim Rao Ambedkar College, University of Delhi, Delhi. **E-mail:** *kumar.satyam@bramb.du.ac.in*

Lokender Prashad, Ph.D. Research Scholar, Tata Institute of Social Sciences, Mumbai. **E-mail:** *lokenderlokender@gmail.com*

Manju Goel, Assistant Professor, Department of Social Work, Aditi Mahavidyalaya, University of Delhi, Delhi. **E-mail:** *goelmanju12@gmail.com*

Nita Kumari, Teaching in Deptt. of Social Work, Dr. Bhim Rao Ambedkar College, University of Delhi.
E-mail: *nitasharma.nn@gmail.com*

Pankaj Gupta, Ph. D. Scholar, Department of Social Work, University of Delhi, Delhi. **E-mail:** *pankajdsw06@gmail.com*

Puneet Kumar Ojha, Ph.D. Scholar, Department of Social Work, University of Delhi, Delhi.

Ravindra Singh, Assistant Professor, Department of Social Work, Dr. Bhim Rao Ambedkar College, University of Delhi, Delhi.
E-mail: *singhravi30@gmail.com*

Sayantani Guin, Assistant Professor, School of Social Work, Indira Gandhi National Open University, Maidan Garhi, New Delhi.
E-mail: *sayantaniguin@ignou.ac.in*

Sheeba Joseph, Associate Professor, Department of Social Work, BSSS, Bhopal. **E-mail:** *sheejose03@yahoo.com*

Shreshti Sharma, Ph.D. Scholar, Department of Social Work, University of Delhi, Delhi. **E-mail:** *shreshti101290@gmail.com*

Sushma Batra, Former Head, Department of Social Work, University of Delhi, Delhi. **E-mail:** *sushmabatra18@gmail.com*

Swati Bist, Assistant Professor (Guest), Department of Social Work, Dr. Bhim Rao Ambedkar College, Delhi University, Delhi.
E-mail: *swatibist09@gmail.com*

Part One

1
Introduction to Social Work

Nita Kumari

Introduction

Social work as a profession was recognized and developed initially in the Western World. It began in England and moved over to America. Social work as a profession had its beginning in charity, social services, reform and welfare services. It has travelled a long way from welfare approach to development and empowerment approach. Now the profession has given emphasis to the rights based approach thereby protecting and promoting the rights of individuals. As a professional discipline, it promotes the well-being of individuals, groups and society as a whole and requires the adequate knowledge and understanding of human behaviour and development. It basically focuses on the interaction between individuals and systems in various social situations to actualize their aspirations and to help them cope with their life tasks.

According to Friedlander, social work is a professional service based upon scientific knowledge and skills in human relations, which assists individuals alone or in groups, to obtain social and personal satisfaction and independence. It is usually performed by a social agency or related organisation (Friedlander, 1955). Historically, the goal of professional social work has been to enhance the well-being of human race. As mentioned above, it operates within the three paradigms of welfare, development and empowerment to achieve its ultimate goal of human welfare. The welfare paradigm emphasizes external support to the individuals to cope with their problems; while in the development paradigm self-reliance is emphasized. On the other hand, in the empowerment paradigm the people's involvement in determining the decisions that affect their lives are emphasised (Sarathy *et al.*, 2013). The profession of social work is constantly committed to promote social and economic justice, affecting changes in societal values and policies that limit or forbid the free and full participation of individuals. It works for changes in discriminatory or else restrictive practices that limit opportunities and prevent maximum social functioning.

Social work is considered a unique blend of science and art. It derives the knowledge from various disciplines such as psychology, sociology, political science, economics, biology, counselling, and anthropology. It is considered a science because it adopts systematic approach in making use of knowledge (assumptive, validated and hypothetical). On the other hand, it is also reckoned as an art because it requires various skills and techniques as per the need of different situations.

Definitions of Social Work

A number of authors have given various definitions of social work. Some of the definitions are cited below:

According to Anderson (1945): "Social work is a professional service rendered to the people for the purpose of assisting them, as individuals or in groups, to attain satisfying relationships and standards of life in accordance with their particular wishes and capacities and in harmony with those of the community."

In the words of Clarke (1947): "Social work is a form of professional service comprising a composite of knowledge and skills, parts of which are and parts of which are not, distinctive of social work, which attempts on one hand, to help the individual to satisfy his needs in the social milieu, and on the other, to remove, as far as possible, the barriers which obstruct people from achieving the best of which they are capable."

According to Youngdahl (1949): "Social work seeks two things for people: economic well-being and deeper source of happiness, that is self-realisation, but subject of its concern is human behaviour and relationships, its focus of attention are the individual and his adjustment to a recognised reality."

Konopka (1958) defines "social work as an entity representing three clearly distinguished but interrelated parts: a network of social services, carefully developed methods and processes, and social policy expressed through social institutions and individuals. All these are based on a view of human beings, their interrelationships and the ethical demands made on them."

The National Association of Social Workers (NASW), the largest professional association of social workers in North America, describes social work as: "the professional activity of helping individual, groups, or communities to enhance or restore their capacity for social functioning and to create societal conditions favourable to this goal. Social work practice consists of the professional application of social work values, principles, and techniques to one or more of the following ends: helping people obtain tangible services; providing counselling and psychotherapy with individuals, families, and groups; helping communities or groups; provide or improve social and health services; and participating in relevant legislative processes. The practice of social work requires knowledge of human development and behaviour; of social, economic, and cultural institutions; and of the interaction of these factors" (NASW, 1973). Similarly, the Social Work Dictionary (Barker, 1999) defines the profession of Social Work as "the applied science of helping people achieve an effective level of psychological functioning and effecting social changes to enhance the well-being of all people."

In the year 1982, the first International Definition of Social Work was developed by IFSW and IASSW which says "Social Work is a profession whose purpose is to bring about social change in general and in its individual forms of development."

In the year 2000, further improvements have been made in the definition, according to which, "The Social Work profession promotes social change, problem solving in human relationships, the empowerment and liberation of people to enhance well-being. Utilizing theory of human behaviours and social systems, social work intervenes at the points where people interact with their environment. Principles of human rights and social justice are fundamental to social work" (IFSW & IASSW, 2000).

In July 2014, another global definition of Social Work was approved in the general meeting of IFSW and General Assembly of IASSW. According to the definition "Social Work is a practice-based profession and an academic discipline that promotes social change and development, social cohesion, and the empowerment and liberation of people. Principles of social justice, human rights, collective responsibility and respect for diversities are central to social work. Underpinned by theories of social work, social sciences, humanities and indigenous knowledge, social work engages people and structures to address life challenges and enhance well-being.

On the basis of above given definitions, we may analyse that:

- Social work is a professional service based on skills, techniques and scientific knowledge.
- It creates such social conditions that enhance the well-being of individuals and try to prevent problems in social functioning.
- Helps people to improve their social functioning for the purpose of obtaining personal as well as social satisfaction.
- It can be undertaken by an individual, group or any organisation.
- It is based on democratic and humanitarian philosophy.
- Always strive to induce positive change in human personality.
- Believe in enabling people to develop capacity for self-help.
- Gives emphasis on empowerment, promote human rights and social justice to enhance well-being.

Objectives of Social Work

The purpose of social work is to provide vision, direction and motivation for addressing social problems for resolving interpersonal conflict, and meeting human needs. Improvement of the quality of life in the human condition is envisioned as an explicit goal of the profession. Promoting adaptive functioning in the relationship between individuals and social institutions is central to the purpose of social work: "Historically, social work has contributed to the development of these relationships in such a way as to promote social and economic justice and protect the opportunities for all people to live with dignity and freedom" (CSWE, 1988 : 120).

Brown (1942) has mentioned four objectives of social work,

viz. to provide physical help; to provide help in establishing adjustment; to solve psychological problems, and to provide facilities to weaker sections of people to lead a good standard of living. However, Hamilton (1951) has specified availability of opportunities for social growth based on healthy and good standard of life and satisfying relationships and experience.

According to Friedlander (1955), there are three objectives of social work, i.e. Change in oppressive social conditions, development of constructive forces, and help in getting opportunities for democratic principles and human behaviour. According to United Nations Organisation (1958), Social work helps individuals, groups, and community to reach high level of social, mental and physical well-being.

The Council on Social Work Education (CSWE, 1994) lists four purposes of Social Work Practice: (i) the promotion, restoration, maintenance and enhancement of the social functioning of individuals, families, groups, organisations and communities by helping them accomplish tasks, prevent and alleviate distress and use resources; (ii) the planning, formulation and implementation of social policies, services, resources, and programmes needed to meet basic human needs and support the development of human capacities; (iii) the pursuit of policies, services, resources, and programmes through organisational and administrative advocacy and social or political action, so as to empower groups at risk and promote social and economic justice; and (iv) the development and testing of professional knowledge and skills related to these purposes (Thomas, 2009).

According to the National Association of Social Workers (NASW), the primary mission of social work is to enhance human well-being and help meet the basic needs of all people, with particular attention to promoting social justice, addressing the needs and empowerment of people who are vulnerable, oppressed, or living in poverty...(Social workers help people) identify and manage the environmental forces that create, contribute to, and address problems in living (NASW, 2006b: 1). Social work is an activity that seeks to help individuals, families, organisations, groups and communities engage resources that will alleviate human problems. Social work is concerned, too, with enabling clients to develop capacities and strengths that will improve their social functioning. As the NASW definition indicates, social work is an active, "doing" profession that brings about positive change in problem situation through problem solving or prevention.

The purpose of social work profession (CSWE, 2010) is to promote human and community well-being. Guided by a person and environment construct, a global perspective, respect for human diversity, and knowledge based on scientific inquiry, the purpose of social work is actualized through its quest for social and economic justice, the prevention of conditions that limit human rights, the elimination of poverty, and the enhancement of the quality of life for all persons.

The purpose of Social work is achieved through the application of professional social work values, principles, and practice methods. Social workers may, for example, confer with individuals and families, enabling them to deal with stress and resolve interpersonal problems. Social workers also help communities and society prevent social problems and provide or improve health and social services. They actively participate in legislative processes and policy advocacy to formulate fair and equitable social policies. In sum, social workers offer counselling services in times of personal crisis, advise policy-makers on critical issues, and advocate for a better society. These social work activities illustrate that the concern of the profession lies in the interconnections among and between persons and society. No other profession considers the interactions between humans and their social and cultural environment to the extent that social work does (Dubois, 1992: 6).

There are several specific objectives cited in *Encyclopaedia of Social Work* which includes:

- To make social relationships cordial and pleasant and inculcate democratic values in personality.
- To solve psycho-social problems of the people and satisfy unmet felt needs as well (see Box 1).
- To create social awareness among people on various issues and make healthy and people friendly environment.
- To work towards new laws enacted in accordance with the social situations and bring about desired amendments in existing laws, if required.
- To develop capacity for self-help and adjustment among people.

Box 1: Roles played by Generalist Social Workers

Advocate: Without being aggressive, an advocate fights for the rights and dignity of people in the need of help.

Analyst or Evaluator: Gather information to assess the effectiveness of work with clients or client systems and make recommendations for change as needed.

Broker: Link client systems with existing resources. He also ensures that those resources treat client systems in a humane and effective way.

Educator: Convey information and knowledge with the goals of developing skills.

Enabler: Provides encouragement, offers hope, helps clients identify and focus on goals. He also enables clients to make choices that improve their functioning.

Facilitator: Facilitates changes by bringing together groups of people and helping them use their own talents as well as other resources to create positive change.

Manager: Assumes administrative responsibility for a specific project, programme, or agency.

Initiator: Calls attention to an unaddressed problem or need.

Integrator or Coordinator: Brings together various components of a system into a unified whole to create positive change.

Mediator: Helps in resolving conflicts between clients systems at one or more levels of the environment while playing a neutral role.

Mobiliser: Assembles, energizes, and organises new or existing groups.

Negotiator: Advocates on behalf of a client system. The negotiator brings together those who are in conflict to bargain compromise and find an agreeable solution.

Outreach Worker: Identifies specific client systems and reaches out to provide assistance.

Source: Adapted from Kirst-Ashman, K. & Hull, G. (2009). *Generalist Practice with Organisations and Communities* (4th ed., pp. 21-27). Belmont, CA: Brooks/Cole.

- To promote social cohesion and harmony among people.
- To promote law and order in the society and foster unity and solidarity among people.
- To work for minimising the feelings of casteism, communalism, regionalism and linguism and create and enrich positive thinking among people (Singh, 2012).

Functions of Social Work

Generally there are four types of functions of social work, namely Curative, Reformative, Preventive and Developmental.

Curative Functions: Services given to the people in order to treat a particular problem is called curative functions. It includes medical services, health services, psychiatric and mental health services, services for crippled and differently abled and rehabilitative services.

Reformative Functions: They are related to individual reform services such as prison reform services, probation and parole, and legal services. It also includes services related to improvement in social relationships which consist of family welfare services, school social work and industrial social work. Social reform services include employment services, dowry prohibition, restraint on child marriage, prevention and control of immoral traffic, beggary, drug abuse, domestic violence etc.

Preventive Functions: It comprise programmes like adult education, continuing education, population education including sex education, non-formal education, awareness generation programmes creating knowledge and understanding of social policies, social legislation, varied kinds of plans, procedures, programmes/services started for the benefit of weaker and vulnerable sections of society.

Developmental Functions: It include various types of programmes related to economic development such as increase in productivity, per capita income, gross national product etc. and social development, e.g. nutrition, water supply, health, housing, education, training, employment, removal of poverty, sanitation etc.

Methods of Social Work

Social work seeks to assist individual, groups and communities with the help of various methods to promote their well-being. The use of primary methods (social case work, social group work and community organisation) and secondary (social welfare administration, social action and social work research) methods of social work makes this profession unique from other professions.

Social Case Work: It is one of the methods that aims at working directly with individuals or families. With the use of this method, social worker helps individuals and families identify solutions to personal or other problems related to difficulty with social functioning. In many cases, problems related to emotional conflict, social stress, lack of familiarity with the available resources may cause dysfunction in individuals. With the use of social work skills, social worker assesses the problems and makes intervention strategically to ameliorate these problems.

In the words of Mary Richmond, social casework is the art of doing different things for and with different people by cooperating with them to achieve at one and the same time their own and society's betterment (Richmond, 1922).

Social Group Work: It is a method of working with people in groups. Through this method, individuals are helped to develop their inherent potential and identify their innate abilities to cope better with their environment. Group work stresses the value of self-development through structured interactions with other group members.

Trecker has defined social group work as a method through which individuals in groups in social agency settings are helped by a worker who guides their interaction in programme activities so that they may relate themselves to others and experience growth opportunities in accordance with their needs and capacities to the end of the individual, group and community development (Trecker, 1955).

Community Organisation: Community organisation is a macro method in social work. The community organiser possesses required qualities and skills to work with the people and conveys information to the community people in an effective way. The community organiser has essential knowledge, skills about the principles, process and steps of community organisation and applies the same while working in the community.

According to Ross, community organisation is a process by which a community identifies its needs or objectives, orders (or ranks) these needs or objectives, develops the confidence and will to work at those needs or objectives, finds the resources (internal and/or external) to deal with these needs or objectives, takes action in respect of them, and in doing so extends and develops cooperative and collaborative attitudes and practices in the community (Ross, 1955).

Social Welfare Administration: According to Friedlander (1958) "administration of social agencies translates the provisions of social legislation of social agencies and the aims of private philanthropy and religious charities into the dynamics of services and benefits for humanity."

For example, social welfare agencies play a pivotal role in rendering services to HIV/AIDS patients. HIV/AIDS is a very sensitive issue and needs professional competence on the part of the service provider organisation to achieve desired objectives. The social welfare organisations employ professionally trained social workers. The social workers have in-depth knowledge and make use of available resources together with active community participation in order to achieve the goal of the programme properly.

Social Action: Social action is an individual, group or community effort within the framework of social work philosophy and practice that aims to achieve social progress, to modify social policies and to improve social legislation and health and welfare services (Friedlander, 1977). Through social action, social worker addresses the issues pertaining to any social problem. For instance, they advocate by raising the voice on behalf of the people living with HIV/AIDS (PLHAs). It is widely accepted that the rights of the PLHAs are being violated in a great way. They are being stigmatized and discriminated in the health care setting. Through advocacy social workers influence, motivate and encourage democratic powers to take decisions for the welfare of PLHAs. They fight to bring desired changes in the policies with the aim to ensure equitable distribution of resources in the social system, protecting their rights and provide justice. Social action is one of the most effective methods of social work, which social workers can use in fighting for the rights of the PLHAs.

Social Work Research: According to Fanshel (1980), every profession must systematically carry out high quality research about its practices if its performance in the service of clientele is to remain effective and up-to-date. The role of social work research is very important for the effective implementation of any programme initiative. Research studies provide useful information about the different dimensions of the problems and facilitate effective planning, policy formulation and implementation of the programme. Competent social work practitioners keep abreast of professional research and make use of research findings in their practice.

Values and Ethics in Social Work

The profession of social work is based on values, ethics, and a common body of knowledge. The social workers are committed to the dignity, worth, and value of all human beings irrespective of their class, caste, race, ethnicity, colour, gender, sexual orientation, age, physical and mental capacities. Social workers always emphasise that a client must be accepted as they are, with no strings attached. They always make it a point not to judge an individual in order to maintain client's dignity and privacy. Apart from this, a social worker always works towards equality, justice, development, and empowerment of his clients. They always favour that in the society, all the members should have access to the same rights, privileges without any differences which is very much essential for the establishment of a non-discriminatory society. NASW has established a code of ethics (see Box 2) for its members, incorporating these values.

Generic Principles of Social Work

There are seven principles of social work which have been widely accepted in the profession of social work and discussed as below:

Principle of Acceptance: The social worker accepts and deals with the client as he really is, including his weaknesses and strengths, his positive or negative feelings, his different attitude or behaviour.

Principle of Confidentiality: It is the preservation of secret information which concerns the client and can be disclosed in the professional relationship. Applying principle of confidentiality is crucial for maintaining positive working relationship with the clients and winning their trust.

Principle of Individualisation: It recognizes and understands each client's unique qualities and treats them not just as a human being but as the human being with his personal differences.

Principle of Client Self-determination: It gives the freedom to the client in making their own choices and decisions in the problem solving process. Social worker always tries to stimulate the client to think independently and rationally about his own problem and arrives at a decision for himself.

Principle of Communication: The social worker always tries

Box 2: NASW Code of Ethics

Preamble

The primary mission of the social work profession is to enhance human well-being and help meet the basic human needs of all people, with particular attention to the needs and empowerment of people who are vulnerable, oppressed, and living in poverty. A historic and defining feature of social work is the profession's focus on individual well-being in a social context and the well-being of society. Fundamental to social work is attention to the environment forces that create, contribute to, and address problems in living.

Social workers promote social justice and social change with and on behalf of clients. "Clients" is used inclusively to refer to individuals, families, groups, organisations, and communities. Social workers are sensitive to cultural and ethnic diversity and strive to end discrimination, oppression, poverty, and other forms of social injustice. These activities may be in the form of direct practice, community organising, supervision, consultation, administration, advocacy, social and political action, policy development and implementation, education, and research and evaluation. Social workers seek to enhance the capacity of people to address their own needs. Social workers also seek to promote the responsiveness of organisations, communities, and other social institutions to individual's needs and social problems.

The Mission of the Social Work Profession is rooted in a set of core values. These core values, embraced by social workers throughout the profession's history, are the foundation of social work's unique purpose and perspective:

Service: The primary goal of social workers' is to help the individuals in need and to address social problems.

Social Justice: Social workers strive for social change, particularly in the lives of vulnerable and oppressed sections of the society.

Worth and dignity of the person: Social workers treat each individual in a caring and respectful manner, accept individual with differences and cultural and ethnic diversity.

Importance of human relationships: Social workers always recognize the central importance of human relationships and engage people as partners in the helping process.

Integrity: Social workers behave and act honestly and responsibly. They abide by the rules, regulations and ethics of the organisation with which they are associated.

Competence: Social workers practice within their areas of competence and develop and enhance their professional expertise.

Source: National Association of Professional Workers (2008) cited in Ambrosino *et al.*, 2015.

to have an adequate and clear communication between him and the client. The social worker creates such an environment by giving due importance to the client in which he feels comfortable in expressing himself. In order to communicate effectively with the client, social worker develops an understanding about his background.

Principle of Non-Judgemental Attitude: The social worker should not be biased or prejudiced, neither should be guided by any preconceived notion nor should be governed by his past experiences while helping the client. The social worker should take every decision keeping in view the best interests of the client.

Principle of Controlled Emotional Involvement: While working with the client, the social worker can empathise with the client but should not be emotionally involved as such behaviour will adversely affect the worker's ability to work objectively.

Scope of Professional Social Work

Social work is a professional discipline, and at present, is being practised in numerous settings. The social workers today are employed in governmental, non-governmental, private and industrial settings as well as work as private practitioners. Some of the major fields of social work are as follows:

Social Work with Families: Problems in the families may occur between parents and children, between the spouses. The problem could be related to the high expectations of children from the parents or complain of favouritism or over-protectionism of parents, parents may observe disobedience or emotional outbursts as problems from their children, fight between the spouse on the issues of child rearing, distribution of duties. In some cases, the spouses indulge in physical or verbal abuse that may even lead to the breakdown of communication and ultimately the relationship. A social worker closely works with the individuals and families and adopts a number of theoretical approaches in order to understand the human behaviour and for making an intervention. Social worker uses the behaviour therapy with children and ego psychology with adults that can enable the individual to develop more adaptive coping skills. The social worker uses the eclectic approach which is knowledge of many theories and several skills for selecting the right approach and techniques with reference to clients.

Social Work in Correctional Setting: Every democratic society has created a system of correctional agencies to deal with People in Conflict with Law. These agencies administer the penalties assigned to such clients. In correctional settings, people from social work background are designated as social worker, probation officer, welfare officer, treatment officer, superintendent etc. The social workers' main role in the correctional setting is to help the offender in getting rehabilitated rather than punishing him/her.

The social worker gives a space to the offender to ventilate their feelings as an offender like any other individual too wants to share their inner feelings, fear and frustrations, their hopes and aspirations with the person to whom they trust. A social worker provides a safe emotional climate in which offenders can express themselves. He assists the offender in modifying his/her environment. He uses the knowledge and skills of the profession in a corrective manner, to rehabilitate the offender. He helps the client to lead a constructive life after getting relieved from the institution.

Social Work in Educational Setting: The leadership in education rests with teachers. The skills of social workers are used in improving efficacy of education sector. By maintaining the school-home-community linkage, they help education achieve its central purpose. They prevent or deal with behavioural, economic, familial and scholastic problems, which interfere in learning. Relieved off the pressure, the learner then makes the maximum utilisation of learning experiences. In short, social work represents the human factor in education (Gandhi, 2010). The social workers in the educational setting helps the children having problems related to emotional disturbance, learning, and students in conflict with family members, peers, or school authorities. Apart from this, they also deal with the problems of substance abuse, violence and issues of gender and sexuality. Career counselling has also been provided by social workers in schools. School social workers are members of intervention teams that work with children who have developmental disabilities and other special needs. They often liaison with parents and the community when special services are needed. If a social worker is employed in a school where the education is provided to the disabled students as well, the social worker creates awareness among the children and parents about the rights of those children. He protects their rights and helps them with an opportunity for development without any discrimination. They make social work intervention with the children and parents, if need arises. They render needed help to the teachers and network with outside agencies for referral or economic rehabilitation of children with disabilities.

Social Work in Health Care Setting: The role of a medical social worker in a medical team is as important as that of a physician. While the medical practitioner's role is limited to treatment of a patient, the social worker deals with the social, physical and psychological aspects of the patient who is under treatment. They deal with the patients within the framework of a democratic and humanistic way and help the patient in restoration of health and to prevent personal deterioration as a result of the disease. The social workers get involved in providing education and counselling services to the patients and their family members. Social workers enable patients to regain their emotional equilibrium and help them towards an adjustment to their situation. They provide crisis counselling to patients like in case of HIV infection and help family members to have better problem solving and coping skills to get used to with the stressful situation in order to maintain the family functioning in normal manner. The prolonged sickness makes the patient isolated. Family and friends may become less cordial. In such situations, social workers provide emotional as well as social support in order to help the patients to have access to other resources and assistance. Honest listening without non-judgemental attitude is one of the best medicines which a social worker offers to his/her client. Social worker shows an unbiased, friendly and understanding attitude towards the patients. Social workers play the role of a mediator, enabler, coordinator of services, mobilizer of the resources being a member of team of professionals. He/she can mediate/facilitate between doctors and patients and administration and patients in order to avail the facilities of the hospital exclusively meant for the patients.

Social Work with Elderly: The younger generation earlier used to rely on their older family members for skill, expertise, and guidance. However, the elder's status in the society has gradually declined. Formerly, the family served as the primary system for meeting all the needs of their elder members, including emotional, physical, financial, and mental support but now it has been replaced by the old age homes. Older adults have many of the same problems that are evident at other stages in the lifecycle such as personal adjustment problems, marital problems, relocation, family conflict, adjustment to separation and loneliness, anxiety about limited income, mental illness, and interpersonal loss, among others. The most common form of social work intervention with the elderly population is generalist practice at the micro-level. Social workers used to work with older adults and their families on specific problems, such as enhancing personal adjustment, securing resources to meet their needs, providing emotional support in decision making, dealing with death and dying, and managing family conflict. Intervention often involves a counselling and guidance approach, stresses problems clarification and the development of options and priorities, and provides an opportunity for the client to express anxiety and emotions. Social workers work with great sensitivity and take their clients' issues, concern and experiences with warmth.

Social Work in Industrial Setting: Social workers have plenty of scope in industry. In larger organisations, employees face more complex problems as they do not have direct access to the managers and everything has to go through proper channels. In such situations their problems cannot be heard and sorted out early. A social worker can be of great help to the employees to overcome their problems and continue to function as productive workers. Social workers can intervene in industrial setting at micro and macro level. At micro level, the social worker can provide treatment to the worker, his family, employer and union members. Their problems related to job performance, job satisfaction, conflict situations, absenteeism etc. can be looked carefully and solutions can be found out. Social workers also attend to the problems such as anxiety, depression, mental disturbance, phobia, substance abuse, marital and family conflict, sexual harassment, domestic violence etc.

At the macro level, it can be organisational intervention where the social worker can provide individual and group consultation to supervisors and managers at all levels regarding understanding of human behaviour. The intervention may be in the form of proposing a new job design. Organising and planning of the services at the preventive, developmental and curative levels requires a basic study of the organisation. It is through an open and sensitive approach, rather than a predetermined blue-print that the intuitive social worker can positively integrate the social work objectives with the management objectives (Sehgal, 2010).

Social Work among Communities: Working with the communities, whether it is urban, rural or tribal is very challenging. A social worker uses his skills of creativity, innovation, and ability to influence community members to mobilize in meeting their needs. A social worker involves himself at the individual client level and identifies community strengths to create healthy communities that use everyone's capabilities. Social workers often provide community people with services, support, and hope while helping simultaneously to change the environment to provide better transportation, improved medical care, and a more responsive community. A social worker may be helping a family in locating a nursing home, securing resources for a child with a disability, providing counselling services to the community people, collaborating with local stakeholders/authorities in developing something useful for the community people, sensitising people about various social issues, programmes and services available for them. A social worker works with flexibility, use good communication skills, engage both private and public resources and develop basic understanding of community values and practices in order to work effectively. A social worker very appropriately facilitates the problem-solving process. Knowledge of existing resources, resource development, methods of linking clients with resources, and case management skill is very much required of a community worker.

Social workers are providing their services very dynamically to various organisations working for the welfare of the Scheduled Castes, Scheduled Tribes and Other Backward Classes: child welfare; youth welfare; welfare of the disabled; environmental conservation and development; and providing legal aid. They advocate for the social and economic justice by working to expand individual access to resources and opportunities at all levels of the environment, including adequate education, food, clothing and shelter, employment, health care etc. Apart from this, they are also involved in policy making, planning and developmental issues.

Conclusion

Social work is a practice based profession, which has developed special knowledge and skills to deal with individuals, groups and the communities. It focuses on social justice, fairness, development, empowerment and humanistic and right based approach. As a profession it is assisting people who are in need by using the unique skills of the profession and other helping professionals as well. The profession gives emphasis on motivating and encouraging people to fight for their rights and use their capacities in working towards desirable goals and finding a solution for their problems. Social work is considered as a combination of science and art.

References

Ambrosino, A.; Heffernan, J.; Shuttlesworth, G. and Ambrosino, R. (2015). *Social Work and Social Welfare: An Introduction* (7th edition), Cengage Learning India Private Limited, India.

Anderson, P. (1945). *Social Work as a Profession. Social Work Year Book.* New York: Russell Sage Foundation.

Barker, Robert L. (1999). *The Social Work Dictionary* (4th ed.). Washington, DC: NASW Press.

Brown, E.L. (1942). *Social Work as a Profession.* New York: Russell Sage Foundation.

Clarke, H. (1947). *Principles and Practice of Social Work.* New York: Appleton Century Crafts.

Council on Social Work Education (2010). Educational Policy and Accreditation Standards (p. 1), Washington, DC: Author.

Fanshel, D. (1980). Future of Social Work Research, Selected Papers. National Conference on the Future of Social Work Research, October 15-18, 1978, San Antonio, Texas. NASW, Inc., Washington, D.C.

Friedlander, W.A. (1955). *Introduction to Social Welfare.* New York: Prentice Hall, Inc.

Friedlander, W.A. (1977). *Introduction to Social Welfare.* New Delhi: Prentice Hall.

Gandhi, Anjali (2010). "Social Work in Educational Settings." In Gracious Thomas (Ed.), *Social Work Intervention with Individuals and Groups.* New Delhi: IGNOU.

Global Definition of Social Work, 2014, retrieved from http://ifsw.org/get-involved/global-definition-of-social-work/

Hamilton, D. (1951). *Theory and Practice of Social Casework.* New York: Columbia University Press.

Konopka, G. (1958). *Social Work Philosophy.* Minneapolis: The University of Minnesota Press.

National Association of Social Workers (2006). *The Power of Service.* Washington, DC: Author.

Richmond, M. (1922). *What is Social Casework?*. New York: Russel Sage Foundation.

Ross, M.G. (1955). *Community Organisation: Theory and Principles*. New York: Harper and Brothers.

Sarathy, K.; Kanagaraj, E. and Devendiran, C. (2013). "Social Welfare, Development and Empowerment: Fields, Perspectives and Paradigms in Social Work Research in Mizoram", *Social Work Journal*, Vol. 4 (2), 81-96.

Sehgal, R. (2010). "Social Work in Industrial Sector", In Gracious Thomas (Ed.), *Social Work Intervention with Individuals and Groups*. New Delhi: IGNOU.

Singh, S. (2012). "Social Work: Concept, Objectives, Functions, Approaches and Principles", In *Encyclopaedia of Social Work in India* (3rd Edition, Vol. 4), India: New Royal Book Company.

The National Association of Social Workers (1973). Retrieved from http://socialwork.iu.edu/about iussw/what is social work.php on 3/4/2012.

Trecker, G. (1955). *Social Group Work: Principles and Practices*. New York: Association Press.

United Nations. Department of Economic and Social Affairs (1958). *Training for Social Workers—Third International Survey*. New York: United Nations.

Youngdahl, B.E. (1949). *Social Work as a Profession. Social Work Year Book*. New York: Russell Sage Foundation.

2

Social Work and Its Relationship to Other Disciplines

Puneet Kumar Ojha

Introduction

Social work is called a helping profession, a problem solving profession or an enabling profession. To qualify to be a profession, social work should meet several criteria. One of the major criteria is that it should have its own knowledge base (Greenwood, 1957: 44-55). It should be able to produce knowledge and its practice should repeatedly validate. Theories and concepts should be formulated which explain the relationship between various factors that influence human behaviour. Models for interventions should be formulated to solve problems. However, social work, as it is a helping profession, has a major limitation in this area. Most social workers are engaged in practice with little time for developing theoretical perspectives. Social work academics are often criticized for producing research (knowledge) which is not of much use to practicing professionals.

Social work in the early period of growth depended to a large extent on knowledge derived from other disciplines like psychology, sociology, economics and political science. However, since 1970s social work scholarship has broadened and deepened its scope. The profession's self-generated fund of knowledge has expanded substantially (Reamer, 1994: 1). But, this does not mean that social work's engagement with other disciplines has reduced or limited. This chapter will give you an overview about the relationship between social work and other disciplines.

Evolution of Social Work as an Academic Discipline

Modern social work evolved in the nineteenth century to address the problems created by the emergence of the industrial society (Friedlander, 1967: 3). While it is true that all religious traditions had a history of individuals and institutions helping the lesser fortunate, it is only in the modern society that 'helping' became a profession and professional social work emerged. Professionalizing of the helping profession was both a consequence of change and a cause of social change.

The major changes that influenced the emergence of social work in the West were social, political and economic. The industrial society gave birth to a number of problems not seen earlier. Urbanization, and large scale migration of people from rural to urban areas in search of employment were some of the important consequences. Rural communities declined and so did the traditional forms of social control. People in the city often suffered from moral and material problems. Institutions like the family and churches which were earlier responsible for the welfare could no longer cope with the social problems. Modern social work had its roots when volunteers, mainly middle class white women, worked among the poor and the destitutes to alleviate their social and financial problems. However, there was a growing realization that charity needs be organised to reduce costs and made more humanitarian (Desai, 2002). The Charity Organisation Societies (COS) and settlement house were the pioneering efforts in this direction. The COS was founded in 1869 in UK and in 1877 in the USA. The COS used a number of 'visitors' to investigate the clients who were considered needy by the voluntary agencies.

This system introduced some form of order in the then prevalent chaotic situation in dispensing aid to the poor. Secondly, the issue of treatment was introduced as the COS did not simply distribute aid but also provided social and psychological support. Therefore, the COS visitors can be called as forerunners of the method —case work. Thirdly, the formation of specialized agencies for coordinating and administering welfare services were widely used. The beginning of using a systematic method to deal with the poor can be traced to these movements. The settlement houses were started in 1889 in the USA. Settlement houses were agencies in which university students stayed with the poor to support them and at the same time learn about their life. The methods used by these houses can be termed as three Rs—Residence, Reform and Research. Living with those who needed help reduced the distance between the client and the practitioners. The COS's major objective was to reform the poor by counselling and support while the settlement house aimed at understanding the poor and trying to address the conditions that caused poverty.

Another major influence was the growing social movements which took place during the nineteenth and twentieth century. Labour movements, socialistic movements, women's movements and movements for racial justice were some of the most prominent of them. There was growing recognition of the rights for physically and mentally disabled, children, refugees and the homeless. Several social workers gave lead to these movements or were very much influenced by them. For example, Jane Addams, who started the settlement houses in Chicago, won a Nobel Prize for her contribution for the peace movements. Social workers were in the forefront of the efforts to pass legislations to protect the rights of the disabled, minorities and women. Another important factor in the emergence of professional social work was the growing role of the state in welfare programmes. The Social Security Act, 1935 gave the responsibility of providing financial support to the vulnerable sections to the government. The welfare component in the government increased in most of the European countries. Professional social workers planned and implemented the welfare programmes giving the profession greater visibility and legitimacy.

Social work's increasing role in the society made it imperative that a formal system of education should be created that would train social workers to perform their functions effectively. The first university to introduce formal education was Columbia University which offered a six-week training programme in 1896 for the volunteers who were working in the welfare sector. Gradually, number of courses being offered increased. The duration was also increased as subjects of study went up. Newcomer (1959) cites three developments that took place which facilitated the rise of social work education in USA: (i) the development of social sciences as academic disciplines, (ii) the establishment of the National Conference of Charities and Corrections, and (iii) the establishment of privately sponsored women's colleges and co-educational public universities (Desai, 2002). By the early twentieth century, social work courses became part of university system in USA. However, the content and duration of the social work courses were the subject of debate. In 1932, the Association of Schools of Social Work (AASSW) adopted a minimum one year curriculum that included prescribed courses of subject areas such as medical and psychiatric information research, social legislation and legal aspects of social work (Dnnear, 1984 quoted in Reamer). In 1944, the AASSW identified eight areas which should be taught in social work courses, such as public welfare, social case work, group work, community organisation, medical information, social research, psychiatry and social welfare administration. The Council of Social Work Education (CSWE) was started in 1952 to regulate social work education. In 1962, it formulated the first formal curriculum policy which divided the curriculum into three areas like social welfare policy and services, human behaviour and the social environment, and methods of social work practice. The next review in 1982 clarified the important role of liberal arts in the syllabus and identified five important areas: human behaviour and social environment, social welfare policy and services, social work practice, research and field practicum. Again in 1992, some new areas of concern were stressed including values and ethics, cultural and ethnic diversity, population at risk, human behaviour and social environment, social welfare policy and services, social work practice, research and field practicum. Presently, there is a broad consensus in the US on the topics that need to be part of formal training in social work. (Reamer, 1993: 1-12).

The International Association of Schools of Social Work (IASSW) and World Census of Social Work Education 1998-1999 have given a global picture (Not including US) of the topic of study in social work courses. Four courses, namely research, social policy, personal and interpersonal intervention and community intervention were offered by 68.7 per cent of the schools and Social and Public Administration, Social History and Philosophy, Ethnic and Cultural Focus, Bio/Psycho/Social Theory, and Organisational Theory were offered by 50 per cent to 54 per cent of all schools outside the US. Social work curriculum represents the knowledge that has to be transferred to new entrants to the profession and maintains the standards of services. The existing curriculum can be divided into four components: (1) Human behaviour and social environment which will include the theories that explain social reality. This section of social work knowledge relies more on social science disciplines like sociology, psychology, history and economics, (2) Social policy, social welfare policy and social welfare administration. This section enriches itself from the policy sciences and public administration, (3) Social work practice: This section depends largely on the methods of social work namely case work, group work and community organisation. Within these models, social work has evolved many intervention methods, like task centred ecology model, and (4) Social work research which centres around evaluating and assessing the effectiveness of the various means of intervention unlike the social sciences research which aims at dispassionate search for truth.

Along with the gradual recognition of social work as a discipline, there has been an increase in the number of books and articles related to its practice. Mary Richmond wrote 'Social Diagnosis' which described methods to understand and diagnose social reality. It influenced social work practice as it was among the first text to systematically describe the methods for practice. Similarly, contributions by Grace Coyle, Mary Follet and others helped the growth of group work knowledge.

Social Work and its Relation to Other Disciplines

Social work is related to various disciplines. The areas like sociology, psychology and social policy are considered cognate disciplines of social work which has influenced social work (Central Council for Education and Training in Social Work, 1976 quoted in Dominelli, 1997).

Sociology and Social Work

Sociology (Latin "socius" meaning companion and Greek logos the study) is the scientific study of the human society. It is called the science of society. All social sciences study human behaviour, but the content, approach and the context of sociology are very different from other disciplines. According to Inkeles (1999: 14-15) sociology has three distinctive subject matters. Firstly, sociology is the study of society with society as the unit of analysis. Here it studies the internal differentiations and how they interact with each other and how they influence each other. It studies the allocation of functions to the different structures of the society. Max Weber, for example, studied the relationship between religion and capitalism and how the later helped capitalism emerge. Sociology also studies the external characteristics of the population and the rate and stage of its progress. The problems of the society are explained using these factors. Secondly, sociology as the study of institutions — political, economic, social, legal, stratifications etc. It studies the features that these institutions share and the features that are different. Their degree of specialization and level of autonomy are also studied. Durkheim, one of the pioneers of sociology, called sociology as the study of social institution. Thirdly, sociology is the study of social relationships. By social relationship we mean the interactions between individuals. Interactions between individuals are mediated by norms and values of the society and are intended to achieve goals.

The subject matter for sociology was collective behaviour of human beings. Society, community, family, religion, nation and groups are concepts that sociology investigates and studies. Its methods are considerably influenced by natural sciences. Even more importantly sociology studied the European society that was polarized and divided on ideological lines. The society was in danger of being disintegrated. Sociologists through their theoretical contributions were responding to this major crisis that they saw around them. They were suggesting the ways and means that societies could adopt to face the problems caused by modernity. Professional social work and sociology emerged in the European society in the nineteenth century which was the period of great changes in the society. Both responded to the crises caused by the changes in the modern society. They used the scientific methods to validate their means of work, gain acceptance and popular support. There were hard fought ideological debates within the adherents of each discipline so as to the best way to solve problems. For example in social work, the COS approach and the settlement approach influenced the direction of social work. The COS favoured the person centred approach which depended on case work to resolve social problem while the settlement house favoured a structural change to resolve the problem. In different forms, the debate continues so as to find the best way to resolve social problems (Dominelli, 2004: 47).

But sociology and social work differ in many aspects. In

Sociology, the approach to society is theoretical and theory building is its major concern. Social work on the other hand has to be practical and deal with problems. So social workers spend more time in the field with people rather than in the libraries with books. Sociological theory is based on facts drawn from complex social reality. They offer precise cause to explain social phenomena. Often these theories are of little value to the practitioners as many other factors come into play which should be taken into account to reach a realistic solution. On the other hand, sociologist find social workers' work to be fragmented and oriented only towards the problem at hand. Another important distinction between social work and sociology is that the latter made claims to be a value free discipline. Being objective and free from bias was considered a virtue. Social work on the other hand is a value based profession based on humanitarian principles (Johnson, 1998: 14).

Sociology has a significant influence on social work. The work of Charles Booth on poverty gave new perspectives to the society. Sociological analysis provides theoretical perspectives that can subject policies and the work which practitioners do to systematic analysis thereby enhancing our understanding of what is done and why (Dominelli, 1997: 5). The following are the areas in which contribution of Sociology is significant:

1. The systems theory in sociology has been used in the ecological model of social intervention in which the client systems are seen as being part of the environment and being influenced by it. (Germain, 1994: 103)
2. The major three approaches of sociology — structural functionalist, Marxian and interactionist — have influenced social work practice. Marxist theories have helped social worker understand that conflict is part of society and that different sections in society have conflicting interests. These perspectives have helped social workers look critically at its own methods and see whose interests the profession is serving. Further, they have enabled social work professionals to influence social policy by advocating for legislations and programmes. The integrationist school has contributed to the understanding of sub-cultures and delinquency. Some of the key theorists and their concepts that have been significantly used in

social work include Foucault concept of power, Marx's class relationship, and Goffman's closed institutions. (Dominelli, 1997: 82)

3. Sociological concepts like role, status, authority, power, rights, responsibility, groups, communities and nations are used in casework, group work and community organisation which has enriched social work practice.
4. The study of family, types of families, changing roles of family members, changing functions of family and its members, the problems and means to resolve these problems.
5. Problems of elderly and their solutions.

Psychology and Social Work

Psychology (Latin psyche—soul and logos—study) is the study of mental processes and human behaviour. Psychology can be defined as the science of human and animal behaviour; it includes application of this science to human problems (Morgan, C.T. *et al.*, 1993: 30). Being a science it uses the tools of observation, measurement and classification to study human behaviour.

Three main approaches dominate the field of psychology: (1) Freudian and neo-Freudian approaches. This approach gives importance to the unconscious part of the mind which plays an important role in determining the behaviour of the individual. Sigmund Freud is the main proponent of this approach but since then many others like Carl Jung etc. have contributed to giving new direction to this approach. (2) Behavioural approach which takes behaviour as being learnt. Skinner the proponent of this approach advocated the use of empirical methods to study human behaviour. (3) The third approach is the Gestalt approach which takes a holistic approach to the study of human behaviour.

Psychology is further divided into various specializations — clinical psychology, abnormal psychology, industrial psychology, counselling psychology, developmental psychology and sports psychology. While much of psychology is descriptive and analytical in nature, psychology is also a practice profession. A variety of agencies employ psychologists for work related to recruitment, counselling and training. Clinical psychology provides diagnosis to mental disorders and prescribes therapies for their cure. The area of social worker and the clinical psychologist overlaps even in other areas like child development and there are common areas of concern also. Often social work and psychology expand their perspective spheres of influence.

Along with sociology, psychology had a major influence on the social work profession. The emergence of Freud's psychoanalytical approach gave a major impetus to case work in the earlier part of the twentieth century due to the following reasons:

1. Case work in its initial stages was an ordinary method which needed only common sense and logical thinking to practice. The psychoanalytical approach gave it an established (medical) base on which it could develop into a specialized method.
2. The need for knowledge to explain difficult phenomena with which practice was involved.
3. The entrance into the general culture of psychoanalytical ideas.
4. Political and economic contexts that, time to time, emphasized individual culpability over social justice and societal responsibility (Reamer 1983, quoted by Germain in Reamer, 1997).

Social workers trained in this skill extended the clientele of social work profession from the poor to middle class and the rich classes. Social work profession's total identification with poor, destitute and the disabled was reduced when clients from other section of the society started using their services. Most of these clients were well off and were part of the mainstream of the society. They mainly suffered from psychological ailments rather than from poverty. Thus social work came to be seen as a helping profession rather than solely caring for the poor. This new role of the social work was also better paying than those on other positions. Even now the categories of social work professionals who are the highest incomes are who offer individual and privatized care to their clients.

Psychology contributed a number of techniques to social work profession:

1. Behaviour modification theories, psychoanalysis techniques like dream analysis etc.
2. Child development with emphasis on role expectation at every stage.
3. Abnormal psychology and the various classifications of mental illness.
4. Counselling psychology.

Social worker often used these techniques in their practice to increase their effectiveness. But social work engagement with psychology has its critics. The adoption of psychology methods removed social work from its original mission of helping the poor (Dominelli, 2002, Wootton, 1959:271 quoted in Lymbery, 2005: 40). Further, this view also influenced the way social work saw the problems of society. Seeing social problems as being created due to the individual's incapacity diminished the part unjust social structures played in perpetuating injustices.

Medicine and Social Work

The social work had a strong presence in the health sector. Consequently, knowledge about the various diseases, their causes, diagnosis and cure are necessary for the social worker. Social workers should be aware of the social implication of these illnesses. The impact on the family, the resources available to the client, governmental and non-governmental resources available to support the client are areas of concern for the social workers.

Psychiatry and Social Work

Psychiatry is the diagnosis and treatment of psychological disorders. Psychiatric social workers are specially trained social workers skilled in interviewing, in assembling family histories of their clients and assessing social factors involved in psychological disorders (Clifford *et al.*, 1999). Social work and psychiatry have close relation, as one vary important area of intervention in social work is the mental health field. Social work gained a significant amount of information from psychiatry-types of mental illness, their classification, causes, effects and treatment methods. They rely on medical model, sometimes called disease model, which seeks to explain mental illness through organic and biomedical causes (Golightlry, 2004: 22). Consequently, psychiatrists deal with the biological and medical aspects of mental illness. They diagnose the illness and prescribe the necessary medication for the problem. Though the medical model is frequently used and accepted by the medical fraternity and the public at large its effectiveness has been contested.

Social workers on the other hand deal with social aspects of the illness. They mobilize resources within the community to support the patient. It may be a job from the recovered person or getting funds for his livelihood. Social worker will also help his family cope with the difficult situation they find themselves in. Social worker views the mentally ill as a total person rather than a patient. The cooperation of social worker, psychiatrist and other health professionals are needed for the holistic treatment of the patients. In USA, the American Psychiatric Association, earlier known as Association of Superintendents of American Institutions of the Insane, looks after the curative and rehabilitative needs of the mentally ill. There is no similar body in India as of now.

History and Social Work

In simple terms, history is the record of past events. However, history has been able to discover underlying forces that have influenced those events. History is divided into following specializations—political history, social history, and economic history, history of ideas and world history. For social work, history is very important because the new methods in historiography have enabled us to go beyond the approaches that have been seen earlier. This has allowed new light to be thrown on some of the problems that the profession is facing today.

Public Administration and Social Work

According to Luther Gulick, "public administration is that part of the science of administration which has to do with the government and thus concerns itself primarily with the executive branch where the governance is done." Public administration is also a discipline that studies the functioning of this part of the government. Public administration has many branches but Social work is concerned with welfare administration as it deals with the provision of social welfare services and correctional services.

The scope of social welfare administration is: (1) the analysis of social problem and determining the administrative response to the problem, (2) the planning and execution of social services, (3) organizing social security programmes, (4) administering social welfare agencies, and (5) formulation of social policies.

The discipline of social welfare administration includes the study of organisational and administrative structure at the various levels—local, regional, state, national and international; the role of social welfare administration at different levels; Financial administration; Personnel administration; Public relations; Administrative task, like-vision building, planning, coordinating, control, communication etc.; research and evaluation (Sachdeva, 2003: 97). Further, social workers are increasingly aware that participation in the formulation of policies is an important means to bring about social change in line with their values. Policy science is itself a multidisciplinary subject, which deals with how policies are made and how policy analysis can be done. The knowledge about both these aspects are important to the social worker. The need for participation in policy formulation has made knowledge about social policy important.

Law and Social Work

There is a close relationship between social work and law. These are as follows:

(1) In many countries especially in the Western countries, social work has a special status and social worker has been given statutory powers to intervene in selected areas of social life, for example—the family to protect children or prevent domestic violence.
(2) Due to scandals in the social services regulation through law has increased in these areas.
(3) The limitations in law and the legal system has made it difficult for common people to get justice. Social workers have understood this chronic malady afflicting the legal system. Therefore, law has an ever increasing importance in social work education as well as professional service (Cull and Roche, 2001; 12).

Another important development that has made law important for social work is the emergence of human rights based practice. (Johns, Roberts, 2005: 20).

The need for knowledge of law is of paramount importance to the Indian social worker. Indian social legislations are often attempts to bridge the gulf between consensual values and their apparent incongruence with prevailing patterns of behaviour. It creates a legal framework for the new situations and provides opportunities for change in the desired direction (Gangrade and Batra, 1987: 72).

Social workers need the knowledge of law when they perform their roles as counsellors. Secondly, social worker as mentioned earlier performs a number of quasi-judicial functions in the correctional field, childcare, adoption and mental health field. Thirdly, in developing countries like in India the social worker need the knowledge of law to protect the poor from the misuse of law by the powerful. PIL is a tool to ensure rights to those whose rights are violated.

Hence, the social work has to get a basic understanding and knowledge of the following:

(1) Constitution with special emphasis on rights and directive principles.
(2) Legal aid.
(3) Legislations related to marriage, divorce, maintenance, adoption and succession.
(4) Special legislations to protect disadvantaged sections like: Dowry Prohibition Act, People with Disabilities Act, Prevention of atrocities of SCs & STs, Juvenile Justice Act.
(5) Public Interest Litigation.
(6) Basic procedures related to arrest, bail, first information report, charge sheet etc.

Philosophy, Ethics and Social Work

Social work is a value-based profession that deals with the life of human beings. Hence its relationship with philosophy especially moral philosophy is very important. Moral philosophy also called ethics, aims at determining 'what ought to be' in any given situation. In simple words, it helps in distinguishing right from wrong. The study of Ethics can be divided into three: (a) Meta ethics that deals with the ultimate questions of human life. What can be called good? What should be the basis of all decisions? (b) Normative ethics deals with how Meta ethics can be formed into principles that can govern the social life. (c) Applied ethics is applying this knowledge to everyday life situation. Social workers work with human beings and with human relationships. Often social workers are confronted with decisions that have to be ethically sound. The end cannot justify the means. Ethics provides the basis for the right action towards the client. Large sections are increasingly becoming aware of their rights and value systems are constantly changing. Different perspectives and often contradicting opinions are available on different issues based on beliefs in values. For example, on abortion there are number of perspectives and the question arises which is the correct approach.

Ethical problems and dilemmas in professional worker exist in three forms: (a) issues related to individual welfare and rights, (b) issues around public welfare, and (c) issues related to inequality and structural oppression (Banks, 2001: 11-12).

Social work's professional bodies formulate ethics for its members. It regulates the relationship between the professional and the client, professional and fellow professionals, professional and the society (NASW Code of Ethics). Social work will increasingly depend on philosophy and ethics to answer new questions and resolve dilemmas arising in the profession due to new issues like—same sex marriage, euthanasia, cloning and stem cell use.

Economics and Social Work

Economics is the study of how the goods and services we want get produced and how they are distributed among the society. Economics has a number of branches—agricultural economics, development economics, financial economics, industrial economics etc. Economic policy is how the system of production and distribution works better. No area of society is free from the influence of economic policy. Many issues related to social work like—income, poverty, unemployment, migration are directly related to the economic situation. Social worker has to understand the situation, has to adopt a thorough analysis of the situation which often includes the study of economic factors. Often individual and relationship problems have its root in the economic condition that in turn is created by factors beyond the control of people affected by it. For example, unemployment can increase tendency to divorce and depression. Amartya Sen's concept of entitlements and Mahbub-ul-Haq's Human Development Index (HDI) have given social work a sound basis for the provision of services to individuals. It has clear evidence that these measures are not only the rights of the people but has benefits for the whole society.

Interdisciplinary Relationships

Professionals, paraprofessionals, and volunteers from disciplines other than social work are part of the environments our clients live in, and because social workers focus on the interaction between people and their environments, we must work effectively with people from other disciplines if we are to effectively serve our clients. Learning to work effectively with other disciplines can be a challenge. Each discipline has its own set of assumptions, values, and priorities, and these differences can easily lead to uncoordinated services, or, even worse, to resources being spent on interdisciplinary conflict.

There are many different models of interdisciplinary relationships. Competition and conflict are two examples that are easy to conceptualize. The model most consonant with social work values is collaboration. Collaboration may be defined as working together. It connotes that collaborators share power and that they each contribute special knowledge or skills. Smith (1985) highlights the distinction by using the terms multidisciplinary and interdisciplinary, the former to refer to many disciplines working in the same setting and the latter to refer to members of those disciplines working together as a team. Although this distinction is not standard in the literature, it is a useful distinction.

When individuals from various professions work together day-to-day in one setting, they often think of themselves as forming an interdisciplinary team, and yet interdisciplinary teams may function in other ways. For example, a group of individuals from various disciplines may meet periodically or episodically to review critical incidents. They are an interdisciplinary team even though they do not work together everyday. Similarly, an ethics committee typically consists of individuals from various disciplines and may even include members external to the organisation to assure representation of diverse views. This too is an interdisciplinary team.

And social workers frequently form both brief and ongoing interdisciplinary relationships that do not constitute team practice but that are nevertheless necessary for effective service. Relationships with police officers, probation officers, attorneys, and judges are interdisciplinary in nature. Similarly, relationships with teachers, school administrators, and playground supervisors may be necessary for effective practice. To practice effectively, social workers must be prepared to work with all of the individuals in the client's environment. The focus of this brief review is on relationships with allied health professionals, not because those relationships are most important, but because those have been examined most in the professional literature.

Social work knowledge is influenced by and in turn influences other disciplines. Cheung (1990) reviewed interdisciplinary contributions in professional journals from 1981 to 1985. The top five disciplines cited in social work journals were social work, family studies, psychiatry, sociology, and education. If clinical psychology, psychology, developmental psychology, educational psychology, social psychology, and applied psychology had been counted together, they would have placed second after social work as the source of citations. The same article showed that social work was cited most in social work, education, family studies, clinical psychology, and psychiatry. These findings demonstrate strong interdisciplinary relationships in professional knowledge, and suggest not only considerable overlap in knowledge but also the potential for significant ideas from one discipline to influence another.

Abramson and Mizrahi (1996) examined the characteristics of physicians and social workers identified as important in collaborative relationships. Those rated most important by social workers were, respect for collaborator, similar perspectives, positive quality of communication, social worker's role well understood by physician, and amount of communication was positive. Those items rated as most important by physicians were: the social worker was capable, positive quality of communication, respect for the physician, similar perspectives, and the social worker kept the physician informed.

Abramson and Mizrahi reported that the most common negative variables for social workers were: dissimilar perspectives, poor quality of communication, physician's negative style, lack of respect for the social worker, and negative personal traits of the physician. They reported the most frequent negative variables for physicians were: dissimilar perspectives, amount of communication was inadequate, social worker's feedback was not timely, social worker did not keep the physician informed, and poor quality of communication.

A synthesis of those findings suggests that relationship variables are more important to social workers and that amount, timeliness, and content of communication are more important to physicians.

According to Sullivan (1998), the medical literature on collaboration is extensive. It appears to be most extensive for relationships between physicians and nurses. She cites five attributes as contributing most to an effective partnership: respecting each other, communication, working together, partnership relationship, and trusting each other. She also reports on similar terms and related concepts that illuminate the idea of collaboration: joint practice, shared governance, coalition, cooperation, collegial, working together, teamwork, interdependence, and professionalism.

These ideas suggest that important information about collaboration may be found in management literature that focuses on organisational environments and their contributions to organisational effectiveness, and it makes sense that collaboration can occur most effectively in an environment that supports it. Interdisciplinary teams can occur with a variety of relationships. Creating interdisciplinary collaboration is a goal for social workers to strive for.

Smith (1985) identifies benefits of interdisciplinary team practice: improved organisational effectiveness, improved service to clients, synergistic effects, learning from other disciplines, mutual support, and team maturation as it grows from interdisciplinary tension. Schofield and Amodeo (1999) list the benefits of increased awareness of one's own discipline, more respect and understanding of other disciplines, opportunity for cooperative research, and development of a cooperative mind-set.

They cite additional benefits of improved access to care, improved patient efficacy in self-care, improved role satisfaction for practitioners, reduction in length-of-stay and premature admissions, increased use of team members to meet varied needs, relieved burden for team members, facilitated work with difficult patients, and improved objectivity.

Smith goes on to discuss the importance of role boundaries, role maintenance, role clarity, and role overlap. Good social work practice suggests that these issues be openly discussed among team members. Similarly, obstacles to effective team functioning should be identified and openly discussed. Schofield and Amodeo identify problems in teams that may merit attention: differing status among team members, unequal benefits for participation, variability in the organisation and administration of each discipline that contribute to tension, different levels of personal commitment, disparate jargon and technologies, physician dominance, role confusion and blurring, increased time demands, insecurity about the value of the team approach, shift in professional status among disciplines, and lack of administrative support. They cite additional difficulties: competition for clients, disagreements over leadership and authority, lack of a common value base, frequent rotation of some disciplines, unclear definition of team leader's role, inadequate patient care, ineffective and inefficient communication, and lack of consensus on the prognosis of some clients.

Conclusion

Social work is a practice profession. The first and foremost aim of the social work is to help the clients. The three factors that determine the quality of the professional service, that the social workers, provide, are knowledge, skill and attitude. Knowledge means the capacity to understand, skill is the capacity to perform and attitude is characteristic response to the individual towards an issue. Knowledge is important as it improves the personal ability to comprehend and analyse while skill helps in the delivery of services. Other disciplines have contributed to the knowledge and skill of the social worker. The concepts, theories and ideologies have helped the social worker to go beyond the obvious and to establish cause and affect relationship. Social work knowledge comes from a wider range of sources which includes precedent, experience and common sense. However, social work should and does adapt the various theories to its practice (Young, 1964: 124; Payne, 1997: 39). Often these theories lose their relation with the larger theoretical framework from which it had evolved which is not of great concern for the social worker. He often uses the most suitable means to achieve his objective. This eclecticism has contributed to the effectiveness of the methods. The major methods of social work are its original tools for practice—case workgroup work and community organisation. Knowledge creation for the sake of knowledge is not the aim of social work. In any case there is a growing realization that single disciplinary approach is narrow and limiting. Theoretical subjects like sociology and history are adopting the multidisciplinary approach to study their respective areas of study. It is not uncommon to find historians using the methods of sociology and *vice versa*. The interaction between political science and sociology has resulted in a growing area of study—political sociology. When the theoretical subjects are moving in this direction, social work need not be apologetic about amount their use of knowledge about other disciplines.

Alex Flexner in 1915 termed social work as not qualifying as a profession as it does not have a knowledge base of its own. But over the years social work has accumulated large amount of knowledge. Although it has been accepted that there is no universally accepted theories, but social work as a practicing profession has been able to prove its worth by empowering people to help themselves with the understanding derived from other disciplines.

References

Abramson, J. and Mizrahi, T. (2017). "When social workers and physicians collaborate: Positive and negative interdisciplinary experiences", *Social Work* 41(3), 270–282. Retrieved from https://www.csub.edu/~bhartsell/InterdisciplinaryRealtionships.html

Banks, S. (2001), *Ethics and Values in Social Work*, New York: Palgrave.

Cheung, K. (1990). "Interdisciplinary relationships between social work and other disciplines: A citation study", *Social work research and abstracts* 26(3): 23–30. Retrieved from https://www.csub.edu/~bhartsell/InterdisciplinaryRealtionships.html

Cull Lesley-Anne and Rochs, *The Law and Social Work,* New York: Palgrave.

Desai, M. (2002). *Ideologies and Social Work, History and Contemporary Analyses,* New Delhi: Rawat Publications.

Dominelli, L. (1997). *Sociology for Social Worker,* New York: Palgrave.

Dominelli, L. (2002). *Social Work,* London: Polity Press.

Encyclopaedia of Social Work (1987). New Delhi: Publications Division.

Friedlander, W. (1967). *Introduction to Social Welfare,* Second Edition, New Delhi: Prentice Hall of India (Private) Limited.

Gensler, H. (1988). *Ethics: A Contemporary Introduction,* London: Routledge.

Johns, R. (2006). *Using the Law in Social Work, Learning Matters, Exeter.*

Lymbery, M. (2005), *Social Work with Older People: Context, Policy and Practice,* London: Sage Publications.

Morgan, C.T. and others. (1993). *Introduction to Psychology,* New Delhi: Tata McGraw-Hill.

Payne, M. (1997). *Modern Social Work Theory,* New York: Palgrave.

Reamer, G. Frederic (ed.) (1994). *The Foundations of Social Work Knowledge,* New York, Columbia University Press.

Sachdeva, D.R. (2004). *Social Welfare Administration in India,* Allahabad: Kitab Mahal.

Schofield, R. and Amodeo, M. (1999). "Interdisciplinary teams in healthcare and human service settings: Are they effective?" *Health and social work* 24(3): 210–219. Retrieved from https://www.csub.edu/~bhartsell/InterdisciplinaryRealtionships.html

Smith, N. (1985). "Social work in team practice", In P.J. Lecca and J.S. McNeil (Eds.), *Interdisciplinary Team Practice: Issues and Trends* (pp. 97 123). New York, NY: Praeger Publishers. Retrieved from https://www.csub.edu/~bhartsell/InterdisciplinaryRealtionships. html

Sullivan, T. (1998). *Collaboration: A Health Care Imperative.* New York: NY: McGraw-Hill.

University of Washington, School of Medicine (n.d.). *Interdisciplinary team issues.* Retrieved April 16, 2002 from http://eduserv.hscer.washington.edu/bioethics/topics/team.html

Varghese, Joseph (2010). *Social Work and Its Relationship to other Disciplines.* New Delhi: IGNOU Press.

World Census of Social Work Education, 1998-1999, International Association of Social Work.

Younghusband, E. (1964), *Social Work and Social Change,* London: George Allen and Unwin Ltd.

3

Social Work in India

From Charity to Human Rights

Sayantani Guin

Introduction

Social work in India has existed for a long time. In ancient times, social work was done mainly in the form of charity. The roots of social work have been ingrained in various religions like Hinduism, Jainism, Sikhism, Buddhism and Christianity. Many prominent social reformers in the pre, during and post-independence era fought for the upliftment of the poor and the downtrodden. Social Work took a professional meaning with the advent of establishment of institutions imparting social work education. Post-independence, India took up a series of welfare schemes which broadened the scope of work for social workers. A lot of non-governmental organisations also initiated various development programmes in the fields of health, nutrition, rural development, recreation and education catering to the needs of children, women, rural poor, physically and mentally challenged people, and others in need of care and support. In the current scenario, the social work profession has also seen human rights defenders and activists who work for the protection and promotion of human rights of people. This chapter will throw light upon the transition of the concept of social work in India from charity, reform, welfare, social work as a profession and concerned mainly with the human rights.

Charity

The concept of charity goes back to ancient times. Remnants of the pre-Vedic period are marked with the age of invention. The Harappan and Mohenjodaro culture and later the Indus valley civilization depict a people friendly society with a high level of dignity and respect for women.

In the Vedic period, references to charity have been found in *Rigveda, Samveda, Yazurveda* and *Atharvaveda*. Hindu scriptures, viz. *Mahabharata, Bhagawad Geeta*, Upanishads considered charity as morality and duty and was performed as service to God. It was a moral duty of the priviledged class to serve the poor. It was considered a sin not to give alms to the poor. The 'Pathshala' mode of education emphasized the need for effective listening, which is today considered as one of the essential skills in social work profession.

Another form of social service in ancient India, particularly in the Vedic period was in the form of *Yagnas*. *Yagna* literally means "sacrifice, devotion, worship, offering", and refers to any ritual done in front of a sacred fire, often with *mantras*. Each individual tries to contribute his/her bit towards *yagna*, with the sole intention of common welfare of all. Society functioned as an extended family where everyone's need was taken care by everybody and assistance was mutual (Rampal, 2009).

During the late Vedic period and after, with the development of agrarian society, private ownership of land and class rule came into existence. Earlier, there was common ownership of property by the community. *Dana* (charity) was a kind of social insurance and was a matter of right for the sick, aged and the weak. After the concept of the private property emerged, charity became a voluntary virtue of the kings and the *Kshatriyas*. *Dana* was no longer given in connection with a ceremony, but became a common act of acquiring *punya* (merit).

The evolution of Buddhism during the Mauryan Empire emphasized on peace, dignity and right to livelihood. Charity was considered not only as alleviating the suffering of poor but also as giving of gift to *sanghas*. *Sanghas* were centres of shelter and learning. Also, there were guilds, important corporate organisations which performed welfare functions by setting aside a part of their funds for the welfare of the poor and downtrodden.

The Mauryan king Ashoka, undertook a wide range of welfare activities, which included women's welfare, rehabilitation of prisoners, rural development, free medical care, regulation of prostitution and provision of public utilities like roads, rest houses for travellers, wells etc. Similarly another king, Kanishka, gave donations and grants for the construction of Buddhist monasteries which were the centres of learning and provided help to the needy. During the Gupta period too, welfare of the people was the main motto of the rulers.

Charity is also seen during the Sultanate period and during the Mughal rule. One of the notable kings, Akbar, brought many reforms in the society, viz. equality irrespective of class and religion, and freedom of religion. Money and land was granted for the benefit of Hindus, Jains, Parsees etc. and there was a comprehensive system of poor relief.

In the medieval period, caste system and the joint family system took care of the needy. In caste system, occupations were hereditary and the land owning people took care of the service-giving people in times of distress by offering grants or credits. The joint family system catered to the needs of the aged, widows, orphans and the handicapped.

Charity was channeled through religious institutions and giving was institutionalized. Individuals and communities provided temples and *mutts* with lands. Income from these properties was used to provide one meal to the poor. This system was called *sadavrata*. Sometimes, meals were offered in remembrance of forefathers (Gore, 1965). However, people who were really destitute took to begging.

During the 16th and 17th centuries, the colonial rule was more prevalent. There was a large scale and severe famines which affected the country, leading to widespread starvation and death. There was a need to cater to a huge population of needy and destitute. However, the traditional methods of individual and religious charity prevailed. There was no effort of prevention and mitigation of destitution by the state. There was neither any institutional facility, nor any agency exclusive for the administration of relief.

During the 19th century, the British introduced a uniform system of administration and judiciary, which weakened the stronghold of the local village council, which were unable to impose traditional obligations. In the midst of famines, there was economic insecurity and political defeat which replaced community cooperation with rivalry and mutual distrust. However, the British rule influenced the idea of equality leading many people questioning the negative impacts of the caste system and the position of women in the society (Gore, 1965).

Social Reform

During the 19th century itself, major reform activities began which questioned the ill effects of caste system, and promoted abolition of *sati*, promotion of widow remarriage, education and rehabilitation of the young widow. Social reform movements have a direct consequence in shaping social work in India as it reflects the concerns and sufferings of the underpriviledged group.

During this century, some of the major social reform movements were abolition of *sati*, promotion of widow remarriage, education and rehabilitation of the young widow. Some of the notable social reformers of this period were Raja Rammohun Roy, Iswar Chandra Vidyasagar, Sasipada Banerjee, Ranade, Telag, Lokahitawadi Deshmukh, Bhandarkar, D.K. Karve etc. The various reform movements were also accompanied by acts of social service. After the series of famines that hit the country during the later part of the 18th centrury, Christian Missionaries had already started relief work in the form of relief camps, orphanages, destitute homes etc. These activities were also taken up simultaneously by the reform movements (Gore, 2011).

Jyotiba Phule of Maharashtra revolted against the caste system and upheld the cause of untouchables. Chattrapati Shahu Maharaj's greatest contribution was in the direction of education. Sri Narayan Guru from Kerala, worked for the upliftment of the backward classes, especially the Ezhava community (Dash, 2010).

The reform movements promoted education for boys and girls by establishing schools, which during 1830s and 1840s were no less than act of social service as education was the basic need of the country (Gore, 2011). Apart from schools, orphanages, homes for the widows, aged and the destitute, were also established.

The reform movements through their acts of social service began a phase of institutional care for the needy. Individuals who earlier donated to *mutts* and religious endowments gradually started donating to these institutions. This was the first time that a system of specialized institutions were established, where a group of individuals devoted their time for the organisation and management of these institutions, which took exclusive responsibility for the care of the needy. Thus, the earlier acts of individual charity and outdoor relief by temples and *mutts* were gradually taken over by the social service institutions. However, religious and individual charity continued and it continues even today, but those did not remain the only and main channels for taking responsibility of the needy.

Apart from institutional care, charitable trusts and funds were established during the later half of the 19th century, which provided scholarships and organised cash relief to the poor. However, these were restricted to particular castes or to particular religious communities (Gore, 2011). There was this phenomenon more prevalent in urban India.

During the 20th century, few reformers like B.R. Ambedkar, fondly remembered as chief architect of the Constitution of India, fought for the equal status of the lower castes and untouchables. Sardar Vallabhbhai Patel, through his political involvement, worked for the empowerment of the poor, particularly the peasants. Amrutlal V. Thakkar, popularly known as Thakkar Bapa, worked relentlessly for the upliftment of tribals, and organised cooperative societies for the sweepers and scavengers in Pune and Schools for the children of labourers in Ahmedabad. Vinoba Bhave started the *Bhoodan* (land gift) movement, for which he toured almost the whole of India on foot to motivate landlords to voluntarily donate land to the landless. Sir Syed Ahmed Khan propagated for the Western scientific education of the Muslims and opened various schools in several villages and towns to encourage modern education (Dash, 2010).

Mahatma Gandhi started the community development model, which emphasized the concept of self-sufficient village economy through the revival of the village panchayats. Apart from the problems of the community as a whole, Gandhi also worked for the women, untouchables and the tribal populations of India, who were the specially disadvantaged group within the community. Simultaneously, the number of social institutions multiplied which now provided services for not only the orphan, widow and the aged, but also for the physically handicapped, the beggars, the unmarried mothers, delinquents, mentally challenged and after the post-Independence period, the refugees.

During the first half of the 20th century, apart from the expansion in the social service institutions, the need for training and preparation for social work was accepted. The concept of preparing an individual for a life of social service had existed earlier, in the form of apprenticeship, which was commonly found in the missions where a novice was apprenticed under the guidance of a senior priest or *swami* for a considerable period of time. But formal education in social work was first organised by the Social Service League in the erstwhile Bombay in the 1920s in the form of a short training course. However, this training was meant for voluntary service, and not for a paid position or for a profession. So far, even though individual agencies had paid employees, but they were not called social workers.

Some of the notable social reformers of post-Independence include Baba Amte, Mother Teresa, Medha Patkar, Sunderlal Bahuguna etc. Baba Amte worked relentlessly for rehabilitation of leprosy victims and making efforts towards national integration. Mother Teresa, a catholic nun, was recently crowned 'Saint' for her inexorable work for the poor and downtrodden. She was awarded the Nobel Peace Prize in 1979. Medha Patkar started the Narmada Bachao Andolan and voiced for the cause of the peasant, tribal, *dalits* and labour movements. Sunderlal Bahuguna, an environmentalist, worked for the preservation of forests in the Himalayas as a member of the Chipko Movement. He generated pressure for a national forest policy and preservation of the country's ecology.

It may be noted that the social reformers of the past and the present have been applying social work methods like community organisation, social action, and case work etc. Medha Patkar herself has been a trained social worker from TISS. They have also been successfully working for the cause of empowering people.

Emergence of Professional Social Work and Social Work Education

The need for granting professional status to social work emerged in the West around 1890s among the workers of the Charity Organisation Society (COS) due to variety of reasons as follows (Lobo, 2012):

1. The professional status of medicine and engineering had demonstrated practical solutions to many problems.
2. A professional recognition would enable worker establish their work deserving a decent wage.
3. A full-fledged profession would motivate educated women wanting careers in social work.
4. Education and training were required to deal with complex problems of people.

In India, it was in 1936, social work as an education was started with the establishment of Sir Dorabji Tata Graduate School of Social Work, currently named as Tata Institute of Social Sciences (TISS), in Mumbai by Sir Clifford Manshardt. With the introduction of social work education, the concept of social work, which so far was equated with charity, welfare and unorganised services on a voluntary basis, was now seen as a professional activity with specialized knowledge and skill. Initially social work education was introduced at the post-graduation level. Gradually, a number of institutes, viz. Kashi Vidyapeeth, Delhi School of Social Work, Visva-Bharati University etc. started offering social work education at the masters and bachelors level.

The idea of a profession in social work implied the practice of specialized skills, techniques and methods. The role of professional social workers include case management, medical social work, counselling, community organizing, advocacy, teaching, social science research, human service management so on and so forth. Professional social workers find employment opportunities in a variety of sectors ranging from non-governmental organisations, governmental organisations (e.g. welfare officers in factories and prisons), hospitals, hospices, grassroots advocacy organisations, community health agencies, faith based organisations etc. (Rampal, 2009).

The First Review Committee for Social Work Education was set up in 1960 and the Second Review Committee for Social Work Education was set up in 1975 by the University Grants Commission for the promotion, maintenance of standards of education, coordination of social work education, training, research and practice. The Third Review Committee, set up in 2001, emphasized on relating social work education to the social realities (Pandey, 2010).

The first University to offer Social Work Education in the open and distance learning mode is the Indira Gandhi National Open University (IGNOU), which started with offering Bachelor Degree in Social Work in 2004. Currently, MSW and MSW (Counselling) courses are also offered through ODL (Pandey, 2010).

Generalist Social Work

With the emergence of social work education, the term generalist social work gained prominence. Earlier, social workers were committed for help of the marginalized and poorest groups in society. Gradually, as per the need of time, various specialized social work activities emerged, e.g. war situation created the need for psychiatric social work for people suffering from psychological problems. The demands of the field practice also led to the emergence of specializations like social work with family and child, prison inmates etc. Later, various methods of social work developed, viz. case work, group work, community organisation, social action, social welfare administration and social work research. Since 1920s, the generic-specialization controversy has existed where the former group views social workers with a macro orientation whose skills and knowledge can be applied to various settings. The other group, on the other hand, views that specialized knowledge and skills are required for specific needs of people. There have been efforts to unify the two viewpoints. Majority of social work institutions offering social work education follow the specialization pattern of training.

The idea of generalist social work focuses on the fact that the problems of individuals cannot exist in isolation as human beings are a part of the social and physical environment. Thus social work interventions may spread across a broad spectrum of addressing individual needs to social justice to social policies. In India, the need for culturally relevant social work practice and indigenization was felt and some social work educational institutions revamped social work education syllabus which included subjects such as social action, integrated social work practice, communication and social policy.

With the advent of globalization, social work practice areas have broadened to various other issues like peace, assertion of ethnic identity, ecology, human survival etc. In India, social workers have to address the needs of the traditional feudal society on one hand, and on the other hand the needs arising out of the impact of technological changes.

Generalist social work practice has wide applicability as it can be applicable to all settings, locations and groups of people. A variety of perspectives, viz. systems, ecological, eco-systems perspective, practice theories and sources of information are sought to apply for a wide variety of interventions. It is problem solving process which integrates policy and research. Social workers need to apply appropriate skills in specific situations. Social workers can directly work with individuals, groups and communities and indirectly practice with agencies, institutions and systems by engaging with professionals from other disciplines for problem solving (Narayan, 2012).

The Welfare Approach in Social Work

In a Welfare State, the State has to take care of the people in the form of provision of food, clothing, shelter and medical treatment. Post-Independence, the Government took various measures for the welfare of its citizens. Emphasis was placed on addressing the existing needs and challenges of the era. The scope of social work practice broadened with the expansion of the welfare activities, economy and the service sectors.

The country adopted various welfare and development initiatives by implementing schemes and measures for various sectors through the formulation of the five year plans.

For labour welfare, the Government of India enacted various legislations, viz. Factories Act, 1948, Labour Act, 1951 and Mines Act, 1952, which set standards for health, safety, welfare, employment of young persons and children, working hours for adult and child worker, holidays, leave with wages etc. It was for the first time that the professional social worker was given due recognition in the field of labour welfare. Social welfare officer having qualifications in Social Work, Social Welfare or Social Science were appointed as per the provisions of these Acts.

The Government of India enacted the Scheduled Castes and Scheduled Tribes Act (Prevention of Atrocities) Act, 1989 to integrate the tribal people into mainstream. The provision of Special Officer, whose duties are in tunes to the attributes of a professional social worker, was made.

In the field of rural development, people's participation was emphasized and various Community Development projects were launched, viz. National Extension Service (1953), Intensive Agricultural Development Programme (1964), Intensive Agricultural Area Programme, Tribal Area Development (1972) etc. Panchayati Raj Institutions were created under the 73rd Amendment Act, 1992. At present, the Ministry of Rural Development has been implementing various programmes relating to rural development, drinking water and land resources. All these programmes are in tune with the methods of Community Organisation, Community Development and Social Welfare Administration of the Social Work Practice.

Major health facilities in the form of setting up of primary health centres and district hospitals, training of community health workers etc. were initiated by the Government. Focus was given on the eradication of communicable diseases, strengthening of basic health services, population control and development of health during the five year plans. The need of a trained social worker specialized in the field of medical and psychiatric social work was felt and social workers were appointed in many hospitals.

Child welfare assumed a broader meaning with the aim of all round growth and development of all children, not only for the care of maladjusted, destitute and delinquents, but also for the physical, emotional and intellectual development of children. The Constitution provides for free and compulsory education for children till the age of 14 years, non-employment of children in hazardous employment, abolition of child labour, health immunization, raising the level of nutrition and standard of living.

Several youth welfare programmes have been floated to promote youth leadership, sports, training camps, students study tours and non-students clubs and centres. The young Men's Christian Association and the Young Women's Christian Association provide opportunities for games, recreation and social activities. Leadership amongst youth, helping them realize their potential and confidence building were encouraged.

The other areas of social work practice included work with refugees and victims of partition. In this regard, the Government provided them economic assistance, housing and education facilities. The Ministry of Education provided financial assistance for the establishment of Schools of Social Work at different regions of the country. It promotes research in the field of social work by providing students with scholarships. Several bodies have been set up under the Ministry of Human Resource Development to look into the secondary education and higher education system.

The scope of social workers have been recognized in the correctional settings as well. The Government has taken initiatives for improving the correctional services and prison administration, juvenile delinquency, suppression of immoral traffic, programmes of aftercare etc.

From the above, it may be stated that professional social work has been rooted in all the welfare approaches and there is ample scope and opportunity in the current scenario for a social worker to work. The Government has been relying on several social welfare organisations to implement many of its schemes and programmes. Trained social workers have been employed in these welfare organisations to serve all sections of the population. Thus, the scope of social work in the current scenario has drastically enlarged (Pandey *et al.*, 2010).

Social Work and Social Policy

Social Work practice evolved in another area where the role of social workers extended towards nation building and national development. After independence, India aimed for national development by drafting various policies, which would guide for planning, organizing, implementing and evaluating various components necessary for development. According to Concise Oxford Dictionary, a policy is a "settled course of action adopted and followed by a government or a political party." The Constitution of India, in its Directive Principles of State Policy, has reiterated the welfare of its citizens in their social, economic and political life. Justice to all and inclusion of sections of the society have been emphasized and proposed in the several five year plans.

Social Workers have been engaged in the policy framing activity of the country. Framing of social policy include a series of discussions with a wide range of stakeholders like planners, bureaucrats, voluntary organisations, academicians, politicians and other experts. Social workers, by virtue of their knowledge of the grassroots and experience of working with the people have been considered such experts. Several schools of Social Work and institutions have helped in policy formulation in the areas of education, housing and slum development, adoption and child development, family welfare and women's development, youth programmes, police, prisoners, rehabilitation of displaced people etc. Non-governmental organisations have helped in the identification of issues, advocacy, consolidation of expert opinion, implementation and monitoring and evaluation.

Issues are identified by social workers working in NGOs or academic institutions by conducting research studies. Low floor high capacity buses were introduced in Delhi after a study conducted by a NGO found out that the existing buses were not conducive for the use of people with disabilities. However, there are many instances where mere identification of issues does not help. Thus social work practice have also used advocacy and built pressure on the Government to build suitable policies for the upliftment of the vulnerable and weaker sections of the society. The first National Settlement and Rehabilitation Policy was considered after the efforts of noted social activist Medha Patkar. Eminent Social Workers have served as experts in Planning Commission and in the advisory group of the University Grants Commission in developing curriculum. Social work practice also includes implementation of policies by disseminating information and making the provisions of the policy accessible to the public. With the advent of mass media and information technology, information is spread through television, radio, newspapers, and even through social media (Nalini & Bharadwaj, 2010).

Social Workers are directly getting involved with implementation of policies by becoming members of different schemes. For example, social workers are employed as "Development Workers" in ICDS programmes, and as member in Child Welfare Committees under the provision of Juvenile Justice (Care and Protection of Children) Act, 2015. Some of the other legislations which have provisions for the appointment of social workers are the Immoral Traffic and Prevention Act (1956), Probation of Offenders Act (1955) and Protection of Women from Domestic Violence Act, 2005. Social Workers are also part of the monitoring and evaluation team of various schemes and provisions which ensure that services are reaching appropriately to the target group. Monitoring helps in assessing the physical and financial progress in the implementation of schemes. Evaluation ensures periodic assessment of the impact of the scheme and evaluates the strengths and weaknesses of those schemes so that those can be streamlined and improved. Social workers are appointed as team members for the evaluation of services available in children home. Social Workers are also appointed as consultants in national or international level funding organisation like UNICEF, UNDP, NACO etc. who evaluate and prepare reports regarding the effectiveness of the provisions of the policy (Nalini & Bharadwaj, 2010).

Human Rights and Social Work

Various Human Rights movements have existed in different parts of the world. In the 18th and 19th century, the concept of natural rights was put forward by the philosophers in Europe. Natural Rights were defined as rights which belong to a human being by virtue of being born human. Two great revolutions, viz. the American Revolution and French Revolution contributed to the documents titled, the U.S. Declaration of Independence (1776) and the Declaration of the Rights of Man (1789), which contributed to the human rights movement. A number of issues, viz. slavery, brutal working conditions, starvation, child labour etc. were termed as human rights issues during the late 19th and 20th century. The acceptance of human rights and fundamental freedom were explained in the United Nations charter, the Universal Declaration of Human Rights of 1948, the International Covenants on Civil and Political Rights, the International Covenants on Economic, Political and Cultural Rights and the optional protocols of 1966.

In India, efforts for promotion of human rights started before independence. The attempt to give Indian magistrates to try British subjects in criminal cases, as proposed by Ilbert Bill, failed but became one of the reasons for the formation of Indian National Congress. The Indian National Congress worked towards the promotion of human rights by submitting the Declaration of Rights to the British Parliament in 1918, and passed a resolution on Fundamental Rights in 1931. The Indian Civil Liberties Union was formed in 1936. During the Emergency in 1975, suspension of fundamental rights of citizens led many civil liberties organisations to fight for civil and democratic rights. Post-independence, the Protection of Human Rights Act was passed by the Indian Parliament in 1993, under which the National Human Rights Commission was created.

Human Rights thus, enforce the idea that people's needs are to be met because it is their right since every human being is entitled to them. It is the right of every individual to have some basic minimum rights, like right to food, shelter, clothing, employment etc. Without such rights, one cannot live as human beings. A human rights approach propagates fundamental freedom of an individual to utilize his/her full potential and resources in meeting one's needs. A person unable to do so on his/her own calls for professional help and it is here that the job of professional social worker starts. Thus, professional social workers, who are trained and qualified to provide services to people in need, have to do so while recognizing the inherent dignity and worth of individuals (Kohli, 2012).

Social Work and human rights both aim to protect and empower the weak, the poor, the vulnerable and the oppressed. Human rights have been linked to both micro and macro social work practice. Micro practices focus on the "at risk" population, viz. victims of torture, human trafficking, terrorism, refugees of war and mass human rights violations. Macro practice focuses on the "whole population", fields such as political and legal advocacy, education campaigns, researches etc. which have a larger implication.

Social Work practice in India has evolved along with the evolution of the three generations of human rights. The first generation of rights focused on the civil and political rights and formed the basis of social work advocacy in the areas of political advocacy, refugees and immigrants, forensic social work, prison reform, access to legal representation and collaboration with lawyers. The second generation human rights include economic, social and cultural rights. Here social work practice includes areas of direct services involving policy practice and research. This comprises areas such as provision of adequate standards of living, health, housing, education etc. The third generation rights include collective rights such as right to development, clean water etc. Social Work practice is relevant in all the three generations of rights (Androff, 2016). There have been movements by social workers for the gay rights, and the rights of the transgender to vote, which are few examples of the trend in which social work practice have evolved recently.

Conclusion

The chapter attempts to trace the evolution of social work practice in India from charity to human rights. Before Independence, kings and rulers attempted welfare initiatives for the people in the form of relief, protecting families and dependents, sound administrative policies and other welfare measures. The British rule in India introduced a new outlook in thinking among the Indian masses. With the advent of Christian Missionaries and Western education, the scope of social work practice broadened. The Indian social reformers enlightened by liberal ideas and equality of rights, dedicated their lives for the upliftment of the poor and the downtrodden. After independence, with the inclusion of welfare policies and programmes, the field of social work profession widened. Social Work, first introduced as a programme of study in 1936, facilitated people to gain adequate knowledge and skills for social work practice. Social Work education offered through open and distance learning by IGNOU enabled people from remote locations to pursue the course. The trend in social work practice in present times is towards protecting and promoting the rights and dignity of people. Social work has accommodated rights based approaches to all its dimensions and areas of work.

References

Androff, D. (2016). *Practicing Rights, Human Rights-based Approaches to Social Work Practice,* New York: Routledge.

Dash, B.M. (2010). "History of Social Work: Individual Initiatives", In G. Thomas (Ed.), *Origin and Development of Social Work in India.* New Delhi: IGNOU.

Gore, M.S. (1965). *Social Work and Social Work Education,* Jaipur: Rawat Publications.

Gore, M.S. (2011). *Social Work and Social Work Education,* Jaipur: Rawat Publications.

Kohli, A.S. (2012). "Human Rights and Social Work", In S. Singh and S.P. Srivastava (Eds.), *Enclyclopaedia of Social Work in India.* Lucknow: New Royal Book Company.

Lobo, J.T. (2012). "History of Social Work Education around the World and its Current Trends", In S. Singh and S.P. Srivastava (Eds.), *Enclyclopaedia of Social Work in India.* Lucknow: New Royal Book Company.

Nalini, R. and Bharadwaj, T. (2010). "Involvement of Social Workers in National Development", In G. Thomas (Ed.), *Origin and Development of Social Work in India.* New Delhi: IGNOU.

Narayan, L. (2012). "Generalist Social work", In S. Singh and S.P. Srivastava (Eds.), *Enclyclopaedia of Social Work in India.* Lucknow: New Royal Book Company.

Pandey, N.; Gupta, M. and Patel, S. (2010). "History of Social Work: State Initiatives", In G. Thomas (Ed.), *Origin and Development of Social Work in India.* New Delhi: IGNOU.

Rampal, V. (2009). *Social Work and Community Development,* New Delhi: Alfa Publications.

4
A Glance through the History of Social Work in UK & USA

Sheeba Joseph

Introduction

Social work has developed through centuries like all other disciplines. Social Work as a discipline attained a professional status in USA and UK long back and India is still struggling to acknowledge the professional standards of Social Work profession. It was developed through the practice of charity, philanthropy, social service and welfare measures. In this chapter it is attempted to trace the evolution of social work in the United Kingdom (UK) and the United States of America (USA) to understand the sprouts of professional social work. All the Social Workers should first try to understand the genesis of Social Work before going into the nitty-gritty of the profession. This chapter will help the reader to understand how social work as a profession evolved and the developmental milestones from charity to professional approach has come into force. The first section explains about the genesis of Social Work in UK and the subsequent part will highlight the development in USA.

History of Social Work in UK

In the medieval period in England like other countries, it was the moral obligation of the church to help the poor and the needy. People were helping and giving alms to the people who were destitute, specially abled and the underprivileged out of religious sentiments. The basic objective of this charity was the refinement of the soul. The poors were divided into two categories: able-bodied and the destitute in the beginning of the fourteenth century. In 1349, King Edward III issued the statute of labourers which compelled the able-bodied to work for their livelihood. This statute made a provision for those able-bodied who have no means must work under a master who should be willing to employ them. A direction of not to leave the parish was also given and those who violated were given rigorous punishment.

Another remarkable direction of assistance for the poor was done in 1531 when Henry VIII made a law known as Statute of Henry VIII. The statute directed the strict scrutiny of application of deprived who are aged and unable to do any work by the judges and the priest. The law asked them to register themselves and take the licence to beg in some specified areas. In 1563, parliament passed a resolution which made all the house holders to provide funds every week for the welfare of the poor. In 1572, Queen Elizabeth signed on the statute which levied a general tax for the financing of poor relief programme. Overseers for the poor were appointed which made it very clear that the government is totally responsible for the maintenance of poor.

The Elizabethan Poor Law, 1601

During the reign of Elizabeth I, legislation was passed to deal with the increasing problem of raising and administering poor relief. In 1552, every parish registers of the poor were introduced so that there was an official record of those who fell into the category of 'poor'. In 1563, justices of the Peace were authorised and empowered to raise compulsory funds for the relief of the poor and, for the first time, the poor were put into different categories. In 1572—the first compulsory local poor law tax was made obligatory by making the alleviation of poverty a local responsibility. The idea of a deterrent workhouse was first suggested and nothing remarkable was done at this point in 1576. To raise compulsory funds for the relief of the poor and the post of 'Overseer of the Poor' was created and thus Justice of the Peace once more was authorised and empowered. This happened in 1597. The position continued after the 1834 Poor Law Amendment Act.

The Elizabethan Poor Law of 1601 is also known as "43 Elizabeth", which was to remain in the basis of handling relief for the next 233 years, spelled out the existing practice of poor relief in a more logical way. The law divided the poor into three categories.

The able-bodied Poor	They were sturdy poors who were forced to work in the House of Corrections or in Work Houses. People were not ready to give them alms. They were the able-bodied or deserving poor. They were to be given help either through outdoor relief or by being given work in return for a wage.
The impotent poor or Unemployable poor	They were sick, old, especially abled, people who are having mental illness and were placed in alms houses or given outdoor relief for their livelihood. They were to be whipped through the streets, publicly, until they learned the error of their ways.
The Dependent Children/ those who were too old/ill/young to work	They are children who are orphans and who were deserted by parents or from very poor families whose parents were unable to bring them up. These were the impotent or deserving poor. They were to be looked after in alms houses, hospitals, orphanages or poor houses. Orphans and children of the poor were to be given a trade apprenticeship so that they would have a trade to pursue when they grew up.

When it comes to the dependent children they are given to persons who are willing to take them without any charge. If such "free have" were not available, they were given to the lowest bidder for whom they had to work up to the age of 24 (males) and 21 (females). They were given apprentice and overseers were responsible for the execution of Poor law. On the basis of property the finances were collected by imposing poor tax.

Charles II passed the Settlement Act in 1662 which empowered the justice of the peace to return to free place from where he had come and any such newcomer who in the opinion of the overseers of the poor could become a liability in future. In 1696, the Work House Act was passed which made provision for the training of inmates of the work houses.

Charity Organisation Society (1869)

In the mid-19th century social work originated as one of the solutions to tackle poverty during the epoch of Victorian plenty. The country as a whole was at the peak of great economic dexterity from trade, industry, finance, agriculture, forestry and fishing. This prosperity brought pride and satisfaction among the successful elite citizens who claimed that the achievement was through individual hard work. The existence of poor was not a concern and it was blamed upon an individual. Poverty was hardly noticed by law and was described as self-inflicted and an unfortunate necessity.

The 1834 Poor Law Amendment Act and the Workhouse came into force as a measure to reflect the changes in society and introduced the principle of less eligibility. The previous Poor Law was set up in Agricultural context was based on local parishes relief and was proving inadequate and incompetent with the present societal needs and demands. This was because of the shift from agriculture to Industrialisation and urbanisation. Poor people were to be treated less favourably and harshly so much that if they were genuinely poor they would voluntarily enter the Workhouse. The society which created the 1834 Poor Law Amendment Act was a decentralised rural society derived from private and local agencies existing in the Industrial revolution, with limited resources and techniques in the field of government and administration. This affected their performance and quality of work as they lacked central control, consistency and vision.

The middle of the 19th Century was a period of scientific and humanitarianism awakening. The poor law was criticized by the Thomas Chalmers, a Scottish Minister and his associates the methods and the administration of the Elizabethan Poor Law. He suggested that proper investigation should be made in every case and intervention of NGOs was recommended in the direction and supervision. As a result of this effort although it took time, a scheme similar to the idea suggested by Chalmers was implemented. Thus, the London Charity Organisation Society was formed in 1869.

The ideas underpinning the COS were:

- The giving of doles (alms) should be stopped.
- Relief giving should be coordinated.
- Thorough study of every applicant should be made so that the assistance can be offered to make them self-reliant.

The COS was involved in the following work:

- Interview the applicants.
- Draw up plans for the treatment of their social disabilities.
- Secure the needed funds from already established organisations.

Historians of Social Work stated in this scheme laid the

beginning of the present system of organised social work activities. The two primary methods Social Case Work and Community Organisation were applied in the Charity Organisation Society's activities. The poor were helped by the COS workers to use the assistance effectively. All the assistance was provided to try and put them in a position in which they could dispense with charity. Efforts were made to find jobs, education, counselling for financial gains and encouragement for creative plans was put forth. Public welfare administration was represented by establishing order and efficiency in the distribution of relief. Social action was also contemplated and to some extent carried out in attempting to influence poor relief legislation and also to alter the social and economic conditions that handicapped the poverty-stricken classes.

Settlement House Movement

In 1867 there was a thought which came from Edward Edison that the distribution of alm or relief had no meaning in the context of the solution of the problem. The idea was forcefully put forward by Cannon Samuel Augustas Barnet and it was mentioned that in his memory his friends founded University Settlement House which was named as Toynbee Hall which had three-fold objectives:

- Education and Cultural development of the poor.
- To provide information to the students and their inmates of the settlement house regarding the poor for the improvement of their conditions for social reform.
- To develop consciousness towards social and health problems and the need for enacting the legislation.

The Poor Law Commission of 1905

A huge unemployment problem was faced in England in the beginning of twentieth century. As a result of that most of the coal mine workers became unemployed and started begging for aid. That led to a very difficult situation to solve the problem of poverty through the existing Poor laws. Royal Commission on the Poor Law and Relief of Distress was appointed in 1905 to solve the present crisis which was headed by Lord George Hamilton as its Chairman. Four recommendations were made by the Commission:

- Country Councils should be established in place of poor

law union and board of guardians, so that the local administration could be reduced up to three-fourth.

- To abolish the punishable nature of poor welfare and beginning of public welfare programmes on humanitarian basis.
- Mixed orphanages should be stopped. Specially abled and the people who are sick should be treated in hospitals. Children should be kept in foster homes or in local schools.
- National pension for the aged, free treatment facilities for the poor in the hospitals, public employment services and insurance for the unemployed and invalid be started.

Based on the recommendations of the Commission, very important Acts were passed. The provision of meals Act was passed in 1906. The facility of free school benches was provided under the Act. The Education Act was passed in 1907. Provision for medical examination of school children was made under this Act. Prevention of Crime Act was also passed in 1908 which made provision for the establishment of special courts for children. The Children Act was passed in 1912 which led to the formation of court for the trial and probation services for reformation of juvenile delinquents. In 1920, the Juvenile Court Metropolis Act was passed which empowered the secretary to select qualified and experienced magistrates to deal with the cases in the juvenile courts. Labour Exchanges Act was passed in 1909 and this led to the establishment of employment exchanges to help the unemployed in getting employment. National Insurance Act was passed in 1911 to provide compulsory Health Insurance of workers belonging to lower income groups. The Widows', Orphans' and Old Age Contributory Pension Act was passed in 1925. Local Government Act was passed in 1925 which abolished the Poor Law Unions and Board of Guardians and gave responsibility of administration of poor relief to the country councils. In 1931, National Economy Act was passed which made provision for the payment of unemployment assistance. Old Age Pension Act was passed in 1940 which made provision for the payment of need-based additional pensions to the aged, especially for medical treatment.

The Beverridge Report

An inter-Department Commission on Social Insurance and allied

Services was appointed under the chairmanship of William Beverridge in 1941. The objective of this Commission is to make survey of the structure and efficiency of social services of England and to recommend the proper course of action. The Commission found that there were five giant evils, viz. physical need, disease, ignorance, squalor, idleness; which were responsible for all the human miseries.

Recommendations of Beverridge Commission	*Six Basic Principles of the Programme*
(i) Social Insurance	United Administration
(ii) Public assistance	Comprehensive Coverage
(iii) Children's Allowance	Flat rate of Contribution and benefits
(iv) Comprehensive Free Health	Adequacy of all benefits to meet basic needs of recipients
(v) Maintenance of full employment	Classification of population

British Social Insurance Programme was based on Beverridge Report. Various Legal enactments were made after the submission of the report. Disabled Persons (Employment) Act was passed in 1944 which made provision for the employers of commercial or industrial enterprises to compulsorily employ the disabled persons. In 1945, The Family Allowance Act was passed. National Insurance Act was passed in 1946 which provided a scheme of health, invalidity and old-age insurance. The Industrial Injuries (Workman's Compensations) Act was enacted in 1946. The National Assistance Act was made in 1948.

Major Developmental Milestones in Social Work in UK Included

Year	*Law/Movement*
1601	The Elizabethan Poor Law
1869	Charity Organization Society
1884	Settlement House Movement
1905	The Poor Law Commission
1941	The Beverridge Report

History of Social Work in USA

The following section attempts to trace the genesis of Social Work in USA. In order to understand it thoroughly and systematically, it has been divided into five steps which are as follows:

1. The Colonial Period (1620-1776),
2. Civil War and Industrial Revolution (1776-1860),
3. Industrialism — The Human Side (1860-1900),
4. Social Work seeking Professional Characteristics (1900-1930), and
5. Highly Professionalised Discipline (1930).

In the seventeenth and eighteenth century social welfare services existed in USA after the establishment of the original thirteen colonies on the eastern sea board. The English people settled here, brought with them their customs, laws and ideas. Elizabethan Poor Law served as the basic guidance for extending financial aid to the persons in need. Assistance to the poor in their own homes (outdoor relief) was the initial method followed in the growing colonial towns. The assistance was provided to the persons who were in need of temporary or partial public support, generally temporarily unemployed and disabled members. The assistance was provided to the families to look after the people who were in need.

The first alm house was established in Massachusetts in 1662. It started functioning in 1685 both as an alm-house for the disabled and as a work house for the able-bodied paupers. Their health problems also took care of these alms and work houses. Most of the specialized and advanced general hospitals of USA like Bellevue Hospital in New York and Philadelphia General Hospital were in the form of alm houses in its original form. The former hospitals were for the poor with physical or mental ailments. The Pennsylvania Hospital completed in 1756 and it planned primarily to house the sick poor, admitted the mentally ill who were confined in the building. After the settlement of New Amsterdam several "Sieck entroosters", minor religious functionaries were sent to the colony whose duty was to visit the sick persons in their own houses. To protect the interest and properties of widows and orphans, orphan masters were appointed. The first 'overseers of the poor' were appointed in 1691 in the city of Boston.

Associations for the function of charitable aid and mutual benefit were also formed on the basis of national origins and church affiliations. Scots Charitable Society was the first such association which was established in 1657 in Boston to help the sick aided the poor and to provide burial for deceased countrymen. The outstanding association with welfare activities was the Society of Friends in Pennsylvania members of its own, and other colonies which cared for members of its own sects but later on extended its services to others. The system of poor relief during colonial period in USA reflected Elizabethan Poor Law. The town, the smallest unit of government was responsible for its inhabitants. The primary motive of the town was to protect itself against the poor and the destitute. It was uncommon to auction the poor to the neighbouring farmers to send them to privately run alm houses. Another development during this period was the broadening of the base of responsibility from town to the province of Massachusetts for a special category of the poor. By 1701, there was provision for reimbursement for relief in all cases of unsettled dependent persons ill with dangerous infections of contagious diseases.

The rapid growth of manufacturing industries after the civil war intensified the complexities of social need. People came in large numbers to the urban areas and faced the wrath of poor wages, poor housing, unemployment etc. but on the other hand a wealthy class of industrialists emerged which stimulated voluntary relief efforts through their contribution to private charities.

To solve the problems of social maladjustment in the cities and of the labour class, there developed a settlement movement that had great influence on the evolving pattern of the social services. Beginning with the establishment of 'Neighbourhood Guild' (it is known own university settlement) in the lower east side of New York city in 1880, the Movement spread rapidly through the larger industrial centres. The most important settlement were Jane Addams 'Hull House in Chicago and Mary Simkhovitch's Greenrich House in New York City.' These settlement houses provided direct service to people living in the neighbourhood planning and improvement. An early result of settlement house movement was the development of playground movement in American cities.

By the last decades of the nineteenth century, thousands of immigrants were reaching the eastern seaport, mainly from the countries of southern and eastern Europe. Several new agencies were established to help these immigrants adjust to American ways and to protect them from dangers always prevalent for a stranger in a new country. The Hebrew Sheltering and Immigrant Aid Society, with many branches in many cities and one of the most influential of these agencies was founded in 1884 in New York City. By the turn of the century scores of relief-giving and service centres and societies were founded in most of the metropolitan cities. For the care of the children and patients, the state government also established mental hospitals, orphanages and schools.

There were three important developments in social welfare during this period. The first was the gradual recognition of the social needs of people with particular handicaps. Special institutions, both public and private, were developed for children, for the handicapped and mentally ill. Child labour legislation was enacted. A law was passed in 1813 in this connection to press mill owners to have children in their factories. Massachussets passed a law in 1836 requiring the children under the age of 15 years working in factories attend the school for three months in a year. In 1842 both the states, adopted a law which established 10 hours a day as the maximum work for children under 12 years. Children under 12 years were prohibited from working in textile factories.

In 1797, Massachusetts legislature passed a Bill holding that if a person is mentally ill and very furious mad as to render it dangerous to the peace and safety of the good people, he may be sent to the house of corrections. The less serious and less dangerous were sent to alms-houses, mixed with the paupers, the children and the criminals.

A second important development was the assumption of greater responsibility by the states when local units could not provide adequate relief to these special groups. State government opened the first juvenile reformatory in New York in 1825, the first school for deaf was opened in 1817 and the first school for the blind was opened in Boston in 1830. Soon after other States also provided such facilities. Dorothea Lynde Dix contributed greatly during this period to the recognition of the need of mentally handicapped. Treatment for mentally ill people and the institutional care was popularised by her.

A third important development was the emergence of the private agency. People with humanitarian interest could not remain unmoved from the experience of shock and agony of poor people living in urban slums. Many organisations and associations were founded for the welfare of the children, handicapped and the sick. Around 1850 several maternity homes for unmarried mothers were established by various groups. The motivation for these programmes was highly moralistic. YMCA movement was also started during this period.

The Charity Organisation Society (COS) was one of important forerunners of modern social work. They were first organised in London in 1989 as an attempt to eliminate indiscriminate alm giving by the existing relief agencies and to organise the resources for the maximum benefits for the needy persons. The charity organisation society movement was also started in the United States. The first COS was organised in Buffalo in 1877. Later on Boston, Philadelphia, New Haven had established COS in 1878.

The COS operated on the following four principles:

(i) Detailed investigation of the application,
(ii) A central system of registration to avoid duplication,
(iii) Cooperation between the various relief agencies, and
(iv) Extensive use of volunteer friendly visitor.

The main functions of the COS were three-fold: First and basic, the rehabilitation of families which for any reason fails to be self-sufficient; second, the education of the community in correct principles of relief and third, aid in the elimination of the causes of poverty.

In early efforts of COS one sees the roots of many present-day programmes and practices. Among these are the Social Service Exchange, the Case Conference, social action and planning. The first Social Service Exchange was organised by the Associated Charities of Boston in 1879. The objective of the Exchange was to serve as a clearing house in order to prevent duplication of services and to save the clients from unnecessary investigation. Period of 1896-1904 pointed out the outstanding characteristic was the emphasis placed by COS upon the prevention of poverty, as reflected in the various movements to change social conditions.

By the end of nineteenth century, the Charity Organisation Societies began to employ paid workers. Many of these societies established training courses for their workers. The New York COS established training centre for their workers. The New York Charity Organisation established the first School for training social workers in the country in 1898. It was called the New York School of Philanthropy and now it is known as the New York School of Social Work, Columbia University.

During the first two decades of the twentieth century, the following major social welfare programmes were developed:

---

1. The rise of philanthropic foundations devoted to health, education, science, research, international peace, social welfare and civic improvement. For Example Rockefeller Foundation[1], Julius Rosenwald Foundation[2], Russel Sage Foundation[3] and the Commonwealth Fund.
2. Public parks and playground, programmes for the conservation of natural resources and the greater expansion of neighbourhood centres and other cultural and recreational agencies. National Service Agencies were established for the Boy Scouts, Girl Scouts and Camp Fire Girls' programme and the Boys' Club Movemnt. The 4-H programme was started.
3. Special wartime programmes which were developed during the First World War (1914-1918) included the home service programme of the American Red Cross Services promoted by a number of national agencies, including the National Recreational Association.
4. Beginning of hospital social service in 1905. Health Centres and Infant Welfare Clinics, other programmes for the reduction of infant and maternal mortality; public health nursing, social hygiene education, special state and voluntary institutions for crippled children and state programmes for rehabilitation (Massachusetts, 1918). In 1920, the federal government enacted its first will for vocational rehabilitation on the basis of matching funds of the state programmes in the fields.
5. Improvment in raising funds and programme planning for voluntary welfare agencies included the rise of community Chest Movement Cleveland Welfare Federations united drive in 1913 and establishment of federations of Charities for Consultation of coordination of effort among the numerous welfare agencies.
6. There was improvement in state institutions for the mentally ill. Social service workers were being added to the staff of the mental hospitals and outpatient clinics both established first Massachusetts in 1913 and 1914. Facilities for the care of feeble minded were being improved and increased.
7. Juvenile Courts were established separately. Only Boston had probation for adult offenders before 1899 but later on other states had enacted such provisions.
8. Civil liberties and inter-group relations were advanced through formation in 1909 of the National Association for the Advancement of Coloured people, followed by the National Urban League in 1910.

The depression of 1929 may be recognized as the turning point in the relief policies in the United States, Federal Government started taking responsibility for welfare activities. Federal

Emergency Relief Act was passed in 1933. This provided the first direct federal grants to states for unemployment relief and created the Federal Emergency Relief Administration to set standards of personnel and relief administration.

A Gaze on the Various Milestones in the Field of Social Work in USA

1662	First alm house established in Massachusetts.
1657	Scots Charitable Society established in Boston to help the sick, poor and provide funeral for deceased.
1797	Massachusetts Legislature passed a Bill holding that severe mentally ill and who are furious people were sent to the house of corrections and others who are less serious and less dangerous were sent to alm houses.
1817	First School for the deaf was opened.
1825	First Juvenile reformatory was opened in New York.
1830	First School for the blind was opened in Boston.
1844	YMCA movement was initiated by George Williams.
1880	Establishment of Neighbourhood.
1869	Charity Organisation Society established in London.
1877	Charity Organisation Society established in Buffalo.
1879	First Social Service Exchange was organised by Associated Charities of Boston.
1889	Establishment of Settlement—Jane Addams and Ellen Gates Starr formed Hull house in Chicago and Mary Simkhovitch Green House in New York.
1898	First School for training social workers was established by New York Charity Organisation Society (Presently New York School of Social Work, Columbia University).
1901	The Chicago School of Civics and Philanthropy was established.
1905	Beginning of Hospital Social service.
1915	Mary Richmond[4] became the first professional Social Worker in USA. She is the mother of Social Case Work.
1918	State Programmes for rehabilitation (Massachusetts).
1919	Association of Schools of Social Work.

Conclusion

The historical development of Social Work in UK and USA was marked by the formation of Charity Organisation Society. From alm houses which were completely for charity to the professional approach took more than a century. The contribution of Dorothea Dix and Mary Richmond cannot be overruled when we make a study on the developmental milestones in social work. The present approach to make the individual competent enough to be productive in the society has evolved as a result of lot of revolutionary legislations and formation and support of welfare organisations.

Notes

1. The Rockefeller Foundation's Mission—unchanged since 1913—is to promote the well-being of humanity throughout the world.
2. Rosenwald established the Julius Rosenwald Foundation for the "well-being of mankind," in 1917.
3. The Russell Sage Foundation is the principal American Foundation devoted exclusively to research in the social sciences.
4. Mother of Social Case Work. She wrote a book called *Social Diagnosis* in 1917. Later she became a practitioner, teacher and theoretician of COS Movement.

References

Cohen, N.E. (1958). *Social Work in American Tradition*, New York: The Dryden Press, p. 66.

Dillick, S. (1953). *Community Organisation for Neighbourhood Development: Past and Present*, New York: Women's Press, pp. 37-38.

Kellog, C.D. (1893). Charity Organisation in the United States, Proceeding of the National Conference of Charities and Corrections, p. 52.

Lurie, H.L. (1957). "The Development of Social Welfare Programmes in United States", *Social Work Year Book*, p. 20.

Schweinitz, K. (1943). *England's Road to Social Security*, Philadelphia: University of Pennsylvania Press, p. 29.

Steiner, J.F. (1930). *Community Organisation: A Study of its Theory and Practice*, New York: Century, p. 155.

Watson, F.D. (1922). *The Charity Organisation Movement in the United States*, New York: MacMillan, p. 94.

5
History of Social Work in India

Charu Sethi

Introduction

Social work is a commonly used term in our daily life as it is taken for granted. But as Nadarajah (2014) observes that all work is social, so what is distinctive about social work? Is social work, work at all? If work is to be viewed as social work should it not be served spiritually and selflessly? O'Brein (2004) says that exploration of social work's 'social' component has three parts. One, an examination of contemporary sociological themes with a view to situating social work theory in a wider framework. Two, assessment of the work that has been done on the historical emergence of 'social' as a discrete arena of intervention. Three, consideration of some recent formulations of these ideas of the 'social' in the social work's literature. Rojek *et al.* (1988) conceptualize 'social' "as the means which allow social life to escape material pressures and politico-moral uncertainties." The 'social', therefore, includes the complete range of allowances and benefits to provide compensation for unemployment, illness, old age, and the practices of assistance associated with social work and other helping professions.

The present chapter attributes to discuss the perspective of social work in India, comprising the history of Indian social work followed by emergence of professional social work in India and the gaps and challenges in the professional social work in India.

History of Social Work in India

The systematic development of social work in India may be grouped into different periods.

(a) Social Reforms in Ancient Period

In ancient India, the nature of social service was charity. The earliest reference to charity is found in the *Rig Veda,* which encourages charity by saying "May the one who gives, shine the most." Upanishad prescribed that every household must practice charity, social welfare activities were performed by *Yagnas*. The intention was the welfare of all. *Yagnashalas* were classrooms where men and women were taught the spirit of working together. *Bhagavat Gita* insists that the privileged class has a moral duty to serve the poor. It was commonly said that persons who served the society with all their ability will be free from all sins. But those who cooked for themselves or produced for their own gain, was eating sin (*Gita,* chap. 3-13).

Charity or *Dana* became the instrument of virtue, of the privileged sections and it was to be dispensed voluntarily. Later in the *Vedic* period "*Dana*" became institutionalized and came to be associated with religious ideology. Kautilya highlights the duties of the king towards the welfare and happiness of his subjects, "In the happiness of the subjects lies the king's happiness."

Buddhism laid great emphasis on *dana* (charity). Guilds were important corporate organisations which performed a variety of economic and welfare functions during Buddhist period. Guilds provided social security to the oppressed class of the society.

Ashoka developed a comprehensive system of social welfare. He appointed a superintendent to look after the welfare of women. Many reforms were introduced in the field of women's welfare, rehabilitation of prisoners, rural development, free medical care, regulation of prostitution and provisions of public utilities like roads, wells, rest houses for travellers etc.

(b) Social Reform in Medieval Period

The duties of a King included the maintenance of peace, protection from external attack and to provide justice. Humayun and Akbar brought about many reforms in Indian society and abolished slavery in 1583. According to Hindu Bhakti cult, all the people were all equal in the eyes of God and birth was no bar to religious salvation. But they refused to believe that Rama and Rahim, Ishwar and Allah were the names of the same God. Most of the reformers preached to the masses through their mother tongue, and therefore, they enriched our modern languages, such as Hindi, Bengali, Marathi, Maithili, Gujarati etc. The period of *bhakti* movement consequently proved to be a golden age in the history of the growth of social reforms. Reformation of Hinduism in the Middle Ages owed a great debt to Islam. It delivered a new social message of the worth of every human being in the sight of God, and urged a reconstruction of the current Hindu thought with a view to making it an efficient vehicle of the new social and spiritual ideals by the pursuit of *Bhakti*. It is true that the *Bhakti* cult was essentially indigenous, but it received a great impetus from the presence of Muslims in this country. This movement not only prepared a meeting-ground for the devout men of both creeds, it also preached human equality and openly condemned ritual and caste. It was radically new, basically different from the old traditions and ideas of religious authority. It sought to refashion the collective life on a new basis, envisaging a society in which there shall be justice and equality for all and in which men of all creeds shall be able to develop to their full moral and spiritual stature. The *Bhakti* saints taught universal toleration and brought about a revolution in the social structure of the society. All the saints loved humanity and were devoted to God. But their disciples failed to rise above personal bias and created sects and sub-sects. As a result, the Indian society came to be divided into a number of new cults based on orthodoxy.

(c) Social Reform in Modern Period

The eminent reformers Raja Ram Mohan Roy was the morning star of Indian Renaissance who sowed the seeds of religious and social reforms. He used his power and influence towards the abolition of *sati* and he was in favour of widow remarriage and female education. Ishwar Chandra Vidyasagar advocated widow remarriage, economic self-reliance, women's education and prohibition of polygamy. It was with the joint effort of Roy and

Vidyasagar that the Widow Remarriage Act, passed in 1856. Professor Bal Shastri Jain Bhaker of Bombay fought against the evil customs like *sati*, female infanticide etc. and tried to frame laws to abolish these customs. Gopal Hari Deshmukh of Bombay promoted modern education, established dispensaries, maternity homes, orphanages etc. Sasipada Banerjee was a notable reformer of Bengal who worked for the cause of women's education and widow remarriage. He arranged several marriages of widows and gave shelter to widows at his residence. Sir Sayyid Ahmed Khan played a prominent role in the education of women and to wipe out social evils among the Muslims.

The important organisations like Brahmo Samaj, Prarthana Samaj, Arya Samaj, Theosophical Society, Ramakrishna Mission, Muhammedan Anglo Oriental Society etc. played a significant role in the development of social work. Brahmo Samaj, founded by Raja Ram Mohan Roy worked towards abolition of *Sati*, promotion of widow remarriage and women welfare. Arya Samaj was founded by Swamy Dayananda Saraswati in 1875. He opposed the caste system and child marriage. Muhammedan Anglo Oriental Society was founded by Sir Sayyid Ahamed Khan. Ramakrishna Mission founded by Swami Vivekananda in 1897 started its programmes with education, treatment and general help. Gopal Krishna Gokhale established the Servants of India Society for social service.

In 1920s, Gandhiji became active in political as well as social fields. He symbolized the integration of political reform with social reform. He worked for the upliftment of women, *dalits* and fought for the equality between men and women. He emphasized the need for freedom from the evils along with political independence. The contribution of Gandhiji like *Sarvodaya*, *Antyodaya*, Non-violence struggle, Panchyati Raj are closely related to the philosophies of social work.

Modern social work was introduced in India by Christian Missionaries in the beginning of the 19 century. When they started making houses for orphans and destitutes, Indian social reformers like Sasipada Banerjee, Phule and Karve too started homes for the widows. Some social and religious associations like Arya Samaj, Prarthana Samaj and Ramakrishna Mission played significant roles in providing institutional welfare service in India. The formal training in the social work, was started in India in 1936 at Dorabji

Tata School of Social Work in Mumbai. Now it is a deemed university named Tata Institute of Social Sciences (TISS). In Delhi, the first school of social work training was started in 1948 at the University of Delhi. The M.S. University, Baroda started teaching of social work as part of university system in 1949. Likewise, Lucknow University started a Diploma in Social Service under the aegis of J.K. Institute of Sociology and Human Relations, which later on was replaced by a two-year course of Master of Social Technique (MST) and finally, Master of Social Work (MSW) in 1954 when the Madras School of Social Work was established. After this, a number of Schools/Departments of Social Work came into existence in different parts of the country. In the early stages of social work education, curricula were usually made up of three areas of knowledge: "(i) knowledge drawn from the social services including the knowledge of social research methods, (ii) knowledge of social work methods including social service administration, and (iii) specialized knowledge relating to individual fields of social work" (Gore, 1968: 256-57): Besides, social work education also involved field instructions and even research methodology, which enabled the students to understand the real nature of social work problems in the country and to know about the methods and techniques of conducting social investigation.

History of Social Work in India narrates that social work grew out of humanitarian and democratic ideas, and its values are based on respect for the equality, worth, and dignity of all people. Since its beginning in India, social work practice has focused on meeting human needs and developing human potential. Human rights and social justice serve as the motivation and justification for social work action.

Present Status of Social Work in India

With the advent of the period of liberalisation, privatisation along with globalisation, brought major changes in human life and society at large, both positive and negative. There are instabilities with rapid changes in every sphere of human life which has affected the practices and thoughts of Indian social workers (Nadkarni, 2011). Professional social work practice involves logical application of its principles, values and skills so as to bring transformation in challenging situations of society and of individuals. Due to privatisation and globalisation, there is an emergence of new forms of repression (Narayan, 2008). Rapid economic socio-cultural changes negatively affect the lives of women, minority groups, underprivileged children and poor (Nadkarni, 2011). Social workers attempt to relieve and prevent hardship and suffering. They have a responsibility to help individuals, families, groups and communities through the provision and operation of appropriate services and by contributing to social planning. They work with, on behalf of, or in the interests of people to enable them to deal with personal and social difficulties and obtain essential resources and services. Social development, social action, policy development, rural development, research, social work education and supervisory and managerial functions are the different fields of social work. The field of practice for professional Social Worker is expanding day by day.

However, the development of social work as a profession has been under debate both within the social work fraternity and outside. Meher C. Nanavaty (1952) has cited four characteristics of a profession as enumerated by Carr-Saunders in the Encyclopaedia of the Social Sciences:

(i) The development of the body of knowledge upon which the skill rests.
(ii) The reservation of functions of qualified by means of licensing or the restrictions of the professional bodies.
(iii) The development of the professional consciousness amongst the practitioners.
(iv) The contribution of the specialised skill and viewpoint to appropriate problems in the surrounding society.

The development of the social work profession in India is in weak state with respect to the first three characteristics. The first characteristic is weak as many educators and students complain that most of the knowledge base of social work is borrowed from the West and is not of much relevance in the Indian context. Till now, the professional bodies of social work were not able to ensure licensing of social work practice in India. Also, in India the professional bodies of social work are rendered almost dysfunctional and there is not much professional consciousness among trained practitioners. The criteria to qualify as a profession, many a time, have been laid out in comparison to universally admit professions such as medicine and law.

Social work, in order to attain a professional status, has also resorted to comparisons. In 1915, Abraham Flexner examined the characteristics of a profession with reference to social work. The characteristics of a profession, as listed by him are still relevant for social work in India, as it is still struggling to establish a professional status for itself. Firstly, professions are intellectual in character, the professional assumes responsibility for her/his decisions, and there is a considerable degree of originality in the decisions that are made by the professional. Secondly, professions are learned in character, that is, they involve a steady stream of ideas. Thus, every profession involves the borrowing of ideas from either natural or social sciences which need to be learnt in order to become a professional in a particular field. Thirdly, every profession involves the component of practice. The knowledge that is learnt needs to be applied by every professional having a definite and practical objective to her/his work. Fourthly, a profession needs to possess an educationally communicable technique which can be imparted through a professional course. Fifthly, every profession should have its own professional body which advocates for a common social interest. Professional bodies are assigned the task of establishing a code of ethics for every profession.

If we examine social work as a profession in India with respect to the characteristics given by Flexner then social work might qualify as a profession. For example, the learned character, the practical purpose, a professional course, professional bodies/organisations all exists in India, but still many do not accept it as a profession. Many social workers argue that, in comparison with the West, the concept of professional social work came late to India and it is a matter of time before the work of social workers will be accepted and recognised as a professional activity. However, there are contrary views both within and outside of the social work fraternity on the acceptance of a professional status by academicians, bureaucrats, Government of India, and the society at large.

Lack of specificity in aim adversely affects the training of social workers in a specialised area. The occupations of social workers are so numerous and diverse that no compact and specialised educational discipline is feasible. Therefore, most of the institutions of Social Work in India offer generic training programmes for social workers rather than specialised ones. People within the social work fraternity, who promote the development of social work as a profession, argue that the reason behind this is not the inability of social work to organise specialised training programmes, but it is the multiplicity of problems in India coupled with limited number of institutions of Social Work to meet the demand that calls for a generic training programme.

There is a world-wide debate today about the education that is imparted to social work students in developing countries. This concern stems from the belief that since much of this education was originally transferred from the West (particularly from USA and UK), it is not culturally, politically and economically suited to meet the needs of developing countries. In fact, many educators are clamouring for the indigenization of social work education. Their quest is based on the idea that students and practitioners face culture conflicts when attempting to apply Western theoretical models to their practice. As a result, huge gap was always felt between the theory and practices of social work in India. Although there has been attempt to modify and develop contextual literature, India being so heterogeneous in culture and other aspects of human life being so varied, a common content would not be sufficient to address the problems of all regions (Narayan, 2008).

Another major hindrance for social work to attain professional status is the job factor. There are hardly any practice areas in the fields of social work that are reserved for social workers. In addition, the concept of receiving payment for doing social work is far from being accepted in India. There is not enough recognition that the work done by social workers involves continuous dedication and, therefore, they do not have the time to be involved in any alternate activity for employment in order to make a living. More so, social workers argue, they need to be remunerated for the services that they offer to the society as they are in the welfare and interests of the people.

Weiss-Gal and Welbourne (2008) mention the absence of the licensing process for the trained social workers in India. There is no restrictions on the use of the designation 'social worker' in the country. A Professional status of social work in India, unlike the

USA and UK, there are no efforts/plans/strategies from official associations of professional social workers to improve/upgrade their image in India (Weiss-Gal and Welbourne, 2008). Consequently, it has become difficult for social workers to correct the notion that 'social work' or 'social workers' do not need any scholarly training to practice (Siddiqui, 2001). This has definitely become a kind of challenge for social workers to deal with during the course of their occupation.

In India, Social Work never got established as an independent profession. The government social welfare departments, hospitals largely employed trained social workers against lower middle rung posts. When Indian labour laws made it compulsory to appoint welfare officers in the factories, Social Work degree became a passport to appointment against these posts. With time, welfare officers saw themselves becoming personnel officers and later human resource development (HRD) managers. People with Social Work background, thus got higher status in society. When management education came to India (also from the USA), HRD became a preferred area of specialisation and management graduates soon replaced Social Work graduates from HRD jobs. A new attractive field opened for the Social Work graduates when some non-governmental organisations (NGOs) adopted corporate culture under the influence of its foreign donors. But these employment opportunities were limited in numbers because how many NGOs in India would find foreign funds? High profile jobs for Social Work graduates were, therefore, ruled out.

Conclusion

The biggest challenge that social work faces for being recognised as a profession is the haziness of its social status. It is still assumed that social work is voluntary in nature and any individual (with a kind heart) who wishes to pursue social work can do so. In India, the lack of governmental support compounds this problem. Some would argue that social worker's efforts are limited to the identification of a problem; solving that problem requires the services of other professionals such as doctors, lawyers, bureaucrats, and teachers. For this, social workers argue that their work involves the intellectual power of analysis and discrimination, breadth and flexibility of sympathy, sound judgement, skills in utilisation of available resources etc. These tasks cannot be performed by people who only voluntarily assume to help the people in need. Thus, there is a distinction between social-service delivery and professional social work activities. Another challenge emphasise that social workers in India are involved in multiple activities and there are no distinct field of social work, that is, social workers are involved in different fields such as disaster management to child welfare to community organisation etc. Professions need to be limited and definite in scope but the high degree of specialised competency required for action cannot possibly go with the social work.

At present, social work profession is seen struggling at various fronts, for instance, to blend international perspectives on social work practices with the indigenous knowledge and to get a professional status. Under such circumstances, the pleas of social workers in the backdrop of cut throat competition, increased job pressure, job insecurity and dearth of resources are ignored by all concerned. As a result, one sees the prevalence of stress and burnout among the professional social workers.

References

Austin, D.M. (1983). "The Flexner Myth and the History of Social Work", *Social Service Review,* 57(3): 357-377.

Devi, P.B. (2014). "Voluntary Sector and Professional Social Work: Trends and Challenges", In T.K. Nair (ed.). *Social Work Profession in India: An Uncertain Future,* Bangalore: Niruta Publications. pp. 148-179.

Flexner, A. (1915). *Is Social Work A Profession? Proceedings of the National Conference of Charities and Corrections.* Chicago: Hildman Publishing.

Gore, M.S. (1968), "Education for Social Work", The Planning Commission, Government of India (Ed.), *Encyclopedia of Social Work,* New Delhi: Publications Division.

Nadarajah, M. (2014). Should We Re-think the Nature of Social Work? In T.K. Nair. (ed.). *op. cit.*: 180-194.

Nadkarni, V. and Desai, K.T. (2012). Report of the National Consultation on National Network of Schools of Social Work for the Quality of Enhancement of Social Work Education in India. Mumbai: TISS.

Singh, S. (2003). "Future Challenges Before Social Work Profession in India and Required Responses." Surendra Singh and S.P. Srivastava (ed.) *Social Work Education in India—Challenges and Opportunities,* Lucknow: New Royal Co.

Vijaya, L.B. (2014). "Let Us Bring Back 'Field' to Fieldwork: An Overview of the Current Scenario of Fieldwork in Social Work Education in India". *Social Work Foot Prints,* 4(4): 17-40.

Wilensky, H.L. and Lebeaux, C.N. (1958). *Industrial Society and Social Welfare: The impact of industrialization on the supply and organisation of social welfare services in the United States.* New York: Russell Sage.

6

Theories in Social Work

Beena Antony Reji

Introduction

Professional Social Work like any other professions has developed its own systematic and specialized body of knowledge. The body of knowledge enables professional Social workers to serve their clients and the society at large. Professional Social work gets its knowledge base from social and human disciplines. Social work is contextually a diverse profession. Social work differs across the historical, geographical and institutional context. There is difference in the environment, culture and population, which also affects the Social Work in that region. The knowledge of Social Work theories provides a better understanding of the profession and provides as well as the complexities of human beings and the environment around us. This chapter is built up on four major theoretical perspectives that form the basis of Social Work as a profession. These are the Psychodynamic theory, Conflict theory, Social learning theory and the Systems theory.

Social work profession has adapted to the changes in social environment, political ideologies and free market and its effect on human beings. Social work advocates the recognition of values of respect, equality and social justices to all human beings. A good understanding of the professional theories is important in understanding the social problems better and further to provide better interventions to the vulnerable populations. Social worker in the field or in academics or as a policy maker acquires from these theories on improved ways of understanding the society and its people, so as to serve them better.

Psychodynamic Theories

In 1920s, the Psychodynamic theory was accepted by Social work body of knowledge. Mary Richmond had contributed to Casework, working with individuals and families. Casework was included as one of the method of Social work. Mary Richmond has also contributed to the systematic diagnosis and treatment procedures in Casework. Psychodynamic theory influenced the understanding of the client in Casework. The theory threw light on the personality and mental illnesses and suggested treatments.

Psychodynamic theories are theories about the mind (psyche) that is very interactive (dynamic) in structure. Psychodynamic theorists study the causes of behaviour in a dynamic interplay of different forces that internally conflict one another. They also focus on unconscious determinants of behaviour. Sigmund Freud was the pioneer to develop the theory on personality and called it the Psychoanalytic Theory. The Psychoanalysis was the most important psychodynamic theory that proposed the inner conflict between Id, Ego and Superego. These are the inner forces or the innate drives or conflicts with the outer pressures or external demands, to create dynamic tensions that influence the human behaviour.

According to Freud instinctual drives generate psychic energy which strengthens the mind and pushes for either direct or indirect release. Freud explains that more of the sexual drives may be direct in the form of sexual activity or indirect in the form of diverse behaviour as sexual fantasies.

Mental events may be conscious, preconscious and unconscious. The conscious mind consists of mental events of the present times. The preconscious mind is of memories, thoughts, feelings and images that we are unaware of but if we recall they can be brought back to our awareness like what did we do on our last vacation. We are aware of our conscious and preconscious mind. The major part of our mind consists of the unconscious, about which we are not aware of. Rarely some thoughts, impulses, dreams, slip of tongues or some behaviour exhibits the unconscious hidden areas of the mind.

Personality

Sigmund Freud has been famous for his explanation of the

personality. He says that personality comprises three interacting sections the Id, ego and superego. The Id is the centre of the personality. It is present from birth onwards and is the origin of the psychic energy. It is situated in the unconscious mind. Id is irrational and away from reality. Id functions purely on pleasure gratification. The ego is the conscious mind and in direct contact with reality. Ego functions according to what is possible in reality. Ego controls the impulses of the id. Freud states "In popular language, we may say that the ego stands for reason and sanity, in contrast to the id which contains untamed passions" (Freud, 1965: 238). The third section of the personality is the superego. This is the last to develop and is the moral part of the personality. It develops at the age of four to five. The superego is the family and societies values and ideals that are socialized to the child. The ego balances between the id demands and the superego restrictions.

Conflict, Anxiety and Defences

Personality is dynamic and balances between the instincts and drives. The id is constantly demanding whereas ego and superego keep the Id in control. When the ego encounters impulses that threaten to get out of control or faces threat from surroundings, it causes anxiety. When the ego is unable to reduce anxiety by realistic ways, it uses defence mechanism. Defence mechanisms are unconscious mental strategies that either deny or distort reality. The commonly used defence mechanisms are repression, denial, displacement, projection, intellectualization, rationalization, reaction formation and sublimation. Defence mechanisms are unconscious mental strategies about which individuals are unaware that they are using these to remove anxiety.

Psycho-sexual Development

Freud proposed that an adult individual's personality was totally influenced by their experiences in the first few years of their life. Freud argued that a child goes through a series of psycho-sexual stages in which the Id's pleasure seeking behaviour is centred on specific pleasure sensitive areas of the body. Either deprivation or overindulgences in these stages result in fixations in those stages. Fixation in a particular stage means that the psycho-sexual development gets fixed. Freud's stages of psycho-sexual development are Oral, Anal, Phallic and Latency stage.

The first stage happens in infancy and is called the Oral stage. At infant stage the satisfaction comes from food and the sucking of breast or thumb or some object. Freud discusses that either excessive gratification or reduced oral needs could effect in fixation on oral themes of self-indulgence or dependency as an adult.

The second stage occurs in the second or third year of the child's life and is called the anal stage. In the anal stage the pleasure is centred on the process of elimination. Freud argues that toilet training is society's first attempt to control the individual's biological demands. Freud explains that strict toilet training causes compulsions, overemphasis on cleanliness, obsessive orderliness and followers of firm rules and rituals. While mild toilet training cause's messy, negative and dominant adult personality.

The third stage is the phallic stage that has brought a lot of criticism to Freud's theory. When the child is around four to five years they start obtaining pleasure from their sexual organs. In this sexual awakening, the boy child feels erotic emotions towards the mother and competes with his father. The boy child also fears the father and feels that the father may come to know and castrate him, thus suffers castration anxiety. Freud called this the Oedipus complex, named after the Greek character Oedipus who kills his father and marries his mother. In this stage, the girls experience a loss of the penis and getting attracted to their father. This was called the Electra complex in which both the children get attracted towards the parent of opposite sex.

The phallic stage lasts for six years then is the Latency stage when sexuality is inactive for six years. This stage is from six years to puberty. There is a reduction in the sexuality and interest in learning skills and playing with same sex friends more.

Then sets in the Genital stage in adolescence in which sexuality becomes most important.

Neo-analytical Theories

The controversial Freud's theory gave rise to various neo-analytic theories who disagreed to Freud. Some of them were Alfred Adler, Karen Horney, Erik Erikson and Carl Jung. They argued that Freud did not focus on the effect of social and cultural factors on personality. They explained that Freud put too much emphasis on childhood experiences on adult personality. Erikson discussed that personality develops throughout the life period. Alfred Adler critics Freud's view that all behaviour is influenced by inborn sexual and aggressive instincts and drives. Adler argued that humans are born to be social and would want to work for social interests and welfare of their fellow human beings. Carl Jung advanced on Freud's view of unconscious. He explained that humans have personal unconscious formed by personal life experiences and collective unconscious formed by the history of mankind like memories of archetypes.

The psycho-analytic theory has greatly influenced psychology, psychiatry and social work and it has been greatly criticized too.

Conflict Theories

Conflict theories are important in social work it is concerned about the society. These theories explain that humans will be in conflict as there will be conflict of interests among human beings on the resources, prestige and power in the society. This conflict will be dealt with by interaction among the different groups aiming for a situation that is best for all. The legal system is a result of the society working for the situation that is best for all. The legal systems and society are described by concepts which explain the attention to fellowship and the absences of an inherit differences in the population. This is also called the functional perspective in sociology. Society's problems are at an individual and community level and are explained as a consequence of insufficient integration of norms. The functionalist like Herbert Spencer, Emile Durkheim, Talcott Parsons and Robert Merton explained that society is a system of interconnected parts that work together in harmony to maintain a state of balance and social equilibrium for the whole.

The conflict theories explain how the society operates. Society is recognized through its difference, conflicts, oppression and change. Conflicts will also bring in struggles between individuals, groups and communities, which will result in victory for some and defeat for the other. Thus, conflict is important to bring in change. Deviations are not seen as faulty rules and regulations. What is of more interest is who has the power to redefine the new norms. Conflict theory explains social consequences in relation to structure and processes of society. The vulnerable individuals and groups are based on their position in the society, are the oppressed and the powerless in the society. The conflict theory explains the terms like 'power',' powerless' and 'control'.

The earliest conflict theories were formulated by Karl Marx, who gave an understanding to conflict in the society. Paulo Freire's contribution with "the pedagogy of the oppressed" has been very important. Freire showed how people in a powerless situation become active and change their own situation and the society they live in. In the Conflict theories in Social Work, individuals and group problems are focused in relation to society. The emphasis is on the power and powerlessness. The focus is directed towards the mobilization of power in each individual by raising the consciousness and moving towards problem solving in the society.

Conflict theories relooked into the importance of community social work in the period of 1970s. It is observed in that 1990s approaches based on the conflict theories started emerging like the "Critical social work", "Radical social work" or "Anti-oppressive social work." These also focused on society reconstruction through problem solving measures.

Social work has been influenced by Marxist theories. Karl Marx (1818-1883) works are described in the subjects of philosophy, sociology and in political ideology. The three most important theories of Marx were the Paid labour's alienation, Historical materialism and the theory of Capitalism. These have together shaped the Conflict theory.

Paid Labour and Alienation Theory

In this theory of Paid Labour and Alienation two conditions are presupposed, one that work expresses human kind's true essence and second that work is preformed as paid labour. Marx argued that human's free and productive work is where they express their special essence and their true nature. How we work and what we do in practice affect our consciousness and our understanding. Our consciousness and our understanding also affect what we do in practice. They are interconnected. Thus, self-realization and knowledge is connected to our work. The individual is in a dialectic relationship to the social world.

Marx observes paid labour as an unnatural form of work. As the paid labour does not decide what, how and why it is to be produced. All these aspects are taken care of by his employer, he is only given a salary to his labour contribution and the production is a matter of indifference to him. As the person making the product is deprived of the product. The reciprocal action between people, their work ethics and the product is interrupted.

Alienation involves people experiencing, feeling or seeing their surroundings as different to them. This is in contrast to humans experiencing one with their surroundings. If humans are deprived of what they are making, then they will feel disconnected. Marx observed that the paid labour and the owners of the production too are alienated to the product and the work.

Historical Materialism

Marx focused on people's production of life's commodities to understand historical changes and development. Marx argued that economic conditions push for development. The production is comprised a base and a superstructure. The base consists of technological requirements such as tools, machines, organisation and ownership. The superstructure consists of political institutions, laws, religions, art and science.

Marx emphasized that the base has a fundamental influence on the superstructure. The material factors linked to the base are seen as very important and as persuading thoughts and ideas. Marx called materialism as 'dialectic' as it is the force behind society's development. Human society is constantly developing through the tensions between the opposites. Revolution causes the society systems to change. In the ancient society, the rivalry was between free citizens and slaves. In the middle ages, in the feudal society, the rivalry was between feudal lords and peasants. Later, rivalry was between aristocrats and citizens. In the modern times, Marx named the rivalry groups as bourgeoise or capitalist and the proletarist or the working class. The rivalry is between the ones that own the means of production and the ones that sell their labour.

Capitalism

Marx expressed capitalism as an historical phenomenon, that had a beginning, a development and an end. In Marxist economy, the core was profits. Worker produces more that what is needed. The surplus belongs to the owner. There is a fight between the owner or the capitalist or the bourgeoise and the working class or the proletariat.

Marxist theory intents to provide tools to understand the driving force in the changes in society. Marx elaborates how capitalistic means of production alienates the worker and also how this influences the interpersonal relations which are valued in accordance with the market.

The Pedagogy of the Oppressed—Paulo Freire

Paulo Freire in 1970s from Brazil contributed to the 'Pedagogy of the Oppressed'. He incorporates Marxist theory to analyse how social conditions affect groups and individuals. Freire argues that the Radicals will fight for freedom of the people and bring in the social change. Freire discussed how conscientization and mobilization of power and change in society is possible. He argues how passive and suppressed people can build consciousness and become critical, active and participate in the construction of society through dialogues. Freire also realized that the education system was a significant tool in maintaining a silent culture of oppression. Freire's work contributed to community based social work.

Social Learning Theory

Social Learning Theory is a theory to understand human behaviour. The Social Learning Theories were proposed by prominent psychologists. The first psychologist who proposed this theory was Albert Bandura and later followed by others. Social learning theory can be defined as an approach that assembles principles of learning and cognitive psychology. It is an organised attempt to discuss how social and personal abilities that are referred to as personality develop from the social context in which learning happens.

Bandura (1971) presented that human nature as different to the dominant American psychologists in the 1950s and 1960s. Social learning theory viewed humans were driven not by just their psychological traits, their unconscious or biological factors. Human behaviour was not controlled only by external environment, according to the theory the "human functioning involves interrelated control systems in which the behaviour is determined by external stimulus events and internal processing systems, regulatory codes and reinforcing responses—feedback systems" (Bandura, 1971).

Bandura included four principles that are important for the theory, these are differential reinforcement, vicarious learning, cognitive processes and reciprocal determinism. Over the years these have been well researched and elaborated with empirical findings.

Differential Reinforcement

Differential Reinforcement is the application of consequences for a behaviour dependent on stimulus conditions. Stimulus conditions mean different settings or environment that individuals come from. Differential Reinforcement means the difference in an individual's behaviour in different setting or environment.

Positive or negative reinforcement or punishment happens directly by the external environment. This can be explained with an example. If suppose an adult individual goes to his friend's house on a Saturday evening and is offered a beer. The individual has the beer and feels good, relaxed and enjoys the evening. This is socially acceptable. If the individual in his office in working hours takes a beer with his friends, feels relaxed but is confronted with his senior or employer, he will be punished for having a beer in the working hours. The same drink of beer in two different settings has two different consequences.

Vicarious Learning

Bandura presented that in Vicarious learning, humans acquire new behaviour through observing others or by communicating in spoken or written language. Social Learning Theory explains that observation of a model being reinforced for a given behaviour raises the possibility of that behaviour in the observer. Likewise observation of a behaviour that causes punishment will have effect in the observer avoiding that behaviour. Bandura explained that vicarious learning allows an efficient manner in acquiring and regulating behaviour patterns than does learning by trial and error or direct experiences.

Cognitive Processes

Bandura discussed cognition as mediating environmental events and behaviour. Cognitive processes such as encoding, organizing and retrieving information regulates behaviour. Bandura explains that environmental occurrences provide the individual with information that is cognitively processed and the result of that processing determine the overt behaviour that will follow. Individuals obtain information from the environment that is the probable consequences for enacting a behaviour in a given setting. The expectancies of behaviour outcomes that are acquired play an important part in guiding later behaviour. Individuals usually behave to acquire sources of reinforcement from the environment. Cognitive processes help individuals to cope with stress present in the environment by using verbal and visual stimuli to process and retain representations of their experiences. These cognitive representations then guide later behaviours. Once behaviour is acquired, self-regulation also plays an important role.

Reciprocal Determinism

Bandura also introduces the concept of reciprocal determinism in social learning theory. Reciprocal determinism explains that behaviour is controlled by the environment and the environment is controlled by the behaviour. There is a mutual action between factors that are seen as causal and determinism. For an example, an alcoholic expresses that he drinks because he feels socially isolated. It could also be that he is socially isolated because he is an alcoholic.

Thus, it can be concluded that Bandura's Social Learning Theory shows how human behaviour is learned from social environment. He has explained various methods by which individual learns from the social environment.

Systems Theory

To understand an individual and plan out an appropriate

intervention when dealing with the individual in Social work we use the Systems Theory. Systems Theory is a way of detailing the complex system that surrounds the person-in-environment. System theory helps us to understand the components and dynamics of the client systems so that we understand the problems and develop an intervention so as to deal with the problems being experienced.

Social work as a profession has struggled to identify an organised framework for practice that puts together what we actually do? Many professionals have identified systems theory possessing that organizing framework. The term system originated from Emile Durkheim's early study of social systems and also from Talcott Parson's work. While in Social Work Systems theory came in with the biologist Ludwig Von Bertalanffy and followed by a social psychologist Uri Bronfenbrenner.

Von Bertalanffy argued dramatic change in an individual occurs because of interactions between parts of an organism that is the wholeness in Systems Theory. His introduction of the Systems Theory changed the framework of looking at the system as a whole, with its relationship and interactions with other systems as a mechanism of growth and change.

Von Bertalanffy stated that all things, living and non-living, are regarded as systems and that systems have properties that can be examined. Systems Theory in Social work involves particular social systems like micro, mezzo and macro levels depending on their size and complexity. Micro System is understood to refer to small size social systems like an individual or a couple or family. Mezzo system centres on the intermediate size systems like extended families, support networks. Macro systems focus on large systems such as communities and organisations. Each system is an unit of wholeness with typical features and structural limitations that distinguishes them from other systems. There are system's boundaries.

Von Bertalanffy's theory believed that there is a single-dimension cause-and-effect relationship between social units within the environment. Uri Bronfenbrenner was against the single dimension relationship and said that Systems Theory is not able to incorporate the complex dynamics that occur within social systems. Thus, Uri Bronfenbrenner came out with an Ecological System Theory.

Uri Bronfenbrenner states that to understand human

development we need to see the entire ecological system in which growth occurs. This system is comprised five socially organised subsystems that help support and guide human growth. These are Microsystem, Mesosystem, Macrosystem and Chronosystem. The ecological environment is conceived as a set of nested structures, each inside the other. The individual is seen as existing in the innermost system that is placed in the outer layers of other systems.

Microsystem

Microsystem is a combination of activities, social roles and interpersonal relations of the individual being examined. The individual's face-to-face setting with physical, social and symbolic characteristics that invite, permit or inhibit associations in sustained progressive interaction with the activities in the environment. Examples of these are family, school, peer groups and work places. The environment that has proximal processes for sustainable development of the individual is included as the individual's microsystem.

Mesosystem

The Mesosystem consists of linkages and processes occurring between two or more settings containing the individual to be examined. An example of this would be the relation between home and school, or school and workplace.

Exosystem

The Exosystem comprises the linkages and processes taking place between two or more settings. In this, one of the setting does not have the individual being examined. But these system's incidents and changes indirectly affect the processes within the immediate setting in which the individual lives. An example of this would be the child's home and the parent's workplace, they have a relationship. The parent's workplace environment has an effect on the parent which in turn has an effect on the child's home environment.

Macrosystem

The Macrosystem comprises the overarching pattern of micro, meso and exosystems featuring the culture and the sub-cultures. This refers to the belief systems, body of knowledge, customs, life styles, opportunities, threats and life options that are prevalent in each of the systems of the individual.

Chronosystem

The final system extends the environment into the third dimension. A Chronosystem covers the changes or consistency over time of the individual's characteristics and the environment in which the individual lives. An example of this would be the family structure, socio-economic status, employment, place of residence, the life-styles all have an effect on the individual. Bronfenbrenner later in 1993 also added the role of individual's genetics in the human development.

Conclusion

Professional Social Work is a practice based course. Professional Social Work has its own values, a body of knowledge, specialized skills and methods to do Social work. There are a number of theories that are incorporated in the body of knowledge that help us understand concepts, explain various occurrences and also help us predict certain outcomes. Theories are based on evidences and reasoning that occur in our social environment and among human beings.

In Social Work there are various theories that are taught to the social work students to broaden their understanding of society and individual human beings. There are various theories like theories of social stratification, theories of social change, theories of conflict, crime, deviance, theories of personality, theories of economic development, theories of group development, dynamics, leadership and theories of political systems.

Some of the theories have been explained in this chapter that are commonly referred to in Social Work. However, the list of theories relevant to Professional Social Work are exhaustive because social work is a multidiscipline course, only four theories have been briefly explained that help us to deal with individuals and society.

References

Anderson, R.E., Carter, I. and Lowe, G.R. (1999). *Human Behaviour in Social Environment.* (5th Ed.). New York: Aldine de Gruyter.

Bandura, A. (1969). *Principles of Behaviour Modification.* New York: Rinehart & Winston.

Bandura, A. (1971). *Social Learning Theory.* New York: General Learning Press.

Bandura, A. (1977). "Self-efficacy: Towards a unifying theory of behaviour change", *Psychological Review,* No. 84(2), 191-215.

Bronfenbrenner, U. (1977). "Towards an Experimental Ecology of Human Development", *American Psychology.* 32(7): 515-531.

Freud, S. (1965). *The interpretations of dreams.* New York: Avon.

Hutchinson, G.S. and Oltedal, S. (2003). *Five Theories in Social Work.* Universitetet I Nordland: Trykkeriet UiN.

Leonard, K.E. and Blane, H.T. (1999). *Psychological Theories of Drinking and Alcoholism.* New York: Guilford Press.

Passer, M.W. and Smith, R.E. (2011). *Psychology of the Science of Mind and Behaviour.* (5th Ed.). New Delhi: Mc Graw Hill Education Private Limited.

Wakefield, J.C. (1996). "Does Social work need the eco-systems perspective? Is the perspective clinically useful?" *Social Service Review.* 70(1), 1-32.

7
Methods in Social Work

Lokender Prashad and *Kumar Satyam*

Introduction

Social work profession is one of the unique and prestigious professions in the world which not only brings out the problem in our notice, but it also carries the specific intervention plan to rectify or solve the problem. It has its own different methods of practice which are being practiced with large theoretical inputs. If we look the origin of this profession, we come to know that this profession emerged as to take responsibility to fight against the social evils and bring social change in the society through the social reforms in the neighbourhood through various activities like charity, poor relief, philanthropy and social services. Initially, the approach of social work was purely philanthropic where its services were concerned to meet the physical needs (i.e. food, shelter, clothing, etc.) of disadvantaged and deprived people. In addition to this, services to medically distressed people are also taken off to get healthy so that they can live a better life. Later on, as per the needs of the society, education and awareness generation activities were initiated against various aspects and to sustain their life or family livelihood activities generation or employment was started so that people can live their life independently with dignity.

Social Work Profession has its six methods of practice which can be classified into primary and secondary methods. While practicing primary methods, the social worker directly deals or intervenes with the individual, target group, community or people who need professional help of trained social workers. These methods are case work, group work and community organisation. In the secondary, it is not necessary to be in direct touch with the people or the community, here they can provide the help or any services from far away. In the secondary methods, the social worker brings social change or improves social and economic institutions through providing organised efforts of people, providing organisational services in the community, analyzing needs and problems with existing information or collecting information about the issues and providing a solution based on the information. These secondary methods are social action, social welfare administration and social work research.

Each method is guided by its theory and further theories are applied in the field, so the application part of this profession brings the gap between theory and the reality. The gap between theory and the practice brings new theoretical dimensions which further practitioners can apply and can monitor for the effectiveness of those dimensions. For the splendors of any profession and effective results, its theory and practice should go hand in hand because practice without theory is blind and theory without practice is lame. Combining theory with practice and *vice versa* shows the significance of combining theory into practice for getting desired outcomes.

In social work, for providing the solution to the particular problem, entire exercises go through the process of social work interventions. Entire intervention process is based on assessment (or psycho-socio-assessment) of the problem *via* applying psychological, sociological, economic, political theories etc. An assessment is the pulsating part of social work practice because entire treatment plan is based on the assessment, hence it should be done very carefully and skilfully. Assessment is carefully done with the observation skill, where social worker analyses and explains the particular situation based on the situation and condition of the target group/individual. During the assessment possible outcomes or hypotheses are being developed so based on them it can be decided which method can be applied to the particular problem in particular setting. After careful assessment and analyzing the situation, a particular method is selected to achieve the desired outcome for our target group or individual. Any intervention method is needed to be carefully implemented. Any effective intervention or assessment cannot be done without proper rapport building with the individual, target group or the community. Here it requires the skill in communication, sustaining relationships and critical reflection at every stage. While implementing the treatment plan, it requires several skills, knowledge of the event or situation and also requires critical reflection in order to evaluate the effectiveness of the intervention using any formal or informal method.

Nature of Social Work Profession

The origin and the nature of social work profession are purely based on philanthropic characteristics and humanitarian drive. There were various angles and purposes of helping people in the early phases of history. It is well known that few of them do help and support for the sake of getting a good life in the next birth; few of them believe that if he/she helps others, God will help them. Mutual cooperation, brotherhood, trusteeship, and cooperation were the elements in the society which encouraged people to help others for getting a return in the form of social support at the time of adverse situations. There were people who believed in the black magic and evil soul; their consideration was like if they do not help the people the negative soul will create dysfunction and discomfort to them. Each and every society in the different timeline of history, it has been found that there was the existence of helping attitude among the populace. Hence people started the practice of *Dana, Dharma,* Assistance and Charity for getting satisfaction in the life. There were certain intentions and motto of this helping drive as well as it was purely heart's call. So in the academic setting, we recognized this phase as the philanthropic nature, which was the oldest form of social work. Gradually, the action of helping assistance changed with the change of purposes and goals. With the advancement of society and cultural transfusion, the society learned to help people in different ways. Economic and political development structured this helping action in refined approach which is usually described as welfare drive in a contemporary time. The state also adopted this welfare approach for providing immediate relief to the disadvantaged and marginalized citizen through different programmes and schemes. After some economic prosperity and social development, the state shifted their approach from welfare to development through the capacity building, providing opportunities and giving minimal aids and assistance. After getting some economic and social development, the profession changed the characteristics and nature. Now the developmental approach not needed anymore, and empowerment approach replaced this approach. In the empowerment approach, we enhance people's skills and capacities so that they can help themselves. The social work profession and the social change go simultaneously in a different timeline, and that is the reason social work profession took a proper and prestigious space in a social setting. So it can be said that social work profession has originated from humanitarian and helping perspective.

Social Work Profession in India

Social work profession in India is not new in a practical and genuine way. The social work approach and intention are inherent in the people of India. This is not the statement only, but we get the evidence from multiple sources. In the ancient time, people of this region practiced communal harmony and lived together. That was the perfect example of community brotherhood where people were cooperative and did social support to all sections of society. The trust of relation and mutual affiliation got a lead of cooperation and collaboration. Community sustained with these parameters and helping nature rooted gravely. There are lots of Vedas and Upanishads which explain and describe the environment of interdependence as well as how these characteristics generate the earliest form of social work. It is true that in some period of Indian history, society deteriorated due to various unavoidable reasons, but the fundamental base of society never changed which were cooperation, social support, mutual aid etc. The evidence of this statement can be searched and found in the political scenario, economic environment and in social climate. The growth of political setting may be the reason of social upliftment, and reciprocally the social harmony helped to make a positive political environment. These all considerations flowed in practice of people's day-to-day life. We can find this oldest form of social work profession in Indian people in their values, culture, norms, taboos, and practices. It was the common perception at that time if we practice social cooperation, social support, donation, helping destitute etc. then we will get a good life in next birth, or we will be welcomed in heaven after the death. That was the philanthropic social work where no particular skills and techniques required for practicing the same. One should not forget the roles of social reformers of India who gave actual results against fighting with orthodox people of our own country against social evils and practices. With mushrooming of non-governmental organisations and some active roles of state, the social work profession started to get some indigenous academic inputs. The formation of new colleges and universities devoted to social work education enhanced the quality of professional practices. At the time of inception of social work education and profession in India, it was not much practical in social setting because the methods of social work profession are borrowed from the West. The Indian community and society were totally different from the society of the West. But after the globalization country like India started to match the pace with the Western culture. So in the current scenario, the methods of social work are more applicable concerning inception in India. There is social inequality and gap due to fast economic growth and development in India resulting gradual social problems and this impact on individual, group and community vary drastically. So in this present situation, it is very significant of application of primary methods of social work. These primary methods of social work may help in reducing social problem and anxiety of individual, groups and community. The secondary methods may act as a supplement and improve instrument of primary methods for enhancing the skills and tools according to the socio-cultural settings as well as present social condition.

Practicing Methods of Social Work

Methods are a systematic process of achieving certain tasks with efficiency and accuracy with following proper procedure. Methods are designed to enhance our practice for handling our job professionally. Different methods are used in different settings, and sometimes practice of a particular method may vary with the specific situation. Hence it is necessary to figure out which settings are most suitable to get the best results and where it may not give you the desired outcomes.

National Association of Social Work (NASW) has described the parctice of social work profession as follows:

> "Social work practice consists of the professional application of social work values, principles, and techniques to one or more of the following ends: helping people obtain tangible services; counselling and psychotherapy with individuals, families, and groups; helping communities or groups provide or improve social and health services; and participating in legislative processes. The practice of social work requires knowledge of human development and behaviour; of social and economic, and cultural institutions; and of the interaction of all these factors."

Social Work Intervention Methods

Social work methods are those methods which a professional or professionally trained social worker use to promote social change and development, social cohesion, and the empowerment and liberation of people in the society while dealing with different sections of the society for getting target specific goals and outcomes.

There are six methods of social work which apply with different circumstances and with different target groups. The very first method is Social Case Work. Perlman (1957) defines social case work as "a process used by certain human welfare agencies to help the individual to cope more effectively with their problems in social functioning." The social case work methods use and apply with resolving or reducing the individual problem and enhances the capacity building. If we talk about the present situation we can find, there are lots of social problems in our day-to-day life which encounter individuals' personality and capacity. Social case work tries to reduce these problems and restore that individual as he/she was in earlier. There are some other areas where social case work can be applied for social upliftment. The fast economic growth is one of the key factors of widening the gap between rich and poor which creates a situation where social case work can spread its wings to normalize the adverse conditions. In these days, poverty has become a big social problem, and due to this poverty, many other social problems arise simultaneously. Poverty could be the reason magnifying various social problems of each and every individual of the family. So in these circumstances, social work profession plays a vital role to employ one or multiple methods for eradicating the poverty and issue related to it. There are some restrictions still prevailing individuals of the family to come up with their problem to a professional case worker. Now it is the responsibility for this discipline to make conducive environment with practicing this profession in a positive way where individuals feel free to consult with a case worker for any help and support.

Social Group work method approach is used for reducing the individual problem in a group situation. Toseland and Rivas (1984) describe group work as a goal directed activity done with small treatment and task groups and at meeting their socio-emotional needs and accomplishing tasks. The group work method in India is more relevant and result oriented. It is accepted that the Indian people are more social concerning than other country's people due to the existence of favourable social fabric. It is an inherent quality of Indian people to support, care and foster to fellow and folks. So in this way organizing social group work is more easy and convenient. But it is important to mention here that with the changing circumstances of present situation the strategy of conducting social group work should be changed. We find the individuals have encountered various new and critical social problems and it could be resolved only in group situations.

Community Organisation is most complex and dynamic method of professional social work. Young Husband defined community organisation as "primarily aimed at helping people within a local community to identify social needs, to consider the most effective ways of meeting them and to set about doing so, in so far as their available resources permit. "It engages various stakeholders for resolving the issues related to the community. It takes sufficient resources, strategies, skills, and expertise for making a proper coordination for the best results. This method revolved around community and its existing discontentment and the needs. A proper organisation of this method could be able to reduce the social problems, social evils, the generation gap and dysfunctioning in the different social system. The other ultimate goal of this method is to create the social harmony and provide social justice to all. In India, the method of community organisation become more useful concerning earlier two methods because at one point of time we can resolve a big issue by which a mass has been suffering. These days people have less free time as well as they intend to invest less resource, so in this case the method could play an important role for normalizing the situation in limited resources.

Social Action is one of the secondary and auxiliary methods of professional social work which deals with the dysfunctioning of society and brings social change for sustaining the society further. M.C. Nanawati (1965) considers social action as "A process of bringing about the desired changes by deliberate group and community efforts. Social action does not end with the enactment and signing of social legislation, but that the execution of the policies was a real test of success or failure of social action." In a country like India, we find various social evils, malfunctioning in the social system, cultural faults and barriers to social development. These hurdles are so much rigid that these cannot be abolished without a great push and of course, social action might be a tool of great push. In Indian society, social action signified and contributed many a times in abolishing social evils. There are many examples we can cite for the performance of social action method. In earlier times social action as a method was used to mitigate the prevailing social evils like the *sati pratha,* widow remarriage and child marriage etc.

Harleigh Tracker (1971) interprets social welfare administration as a "process of working with people in ways that release and relate their energies so that they use all available resources to accomplish the purpose of providing needed community services and programmes." Perhaps the method of social welfare administration is not so much important in current scenario, but for organizing and implementation of different human resource and material resources, we have to employ certainly. In globalized India we can see the economy is shifting from socialist to capitalist, delivery mechanism is shifting in corporate style, policy planning is forming from bottom to top, power is decentralizing, so in this complex situation this method reduced the anomalies and helped us in directing projects and assignments.

Social work research renovates and opens the door of innovation and direction of this profession. According to Friedlander, Social Work research is the systematic, critical investigation of questions in the social welfare field with the purpose of yielding answers to problems of social work, and of extending and generalizing social work knowledge and concepts." Any profession needs the research output for competing in the fast changing social circumstances. Social work research gives direction to the profession in this neoliberal economic environment where its demands gradually have been increasing. If social worker wants to get a prestigious position and rank like other professional discipline, it needs research oriented direction. And, of course, social work research in today's world has provided and contributed for flourishing this profession very adiabatically.

Actions in Social Work Intervention

We can apply different methods of social work profession in various areas adopting following precise actions mentioned below:

- Social justice and advocacy,
- Family planning and Family counselling,
- Counselling and psychological support,
- Relief and Rehabilitation,
- Environmental protection,
- Gender sensitization,
- Social integration, social cohesion, and communal harmony,
- Innovation and research,
- Awareness generation and knowledge building,
- Evaluation of Programme and social policies, and
- Participation, Decentralization and resource mobilization, etc.

Social Work Intervention Plan

Social work professional does not apply the same intervention plan to all similar problems. There are different socio-political and economic considerations behind the issue which makes the similar problem unique which affects the people in its way. Hence, with considering the all socio-political and economic concern, it is required to frame the intervention which is most suitable and acceptable to the situation. Hence, most appropriate interventions are framed according to the community setting, group, client and its surrounding environmental conditions. Social work interventions are designed at different levels—it may be individual level, group level or community level.

While designing our intervention, first of all, the social workers have to identify the problem and set the goals to be addressed and carefully plan what needs to be done. The assessment of the problems should be based on scientific basis, and one has to proceed logically and use the most appropriate tools, techniques and methods for finding the facts about the problem such as one to one interaction, direct observation, personal interview, family visit, group meeting, community meeting, survey, existing records/ history etc. related to the client or the problem. With assessment of the problem, one has to understand and identify the problem at individual, group or community level and based on the target group the social worker inquired to assign the goals. With proper identification of the problem one must prioritize the needs or problems which are needed to be addressed first. After prioritization of the needs and problems it is required to proceed further in a logical manner. It is also needed to identify the individual, groups or the community, for whom behaviours or outcomes should change. In the whole process first, identify the change agent who can help in every stage in achieving the desired goals resourcefully. One of the most important things, the social worker should keep in mind always is to identify the resources. That resource could be an agency/organisation, human, material, service, capital, place or anything which will be very helpful in supporting and achieving the desired goals.

While implementing the intervention or treatment plan carefully be in touch with the target group or the client. Make a proper recording of the changes one observes in every visit in the subject which will help in the progressive evaluation of the client. After the proper implementation of the intervention evaluate at the end, how much one has achieved the desired goals and whether one is on the right track or missed out the track. With all these things keeping in mind the social worker plans his/her interventions according to the target group.

Application of Social Work Method

In the recent era, the application of social work methods

particularly in the Indian setting, it is highly debatable due to various reasons and facts. It is known that there are great diversity and inequality in the country like India. The society is fragmented by caste, class, religion, race, and creed. At the same time, the custom, culture, folkways, mores, taboos, practices and rituals play an important role in creating hurdles in practicing the profession. It is a fact that the social work profession has been facing of more scope and opportunities due to emerging individual and a social problems such as urbanization, industrialization, migration, and inequality. The inequalities based on socio-political and economic reasons propagate various problems to the individual, group, and community. Some social scientists of Indian origin believe that social action is the method which can eradicate and solve all the problems. They think that case work and group work could not be practiced with the people of India keeping various things in mind. They also believe that the case work and group work methods are purely based and applicable in the Western settings, but it is not true at all. The various studies and facts from the society reveal that it is not all true that case work and group work are irrelevant in an Indian setting. In the globalized India, the scope of primary methods of social work gets wider. The contemporary society is matching the frequency with the West. Now there are various individual and social problems which are similar to the Western societies. One can practice case work, group work and community organisation in recent time for getting maximum results to the stakeholders of this profession. India is one of the countries which has fast economic growth, due to this various challenges and opportunities have been encountering. So it is better to say that the primary method of social work will be getting good days rather saying these are irrelevant and ineffective. The recent social change has been done by active social action in Indian milieus such as in the area of environmental protection, social legislation, social justice and alternative politics. These examples and practical suitability expose the relevance of social action. If one sees the preferences and choices of social work research in the academic arena, one finds that there are ample opportunities to explore through the social work research. The privatization opened the door for the private sector to do something with their indigenous knowledge and skills. There are numbers of non-governmental organisations and firms have been working in the Indian setting for individual and community development. Social welfare administration could play an important role to organise and systematize these mushrooming of NGOs and private sectors for getting maximum output and better results. So in this regard, we can profoundly say that the methods of social work are very relevant and essential for welfare, development, and empowerment of individuals, groups and communities professionally.

Summary

So it can be concluded that social work profession in India is new but not irrelevant. In the changing scenario in Indian setting social work profession could be an alternative proposition which has the solution of every hurdles and barriers. The profession of social work not only brings problem in our notice for alternative solutions but also uplift the social life for self-sustenance. The primary methods of social work intervention have been contributing for the immediate relief and action, at the same time, auxiliary methods give direction to the profession for making suitability in the fast changing society. It is urgent to review and recompile all the research findings of social work for its nobility and innovation in upcoming time. In addition to this, one also needs to contribute the indigenous knowledge and practices for expanding the wings of this profession in all segments and sects of the society and community.

References

Bhattacharya, S. (2003). *Social Work: An Integrated Approach.* Deep and Deep Publications.

Chowdhry, D.P. (1992). *Social Welfare Administration.* Atma Ram & Sons.

DuBois, B.L. and Miley, K.K. (2013). *Social Work: An Empowering Profession.* Pearson Higher Ed.

Galtung, J. (1969). *Theory and Methods of Social Research* (No. 1). Oslo: Universitetsforlaget.

Hamilton, G. (1954). *Theory and Practice of Social Case Work* (Second edition). New York: School of Social Work.

Konopka, G. (1963). *Social Group Work: A Helping Process* (No. HV45 K63).

Mathew, G. (1992). *An Introduction to Social Casework.* Tata Institute of Social Sciences.

Prashad, L.; Dutta, M.; Kumar, R.R. and Arya, K. (2016). "Medical Social Work in India: Addressing Emotional and Social Components of Illness", In *Field Work Practice in Social Work Education: Contemporary Areas and Practices* [in Dash, B.M. & Roy, S. (edit)] (pp. 224-244). New Delhi: Atlantic Publishers.

Ross Murray, G. (1955). *Community Organisation: Theory and Principles.* New York; Evanston; London: Harper and Row Publishing.

Roy, S. (2015). *Methods and Development of Social Work.* Delhi: Discovery Publishing House.

Satyam, K. (2013). Social *Work Education and Practice in India: Innovations and Interventions* (pp. 54-59). Pune, Maharashtra: Centre for Social Research and Development.

Shah, G. (2004). *Social Movements in India: A Review of Literature.* SAGE Publications India.

Siddiqui, H.Y. (1997). *Working with Communities: An Introduction to Community Work.* Hira.

Siddiqui, H.Y. (2008). *Group Work: Theories and Practices.* Rawat Publications.

Siddiqui, H.Y. (Ed.). (1984). *Social Work and Social Action: A Developmental Perspective.* Humanities Pr.

Siporin, M. (1975). *Introduction to Social Work Practice.* Collier Macmillan.

Verma, N., Rangnekar, S. and Barua, M.K. (2012). "Team effectiveness in Indian organisations: A comparative analysis of public and private sector", *Delhi Business Review, 13*(2), 43.

Weil, M. (1996). *Community Practice: Conceptual Models* (Vol. 3, No. 3-4). Psychology Press.

Wilson, G. and Ryland, G. (1949). *Social Group Work Practice: The Creative Use of the Social Process.* Houghton Mifflin Co.

8

Roles and Functions of Professional Social Worker in Selected Field Work Settings

Swati Bist

Introduction

Today social work has expanded so much that its presence is felt in all fields of human life. Innumerable organisations have emerged throughout the world, which are engaged in social work for decades. The work conducted by the monasteries and churches is very well known which have been serving the poor and the needy for ages. They hold discussions and organise events in order to expand their services to help the underprivileged. They also document their work which today provides us with innumerable literature regarding the history of Social Work. In course of time, these organisations started providing formal in-service training to the new recruits. The end of the nineteenth century marked the beginning of professional education in social work with the commencement of a short term programme to be offered to the students by New York Charity Organisation. Now, the education in social work profession has become a global attraction.

In the present period, Social Work Profession is performing many activities like providing safe and enriching lives, preventing dysfunction among various units of society and promoting social justice. The goal of social work profession can be summarised as *"enhancing social functioning of individuals, families, groups and communities; linking client system with needed resources; improving social service delivery network; promoting social justice through development of social policy"* (DuBois & Miley, 2002: 11). Towards this end, National Council of Professional Social Work in India (NCPSWI), Bill 1993 defines *"social work professional as person who has undergone prescribed course of study and fieldwork in social work and had passed examination at the undergraduate and/or post-graduate level."*

The first section discusses generic roles and functions of a professional social worker. In the later section, the chapter highlights the roles and functions of a professional social worker in different fields, i.e. in health care system, correctional system, school, disability and mental health setting. Besides, the chapter also focuses on the possible intervention in the non-institutional community set up, in wider horizon.

Roles and Functions of a Professional Social Worker: A Generic Approach

Social work profession appreciates generalist approach. This approach fosters working with the needs of individuals, groups and communities, as well as addressing issues pertaining to policies and legislations to effect necessary changes in the society. The profession requires a worker to develop necessary competencies and be able of broad range of interventions, micro and macro initiatives. The present section reflects the abovementioned approach while enumerating roles and functions of a professional social worker.

Advocate

DuBois & Miley (2002: 236) elaborate the advocate roles of a worker as *"linking clients with available resources or serve as intermediaries to advance clients' cause. A worker uses case management strategies to coordinate the services of multiple providers."* So, it encompasses two important tasks. Firstly, giving voice to the concerns of weaker and marginalised segments of the population and promote social justice. Secondly, case management is another important task a worker is supposed to assume. *"The purpose of case management includes coordinating services and achieving continuity while simultaneously balancing accountability issues such as programme cost and service effectiveness"* (DuBois & Miley, 2002 : 239).

Educator

Education is prerequisite to empower people. Education and awareness generation is one of the core tasks of a social worker. It enables people to take informed decisions in their lives. A worker can help to enhance skills and competencies of the client system which eventually broadens their opportunities and promote self-reliance. Awareness campaign is one of the important aspects of education. The goal of various awareness campaigns is to bring necessary behavioural changes in the attitude and perceptions of the people. The awareness generation campaign is directed to promote safe and preventive practices, to avoid any complications in near future. For example, promoting family health planning, promoting safe sex practices with regard to prevention of HIV, disseminating of information on reproductive health, creating awareness on various socio-legal issues etc. Besides, promoting preventive and safe practices, the awareness campaign also focuses on disseminating information on curative and rehabilitative measures (Kaushik, 2016).

The worker also touches an important domain of education as a trainer. A trainer helps in capacity building of the middle level staff and other formal groups through workshop, in-service training and sensitisation activities.

Facilitator

A worker very often facilitates clients and communities to fulfil the needs and enhance their social functioning. Facilitation is a process of guiding people and providing necessary inputs as per the situation and need of the individuals and groups to undertake certain initiative which could be useful to them or may remove roadblocks in their lives. As facilitator, a worker can undertake following activities:

(a) Facilitation in getting access to various social services and benefits of welfare schemes.
(b) Facilitation to the client in seeking legal recourse to his problems.
(c) A worker can also facilitate in various developmental initiatives and group processes in the community. For

example, facilitation in various income generation activities, self-help groups etc.

Consultant

Though in human service profession, consultation is not restricted to one particular discipline, but often social work professionals are actively involved in consultation. "*Consultation is an interaction between professional persons who explore a problem to find a solution that will best serve the needs of a client. This helps the organisation to extend and improve their services to clients or work effectively for the cause*" (Skidmore & Thackery, 1974 : 117).

Besides social work practitioners, social work educators are often actively engaged in consultation as they come across various social welfare agencies while supervising students of social work during their field work practicum.

Resource Mobiliser

Resource mobilisation is a crucial and integral part of human service profession to successfully carry out a programme or any activity of social significance. Resources are needed to enhance social functioning of the clients and groups, ensuring effective service delivery and maximising participation of the clients and support groups (DuBois & Miley, 2002). Mobilisation of resources is not limited to fund rising. It also includes identification and mobilisation of various other resources. It can be broadly classified as follow:

(a) *Fund Raising:* Arranging Grants and financial assistance.
(b) *Utilisation of Human Resources:* Identifying and motivating people to engage in various developmental and welfare activities as per their competence.
(c) *Material Resources:* Collection of various materials which could be of use to the client system. For example, clothing, bedding, food items, stationery, utensils, furniture, equipment and appliances etc.
(d) *Infrastructural Resources:* Arranging space and buildings, agriculture land, transportations and means of communications etc.

(e) *Natural Resources:* Identifying and mindful use of natural resources. For example, optimum use of natural resources such as soil, water bodies, various plants product and, recognising and promoting beneficial agricultural practices.

A social worker practitioner should be able to recognise various resources which can be employed for appropriate interventions. Social work profession believes in optimum utilisation of community resources. A worker clarifies and motivates people to come forward for a cause, as well as helps to identify resources within the community which can be of use to the people. This process helps in instilling a sense of ownership among community members and recognising their potential. Further, this ensures sustainability of community initiatives and building social capital (Joseph, 2016).

Social Activist

A professional social worker assumes a role of a catalyst in initiating social change. A activist raises the consciousness of the public about the problem and injustice being faced by a certain segment. A social reform can be brought through macro intervention requiring coordinated effort at various levels and efficient networking. A worker mobilises the masses through networking with the groups in the community and strives for reaching out consensus on the shared agenda and possible alternatives to address the existing unrest in the society. A social activist aims at bringing changes in legislations, policies and regulations to ensure justice and harmony in the society.

Planner

As the experience of the worker advances, he can assume role of a social planner. A planner requires knowledge of the society, policies, and problems being faced by various segments and, understanding of administrative and legislative processes. A worker assists communities in planning to resolve problems. A planner should be a person of foresight and possess leadership trait. *"Social planners' activities include coordinating services, developing programmes, evaluating policies' effectiveness, and advocating social welfare reform"* (DuBois & Miley, 2002 : 232). A planner makes use of research and organises consultations with stakeholders, specifically with key persons having specialised knowledge and skills in the given field to enhance their understanding and discover strategies to resolve the problem.

Researcher

Social worker contributes in knowledge production through research. Research can be defined as process of systematic investigation into social phenomenon, the aim of which is to analyse social situations or root cause of the problems and generating theories. Research also helps in evaluating programme effectiveness and social policies (DuBois & Miley, 2002; Kaushik, 2016). In addition, social work profession values their client in the process of knowledge production. Thus, the practitioners very often work with the clients or members of the communities to understand problems, challenges, available resources and possibilities of intervention in the given social situation. This approach is popularly known as participatory research approach (DuBois & Miley, 2002; Kaushik, 2016).

Here we can draw interest to the details of various aspects of social work and their effectiveness.

Health Care System and Social Work Profession

Social work professionals are an integral part of health care system in various capacities. The social worker is visible in hospital and community health care system. There are immense success stories about their contribution in providing community health care and other para-medical facilities.

To begin with **Hospitals:** In hospital set up, the professional social worker extend their services in Out Patient Department (OPD), Wards and Trauma Centres. They engage in the administration mainly as:

(a) plays an important role in drawing up of treatment plan with the doctors and mobilization of community resources and support system,

(b) helps in assessment and making referrals,
(c) assist in preparing 'Socio-Medico history' of the client—collect information on client health history and genetic details of the family as well as seeking information on developmental related history of the client, family history and support system, socio-economic occupational detail of the client,
(d) Facilitates in optimum utilization of health services,
(e) Social worker helps client and family in understanding the illness, its cause and, managing and controlling the illness by bringing changes in lifestyle and stress management to have positive life experience,
(f) They guide family as to how to provide maximum support to the client and encourage co-operation to get treatment,
(g) They also help in dispelling doubts about illness and associated complex situation. The social worker educates both the clients and family as to how to prevent further contraction of the disease in family/community (Gupta, 2011; Skidmore, Thackeray & Farley, 1974), and
(h) "The worker also looks into the aspect of recreational needs of the in-house patients by organizing film shows, video and providing toys to the children" (Gupta, 2011: 23).

Besides that, ***Pallitative Care***[1] is another important area in health care, where social worker provides their services to the terminally ill patients and their family. They focus on providing relief to the patients from pain and depression through psycho-social support and spiritual knowledge. It also offers psychological and social support to the family to cope with complex and difficult situation; social workers are trained in providing counselling and support to people living with HIV/AIDS (PLHA) and client facing life threatening diseases (Nimbiakkim, 2009).

Organ donation: The *All India Institute of Medical Sciences* has set up Organ Retrieval Banking Organisation (ORBO) to encourage organ donation and its optimum utilization of human organ. It also ensures fair and equitable distribution of the services to the patient requiring transplantation. Towards this end, along with medical professional, social work professional plays an important role. He organises various awareness generation related activities to promote organ donation and dispelling myths among masses about the after-effects; The worker helps in coordination and networking with the various hospitals; He provides counselling to the deceased family and motivate them for organ donation.

Community Health: Community health focuses on promotional and preventive measures to improve the health status of a defined population. WHO defines health promotion and prevention as "*The process of enabling people to increase control over, and to improve, their health. It moves beyond a focus on individual behaviour towards a wide range of social and environmental interventions.*" Health promotion and disease prevention programme often focuses on social determinants, namely Physical factors (climate resulting in presence of particular disease, population density of the community etc.); Secondly, Social and Cultural Aspect (gender, social status, belief and traditions); Thirdly, community services; Fourthly, individual behaviour. The activities that come under health promotion and disease prevention programme involves communication, education, formulation of policy and ensuring safe environment.

The social worker can contribute towards well-being of the community in the following ways:

(a) He/she works towards promotion of nutritional diet and reproductive care among adolescent girls and expecting mothers which helps in maintaining a good health of a woman and child after delivery; providing education on ante-natal care in minimising mortality rate among infants. The social worker collaborates with the primary health centres and *Anganwadi* to achieve these objectives.

(b) Promotion of healthy lifestyle in the community and particularly elderly through recreational activities helps in prevention from stress and depression.

(c) Social workers are actively engaged in dissemination of health and hygiene related information among people.

(d) They are crucial link in various public health programmes on prevention of vector; promotion of immunization; ensuring safe drinking water and food and providing safe environment by ensuring proper disposal of the waste in the community (Gupta, 2011; Skidmore *et al.*, 1974).

Therefore, to conclude, that the social worker works at various levels to promote healthy way of living in the community with other stakeholders.

Social Work Intervention in Disability and Mental Health Setting

Persons with Disability Act, 1995, defines disability as "a person suffering from not less than forty per cent of any disability as certified by a medical authority." The Act recognises and classifies disability into seven categories—Blindness; Low vision; Leprosy-cured; Hearing impairment; Locomotor disability; Mental retardation; Mental illness. The Act has broadened the definition of disability and it does recognise mental illness as one of the disability. So, the disability can be categorised for a layman as physical disability and mental health related problem (mental retardation and mental illness) resulting in disability of a person to lead and sustain life.

As per the *Census 2011* over 26 million people in ***India*** are suffering from one or the other kind of ***disability***. This amounts to 2.21 per cent of the total population. Among the total persons with disability in the country, 14.6 million are males and 11.8 million are females. The data for disabled people has been compiled under eight categories, namely seeing impairment, hearing impairment, speech impairment, mental retardation, mental illness, problem in locomotor movement, multiple disability and any other. The statistics show that a sizable number of population is suffering from one or another kind of disability. According to Venketeswaram, Jose & Francis (2014), the most common form of psychiatric disorder seriously affecting quality of life include Bipolar depression, schizophrenia and dementia.

Disability makes a person incapable to participate in day-to-day life and to provide for himself/herself to sustain life, burdening family and caregivers who get exhausted mentally, physically and financially. In the present section, role and function of professional Social worker in mental health problem and other locomotor or neurological problems, resulting in various type of disability can be summed up as—

(a) Social workers, along with other professionals, assist in determining the kind of services needed and motivates families to access these services. The worker helps in liasoning between services and the special needs of the client and his family (Ambrosiono, Heffernan, Shuttlesworth & Ambrosino, 2015).

(b) The workers provide psycho-social support to the caregivers as they get stressed out due to constant attention and pressing needs of the client.

(c) They help in mobilising resources for the client so as to ensure independent living (Morales *et al.*, 2010). This may include, helping in getting financial assistance, life support equipment (e.g. wheelchair, clippers, special shoes) etc.

(d) They also help in rehabilitation of the disabled people and facilitate in making them self-reliant through providing education, vocational training and assisting in getting employment.

(e) In mental health sector, social worker are actively engaged in educating people on self-care and leading stress-free lifestyle (Venketeswaram *et al.*, 2014:286). The worker focuses on preventive measures.

(f) The social worker do provide counselling in mental health setting.

(g) The workers are also involved in early detection of psychiatric symptoms and providing treatment to client. The worker also mobilises resources and community support to ensure adequate and sustain long care to the client (Venketeswaram *et al.*, 2014).

(h) The social workers, along with other professionals, work together to address the multiple needs and services required to the client. Social worker is given responsibility of working with the client family. They either directly provide services or coordinate in providing services to the client (Ambrosino, *et al.*, 2015 : 217). They play a crucial role in case management through monitoring the progress of the client and regular assessment of needs.

(i) Social worker is extensively working towards educating, advocacy campaign to ensure barrier free environment, inclusion of disabled people, e.g. making educational institution more conducive to the needs of physically disabled, providing accessible and affordable transportation etc. (Ambrosino *et al.*, 2015; Morales, Sheafor & Scott, 2010).

(j) helping in getting social security benefits and promote them to get disability certificate to avail various social security benefit.

(k) helping in ensuring educational needs of the children are met (Ambrosino *et al.*, 2015; Morales, Sheafor & Scott, 2010).

The social worker along with other health care professionals and special educators, help in associating the client and his family to get optimum services through his multiple needs and promoting community based care to the client to sustain long and constant support.

School and Social Work

After family, school plays a crucial role in shaping the personality and future of the child, so there is necessity that both of these social institution functions in conjuction with each other. With rapid industrialisation during the last century, there is a drastic change in family organisation, resulting in smaller and nuclear families and weak supervision of parents and elderly of the house over the child, resulting in various psycho-social problems in bringing up of a child.

In such scenario, the professional social worker promotes and strengthens liasoning between the school and larger community, to minimise roadblock in the development of the child and providing positive environment. The role and function of a social worker can be summed up as follows:

I. helping parents to deal and cope with behavioural problems of the children.

II. Assisting teachers in parent-teacher meeting in resolving children's issues.

III. Social worker helps in strengthening parents-teacher cooperation.

IV. The social worker directs his efforts to address the problem of drop-outs and absenteeism in the schools, catering to lower socio-economic classes (Ambrosino *et al.*, 2015; Gandhi, 1990). This intervention is more needed in municipal schools of Delhi. They also look into the matter of poverty and other social issues hindering participation of child into the mainstream. In these schools, they do conduct awareness generation programme and enrolment drive in the community for the disadvantaged and poverty stricken section of the society (Gandhi, 1990 : 216).

V. Social worker conducts various developmental related programmes for teachers and parents to enhance their understanding in dealing with the children.

VI. Social worker organises various life skill programmes for well placed children and sensitise as well as create awareness among children towards diverse social realities through social services activities (Gandhi, 1990).

VII. There are integrated schools where a special child is imparted education with the other normal children. Here, the worker plays an important role in facilitating adjustment of the child and sensitise other children not to discriminate the fellow child with special needs and helps them in accepting the child.

Besides, the social worker regularly organises various diverse social and health related activities, i.e. reproductive health, hygiene and awareness generation or various health related issues as well as focusing on inculcation of moral values. He also organises recreational activities such as sports, and other indoor activities for emotional and mental development of children.

Correctional Services and Social Work Professionals

The correctional institutions are of different categories such as prisons meant for adult offenders both men and women, observation home and special homes for juveniles from the age of 14 to 18 and children's home for those below the age of 14 years. Welfare Officers with the basic qualification of Social Work are recruited for managing the inmates of both prisons and homes. They also act as probation officers and establish relationship between the offender and his family. *The Social Work Dictionary* (1995) defines corrections as "the legal mechanism that seeks to change and improve the behaviour of the convicted law offenders through incarceration, parole, probation and ideally educational programme and social service" (as cited in Dassi, 2012: 1397). The relationship of trust between the worker and inmates motivates inmate to modify their behaviour inconsistent with the norms of the society (Skidmore *et al.*, 1974).

In India, social workers are closely working with police, prison administration and observation/special homes for juveniles. The present section will elaborate on the role of social worker in various correctional institutions, providing treatment to the adult prisoners and juveniles in conflict with law. The section will also elucidate the association of social worker with the police department.

Juvenile Justice and Involvement of Social Worker

The group work process initiated by the social worker helps in developing relationship within the group and managing interpersonal relationship with the help of positive group interaction. In this process, the worker continuously by his presence monitors and supervises the group to provide necessary input to the inmates. According to Dassi (2012), this group process provides medium to introduce desirable changes in the behaviour of the inmates. In Juvenile Justice System, the social worker is also actively involved as the member of Juvenile Justice Board (JJB) and Child Welfare Committee (CWC) to dispose of the case in the best interest of the child and to ensure justice.

He is appointed as a probation officer under Juvenile Justice (Care and Protection of Children) Act, 2000. The probation officer assists the Juvenile Justice Board (JJB) in the social investigation of the child and provides the Board with information of the family antecedent and vicinity from where the juvenile/child comes so as to happily restore him/her back to the society.

The social worker-*cum*-probation officer[2] remains in constant touch with juvenile placed under him as probationee and spends sufficient time in managing his problems and enabling him to adjust in the society (Dassi, 2012; DuBois & Miley, 2002).

Prison and Social Work Intervention

Attending Psycho-social needs of inmates: During initial period of imprisonment, the inmates feel depressed and develop a sense of isolation since their freedom of movement have been curtailed. The worker extends psycho-social support to the inmates so as to adjust in the new ambience and adopt a new way of living (DuBois & Miley, 2002; Shah, 2016).

The communication with the family is also required as the aim of correction is to rehabilitate and re-integrate the offender into mainstream. The worker plays an important role in establishing the contact of inmates with his family to avoid the feeling of alienation in him. The worker conduct counselling session with the family (DuBois & Miley, 2002; Skidmore *et al.*, 1974; Shah, 2016).

Prison, housing women inmates also possess challenge of providing adequate attention and care to the children of female inmates. Female inmates are allowed to keep their children till they attain the age of 6 years. The Tihar Prison in Delhi, has setup a crèche which is being run by a voluntary organisation. The children attend various recreational activities and attain basic education to ensure normal development.

In prison, once the child attains the age of six, she/he is not allowed to stay inside the prison. In this situation, the worker also works towards welfare and development of the child. The worker helps the child in getting education in the boarding school. Shah (2016: 313) elaborates on the engagement of the worker in such situation. The worker ensures that the child gets appropriate and best environment. So, the worker persuades the family members to take care of the child and they are provided necessary support. In the cases where the child is not accepted by the family or any other reason, the worker presents the child before 'Child Welfare Committee (CWC)' for necessary action for the benefit of the child (Shah, 2016: 313).

Besides providing basic health care facility, in Tihar Prison, they have set up Integrated Counselling and Testing Centre (ICTC) to help inmates get their diagnosis for HIV/AIDS. The voluntary organisations are working towards mass awareness generation and prevention of HIV/AIDS among inmates. They have also set up drug de-addiction centre with the support of UNODC.

Preserving and promoting the rights of prisoners: It has witnessed that even after getting bail the prisoner is not being released because of the lack of sureties and bonds. Here, the social worker intervenes and ensures the safety and security of the prisoner and even ascertains the good conduct of the prisoner before the Prison Board, gives sureties on the basis of inmate's good conduct; the worker also helps in processing of the application for parole[3] and furlough[4] through follow-up with the other stakeholders and ensures other requirements are fulfilled. They prepare family to receive the inmate and furnish the sureties of the inmates (Shah, 2016: 312). While the prisoner is outside the jail, the welfare officer remains in his constant touch and helps him to handle any unforeseen difficulties in the family or in the society.

There are problems of under trial and overcrowding in Indian Prisons. Tihar Prison has set up a Legal Aid Cell to address the grievances of under trials and provide them fair opportunity to represent them in the court. In such situations, the social worker are playing active role in imparting information and guidance about the services of Legal Aid Cell. They educate them as to how to file an application to avail the services of Legal Aid Cell. The workers also help in procuring necessary documents required in the court for legal proceedings (Shah, 2016: 310).

Police and Involvement of Social Workers: Social workers are closely working with police in the matters relating to women facing domestic violence and cases of child abuse. Delhi Police has set up Special Cell for Women and Children, a nodal centre, at Nanak Pura, Delhi and Crime Against Women Cell across 11 police districts of Delhi. They have collaboration with Tata Institute of Social Sciences (TISS), National Commission for Women (NCW) and other voluntary organisations.

- The social workers are providing counselling to the couples and other family members to resolve the matter and ensure violence free environment for the woman.
- Facilitating amicable settlement between the women and the respondent.
- The workers guide educates women on socio-legal matter.
- The workers facilitate women to seek consultation from senior advocates of Legal Aid Cell, in Nanaka Pura, Delhi.
- Providing the clients with information on government and non-government agencies and their services as per the client needs like plans and programmes for women and children, de-addiction, mental health etc.

The social workers are a crucial link in the correctional services, addressing the needs and concerns of the inmates. The workers enable the inmates to imbibe norms of the society through meaningful relationship with worker and participation in various recreational and behavioural modification programmes. The social workers are also assisting police in socially oriented problem of domestic violence. The social workers are contributing towards providing community based correction services, reintegration of the inmates in the society, counselling to the inmates, social services for children and families of inmates and the workers are also promoting and ensuring speedy justice to the inmates.

Community—Non-institutional Settings

The efficacy of the social work can be assessed by overviewing specific organisation who are silent workers and are constantly providing services for the upliftment of marginalised groups in the resettlement colonies in Delhi. It is noteworthy to discuss detailed case study of a voluntary organisation working for this target group living in the outskirts of Delhi, in various resettlement colonies. The author came across the voluntary organisation while supervising Students of Social Work.

Lok Shakti Manch, a voluntary organisation is making its prominent presence at Bhalaswa locality, Jahangirpuri in North-East district of Delhi. Lok Shakti Manch is perfect example of neighbourhood development through "Process Orientation Approach" as described by Ross (1967), ensuring participation of people in prioritising need and decision making. They carried out systematic survey to find out their living conditions and problems faced. The community is lacking basic amenities. People are living in highly dehumanising conditions, facing problem of sanitation, drinking water, low land area surrounded by a big mountain of city's garbage (land-fill) being dumped everyday resulting in a high presence of mosquitoes, a highly degrading environment and problem of electricity. The community does not have adequate access to education as there is no school in the vicinity. The community organiser did base line survey to find out the needs of the community and then they shared their findings with people in the community and formed a community nucleus, comprising women and youth volunteers to address the same. Besides this, they were also facing problem of arbitrary hoarding and price hike in the food Rationing System (Public Food Grain Distribution). Community organiser mobilised and organised people to raise voice against corruption, which finally got resolved. The worker also mobilised and organised people to demand for improvement in the basic amenities through negotiation with local administration, resulting in approval for setting up of a state run school and initiation of work to improve sanitation and drainage system.

Presently, the organisation is actively mobilising people living in various settlement colonies across Delhi (Holambi Kala, Jahangirpuri, Bawana, Bhalswa etc.) to fight for their ownership right and change in resettlement policy of Delhi, which sets an example of "System Change Model" to deal with the problem as described by Siddiqui (1997). Towards this end, they are creating awareness and directing efforts towards conscious raising among people and mediating in filing of Right to Information (RTI) to retrieve their ownership status over the land and mobilising people to fight for their ownership.[5]

The above mentioned illustration gives insight into the role of professional social worker. The crucial role and function of a professional social worker can be summed up as—

- ***Conscious raising***, helping people to develop new ideology and perspective towards a particular cause.
- Educating people on various socio-legal-political issues and rights.
- Facilitating group formation and group processes in the community.
- Mobilising and organising people to raise voice against the existing apathy.
- Mediator—Mediating with the demands of the community and local/state administration.
- Guide—Guiding community in various issues and drawing up of planned action, resource identification and maximise utilisation of resources.
- Motivating people to actively participate and assume leadership role to sustain progress and development of the community.

"The professional social worker should be able to develop an understanding of the link between micro and macro realities" (Siddiqui, 1997: 82). In order to successfully work in the broader community set up, the worker should possess certain skills as listed below—

✓ Communication Skill	✓ Observation skills
✓ Interpersonal skills	✓ Listening skills
✓ Organising skills	✓ Interviewing skills
✓ Networking and collaboration skills	✓ Reporting skills
✓ Analytical skills to draw conclusion from the given facts and data collected	

A social worker should have an updated information on various socio-political-legal issues to understand the intricacies of the problem.

A professional social worker working for community/masses should strictly observe Gandhian Principle of non-violence as at times things do not progress as per the expected pace due to disintegration of groups or as per the plan drawn out as authorities do not adequately respond to the apathy of people, but even in these circumstances one cannot adopt aggression and violence. So keeping these situations in the mind; a professional social worker should have patience and adequate *conflict resolution skills* to address the complex situations.

To conclude the present discussion on the role and function of professional social worker, one needs to look into the challenges of the profession. In various social service organisations such as Crime Against Women Cell across Delhi, Prisons and probation services in India, there is huge scarcity of Professional Social Workers due to overcrowding of client populations or weak implementation of social service delivery machinery prescribed under the law. Sanyal (2012) in her report documented the fact that the probation services for juveniles are not sufficiently well in place across India due to inadequate infrastructure. She also shared instances where the district officers are given additional charge of probation officer, subsequently failing in fulfilling the duties of a probation officer. In schools and hospitals, similar situation can be observed where in sporadic manner the social worker are extending their services. This makes various welfare programmes ineffective and fails to reach out the intended beneficiary. The services of social workers are needed to formalise and regularise in the welfare programme to cater the multiple needs of the population.

Conclusion

The professional social workers are constantly working with individuals, families and communities for the betterment of the society both at macro and micro level. The social workers are working with other professionals such as medical professional, psychiatric social worker, special educator, lawyers, prison official and police, school teachers, other para-professional etc. The social work professionals are interface between various welfare agencies and client. They are largely involved in mass awareness generation and mobilisation on various social issues. The workers are providing counselling and guidance in schools, health care and correctional setting etc. They are also linking client to various welfare services to fulfil their varying needs. They help in advocacy and promotion of rights of individuals and people facing incarceration and are integral part in correctional services, facilitating in rehabilitation and reintegration of the inmate through therapeutic interventions. Thus, we can say that jobs of social workers are manifold bringing necessary changes in the service delivery, policies and social systems.

Keeping in view the fact that there is a rising demand for welfare services in the country, social work is not much catered by the students of today. Also there is a sharp decline in the choice of profession by the youth while the social sectors require trained and well skilled professional social worker to effectively implement the schemes and services for the welfare of the common man.

Notes

1. *Pallitative Care:* WHO defines "Palliative care is an approach that improves the quality of life of patients and their families facing the problem associated with life-threatening illness, through the prevention and relief of suffering by means of early identification

and treatment of pain and other problems, physical, psychosocial."

2. *Probation:* Release of offender on probation is non-institutional treatment device prescribed by the court for person convicted of offence against the law. The probationer is allowed to live in the community and regulate his own life under conditions imposed by the court and is subject to supervision by a probation officer.
3. *Parole:* Release from prison after a part of sentence has been served, remaining in custody and under stated conditions until discharged and liable to return to the institution for violation of any of these conditions.
4. *Furlough:* Granting emergency leaves to the convict for short duration.
5. In 2002 a large population from eleven JJ Cluster were forcefully evicted on the pretext of beutification of the city and thrown to these places. Afterwards, the authorities did not pay much attention to the needs of the people and they are living in highly in-humane conditions, devoid of basic amenities. Presently, in the outskirts of Delhi, there is rapid establishment of commercial complexes and malls is taking place, resulting in encroachment of land due to close nexus between the state administration and private builders. In future, since the lease period of 15 years has lapsed, they are facing threat of forced eviction as they do not have ownership rights.

References

Ambrosiono, R.; Heffernan, J.; Shuttlesworth, G. and Ambrosino, R. (2015). 7th ed. *Social Work and Social Welfare—An Introduction,* Delhi: Cenage Learning.

DuBois, B. and Miley, K.K. (2002). 4th ed. *Social Work: An Empowering Profession.* Boston: Allyn & Bacon.

Dassi, A. (2012), 3rd ed., "Social work in Correctional setting", In Prof. Surendra Singh (ed.) *Encyclopedia of Social Work in India,* Vol. 4, (pp. 1397-1407). Lucknow: New Royal Book Company.

Gandhi, A. (1990). *School Social Work: The Emerging Model of Practices in India,* New Delhi: Commonwealth Publisher.

Joseph, S. (2016). "Resource Mobilization." In Gracious Thomas (ed.), *Contemporary Methods in Social Work,* Shipra Publication.

Kaushik, A. (2016). "Awareness Campaign." In Gracious Thomas (ed.), *Contemporary Methods in Social Work,* Shipra Publication.

Kumar, M. (2011). "Medical, Psychiatry and Child Care", In Gracious Thomas and P.K., Gandhi (Ed.), *Social Work Practicum (Social work Practicum in Various Settings, Block 4)* (pp. 17-33). New Delhi: Indira Gandhi National Open University (IGNOU).

Morales, T.; Sheafor, B.W. and Scott, M.E. (2010). *Social Work: A Profession of Many Faces,* Boston: Allyn & Bacon.

Nimbiakkim, R. (2009). "Social work intervention in prevention and control of HIV/AIDS", In Sonny Jose (Ed.), *HIV/AIDS: Stigma, Discrimination and Prevention (HIV and AIDS in Special Population, Block 2)* (pp. 63-79). New Delhi: Indira Gandhi National Open University (IGNOU).

NCPSWI (1993). National Council of Professional Social Work in India Bill, 1993.

Ross, M. (1967). *Community Organisation: Theory, Principles and Practices,* New York: Harper and Row.

Sanyal, S. (2012), A study project on "Reformation and Reintegration of Juvenile in Conflict with Law" sponsored by Ministry of Women and Child Development, Government of India, New Delhi.

Shah, R. (2016). "Criminal justice and social work in India", In B.M. Dash and Sanjoy Roy (eds.) *Field Work in Social Work Education: Contemporary Practices and Perspective* (pp. 302-316). Delhi: Atlantic.

Skidmore, R.A.; Thackeray, M.G. and Farley (1974), *Introduction to Social Work,* Eaglewood Cliffs: NJ Prentice Hall.

Siddiqui, H.Y. (1997). *Working with Communities: An Introduction to Community Work,* New Delhi: Hira Publications.

Venketeswaram, C.; Jose, S. and Francis, A.P. (2014). "Community mental and NGO engagement: The Kerala Experience", In (ed.), A.P. Francis, *Social Work in Mental Health: Areas of Practice, Challenges and Way Forward* (pp. 276-300), New Delhi: Sage Publication.

PWD Act (1995). The Persons with Disabilities (Equal Opportunities, Protection of Rights and Full Participation) Act, 1995.

Web Sources

http://www.who.int/cancer/palliative/definition/en/

https://www.ruralhealthinfo.org/community-health/health-promotion/1/definition

http://www.delhi.gov.in/wps/wcm/connect/lib_centraljail/Central+Jail/Home/Function+and+Services (Date: 17-12-2016)

http://enabled.in/wp/census-of-india-2011-disabled-population/(Date: 10-12-2016)

http://www.orbo.org.in/aboutus.php

9
Attributes and Skills of Professional Social Workers

Sushma Batra

Introduction

Social Work professionals are always concerned with the amelioration of human suffering like other humanitarian professions. However, the social work professionals do not provide instant treatment to cure the problems of their clients, instead they work with the clients with the objective of enabling them to help themselves. Thus it is a very demanding profession which requires professionals having specific type of persona, traits and characteristics. While it is challenging at many levels, it is also very rewarding due to the ultimate satisfaction derived by the social workers after the clients are enabled to find a solution to their problems. Social workers are expected to possess a range of attributes, skills and personal traits to grow as a successful practitioner. It is not important to have the required skills before entering the profession. They can be inculcated while the social workers are undergoing training in an academic setting where they are taught about the required attributes and skills. These qualities can successfully be attained by undergoing training in a deliberate and systematic manner by sustained efforts monitoring one's own behaviour consciously while practicing with their clients.

Social workers work in government agencies, private enterprises, schools, hospitals, courts and much other type of workplaces. The expected personal attributes and skills by and large amongst the professional are as follows:

I. Personal Attributes

Genuine: The social worker should be genuinely concerned with the problem of his/her client. This should not only be depicted by the behaviour but should be communicated to the client verbally. Being genuine is indicative of getting passionately and truly attached with the situation of the client.

Hopeful: The social worker should always be hopeful in all the situations of the client. He should remain optimistic even if it may not be a very happy circumstance from the perspective of the client.

Trustworthy: The social worker should assure the client by emphasizing repeatedly that the communication between them will be dealt confidentially and will not be discussed with any other team member without seeking permission from the client. The client should get the feeling that the worker is dependable. This is likely to reaffirm the confidence of the client in the professional social worker.

Creative/Innovative: The social workers are expected to work with clients having wide range of personalities. It will be a fruitless exercise to use same technique with all of them. Therefore, it is a desired attribute on the part of social worker to be creative and innovative. He/She should be able to adapt as per the need of the client.

Flexible: The social worker should not be a rigid person. He/She must be able to change his plans depending on the priorities of the client and ready to accommodate.

Patient: The social worker should patiently hear the problems of his/her client. He/She should not rush in suggesting solutions/alternatives. Before speaking he/she must make an assessment of the strengths and limitations of his/her client. The client must also be given a chance to open up before the social worker. Being patient with the client is a significant indicator of being democratic and professional as well a good listener.

Empathetic: The most important characteristic of a social worker is their empathy. The majority of the people with whom the social workers work are in a state of crisis and emotional distress. Therefore, offering the clients a caring, understanding and empowering environment for them is an essential requirement of the profession The social worker should be in a position to place himself/herself in the position of their client and then try to visualize the problem from their perspective. Empathizing is both an intellectual and emotional process that makes it possible to understand and help others solve their problems. The common proverb used is that they should wear the shoes of their client in order to understand a situation from his/her perspective.

Resilient: Social Workers see difficult cases everyday and this inevitably disturbs their peace of mind. It is widely accepted that the clients seen by the social workers are in the difficult circumstances which may vary from physical and mental abuse, poverty, financial hardships, bereavement or a number of other life challenges. The social workers have to learn to let it go and should not let them affect their peace of mind. The capacity of resilience helps them deal with following the case with the same enthusiasm and energy.

Self-aware: Self-awareness implies being aware of one's own capabilities and limitations. The social worker should not let his own circumstances take priority or drive the problems of his/her clients. He should be able to evaluate his own performance in an objective manner and work towards improving it. This in fact is an invaluable asset of social workers which adds to the objectivity of the worker.

Persistent and Persuasive: The social workers have to realize that everything may not progress the way in which they think is appropriate. They have to be ready to accept setbacks as a part of helping process. They should not consider these setbacks as defeat and deter from working with their clients with the same vigour and enthusiasm. In fact they should be flexible in trying alternative approaches with their clients. It is one of the innate attributes of the social workers to be able to influence the clients continuously, coax or invite others to take action. In other words, the social workers should be persistent in their approach and be ready to help their clients in a continuous (persuasive) manner.

Relaxed: It is an accepted fact that social work is a highly rewarding profession. However, it can turn out to be stressful if the social worker gets over engaged with his clients. It is essential that the social workers know how to maintain a professional distance between them and the clients by setting their professional boundaries. Being objective and professional while working with the clients is likely to keep social workers relaxed and composed.

II. Skills

The skills are learnt and acquired by regular practice in the field. In social work profession it is always said the trainees can develop skills and competencies if they get a chance to practice which is popularly called 'Learning by Doing—Developing hands on Experience.' These are maneuvered over a period of time under the supervision of a trained and qualified social worker. The process of inculcating desired skills begins when the students desirous of becoming professional social workers seek admission in an academic institution and undergo masters programme in social work. This process of acquiring efficiency in skills (competency) does not stop after two years rather continues as long as the person is in active practice. With the passing of each day the level of competency goes higher. The expected skills in social workers are as follows:

Knowledge about Social Work Profession and related Disciplines: It is very important for the social workers to get an insight into the theories and methods of social work before actually starting to work with the clients. It is also important to understand the theories dealing with human behaviour as well as society. Hence, a required knowledge of Psychology and Sociology is an essential requirement for working with human beings.

Exceptional Communication Skills: Social Workers need to be exceptionally good and effective communicators since their daily tasks include discussions with clients, doctors, family members and other significant others of the client. The skill and care with which these responsibilities are managed can make all the difference in encouraging preferable and successful outcomes among clients (Rutger, 2018). Being a good communicator also includes the ability to listen carefully, asking pertinent questions and retaining verbally transmitted information. This is the first step towards helping the client by being a good listener the initial trust is established and the professional rapport is established between the worker and the client.

Outstanding Listening Skills: Listening actively is regarded as another significant skill of a successful social worker. He/She should give sufficient time to his/her client to express his emotions and problems. It is expected from the social worker to give a patient listening, show to the client by gestures that he/she is genuinely interested in him/her and is ready to provide a helping hand. Only after active listening, he/she will be in a position to analyse the speech and gestures of his clients. Social workers are able to develop this skill by constantly monitoring their behaviour while conversing with the clients.

Organisational Skills: The social workers are expected to handle multiple tasks simultaneously as they are the ones who play the key role in handling the problem of his/her clients. They are required to talk to professionals from different disciplines for the overall betterment of the client. This can be achieved successfully if the social worker is able to organise his/her work systematically and meticulously. This can best be achieved if the worker plans his/her day in advance prioritizing the tasks which are needed to be attended at first. At the end of each day monitoring needs to be carried out so that the left over work could be carried forth to the following day.

Analytical Skills: Social work profession is a practice based profession which believes in the overall betterment of the clients. It aims at improving the situations of clients by trying out different possible solutions though the choice of selecting the suitable solution rests with the client which is popularly called the *'decision making ability'* of the client. Therefore, it is important that the social worker is aware of all the possible interventional strategies which calls for the sound knowledge base and also his/her ability to analyse the problem expressed by the client. The strengths and limitations of the client help the social worker in arriving at the appropriate decision.

Effective Documentation Ability: The ability to take detailed notes popularly called the documentation ability is another essential skill expected to be possessed by the social workers throughout the social work process. It is only after taking the detailed notes that the social worker is in a position to understand all aspects of the problem as stated by the client, arrive at diagnosis and able to plan out the possible interventions keeping in view the abilities and weaknesses of the client.

Commitment to Social Work Code of Ethics: The social workers have to understand that they are helping the clients under the aegis of a profession which is bound by certain code of ethics. This help and the social workers to quickly and effectively establish a boundary in a concise and professional manner. This is not only important for ethical reasons but also justifies the reason of professionalism.

The social work profession deals with the human beings and the person will find himself/herself burnt out quickly if he/she does not rigorously apply and stick to professional boundaries. This also enables the professional in being objective.

Reference

https://online.rutgers.edu/resources/articles/7-traits-of-an-exceptional-social-worker/?program=msw retrieved on 10.4.2018

Part Two

10
Social Work as a Profession

Ravindra Singh

Meaning of Profession

As per nature and scope of the occupation, the word 'profession' has been used to denote an occupation involving special kind of training. According to Cambridge Dictionary 'profession' signifies *"any type of work that needs special training or a particular skill, often one that is respected because it involves a high level of education."* Oxford Dictionary defines 'profession' as *"a paid occupation, especially one that involves prolonged training and a formal qualification."* As per Merriam Webster Dictionary, a 'profession' is *"a calling requiring specialized knowledge and often long and intensive academic preparation."* Collins Dictionary defines *"a profession is a type of job that requires advanced education or training."* Hence, a profession requires a higher educational qualification with special training to deal with a particular occupation. Sometimes, it is thought that occupation involves certain degree of ethical responsibility. After brief perusal of meanings of profession, there are certain attributes, which are common in every definition. Hence, profession exhibits following characteristics:

- A specialized body of knowledge and skills.
- An area of operation.
- A code of ethics and certain degree of organisation among the members of the profession.
- Adherence to a professional code of conduct.

- Provision of training and occupation.
- A professional body to protect interest of profession.

From functional perspective, any profession exhibits following characteristics:

- Profession requires extensive training of an intellectual character.
- Professional services are essential to society's well-being.
- The practitioners of any profession usually have a high degree of autonomy in deciding how to carry out their job.
- Practitioners must undergo a process of certification or licensing by the state in order to be eligible to carry out certain tasks or provide certain services.
- Professionals are usually organised in associations that propagate code of ethics.

So, on this basis we can say all professions must have:

- A systematic body of knowledge, based on scientific theory.
- A mission of service to society.
- The service mission of social work is to enhance social functioning, help individuals, navigate through their society and help society provide resources to its citizens.
- Based on policy and/or legislations professions have authority to make and/or influence decision in prescribed situations.
- Regulative code of ethics.
- Self-regulations and sanctions accountability, licensing and certification.

Thus a specialized body of knowledge, skills, area of operation, code of ethics and certain degree of organisation characterize a profession.

Greenwood (1957) recognized the attributes of a profession of social work, i.e. systematic body of knowledge, community sanction, professional authority, code of ethics and professional culture. Based on these criteria Greenwood (1957) concluded

"Social work is already a profession; it as too many points of congruence with the model to be classifiable otherwise."

Systematic Body of Knowledge

Over the years, there has been a development of systematic body of knowledge in the discipline of social work. It has not only acquired the established knowledge of other disciplines like sociology, social anthropology, social psychology, economics and law to name a few; but it has also developed its own methods of practice with systematic knowledge around it. The theoretical knowledge around methods of intervention in social work has made it a specific discipline. The methods in social work like case work, group work and community organisation etc. provide the solid knowledge base for the discipline. Besides, the philosophy of social work provides a philosophical basis to make it a practice-based discipline. The epistemological basis of social work makes it more logical and distinguishes it from the belief and prejudice. The epistemic model we apply in the social work decides the direction of knowledge production and solution to the existing problems (Garrow & Hasenfeld, 2015). The knowledge production in social work around the problems like poverty, inequality and injustice navigates the practitioners to solutions, which shall be reflected in the social policies. By the passage of time, systematic body of knowledge has evolved and developed. It has identified various core competencies and skills for a professional social worker.

Social Work Competencies

A competency is the capacity or ability to perform a specific task well. The only problem with the competency approach is that one can administer a service competently but the service itself may not be effective.

The social work profession places so much emphasis not only on evidence-based practice, but also practice-based evidence for this they must have followed the same as under:

- Identify ourselves as professional social worker and behave accordingly.

- Professional practice must be guided through ethical principles of social work.
- Professional judgment communicated to client after applying critical thinking.
- In practice, acknowledgement of diversity and difference of client and situations.
- Advances human rights and social, economic justice.
- Engage in research informed practice and practice informed research.
- Apply knowledge of human behaviour and the social environment.
- Engage in policy practice to advance social and economic well-being and to deliver effective social work services.
- Respond to the context that shapes practice.
- Engage, assess, inference and evaluate with individuals, families, groups, organisations and communities.

Engagement—Use empathy and other interpersonal and culturally competent skills to focus on work with individuals, families, groups, organisations and communities.

Assessment—Collect, organise, assess and interpret client data to explore clients' strengths and limitations and develop mutually agreed and appropriate intervention strategies.

Intervention—Implement prevention interventions that enhance client capacities.

Help clients to resolve problems and develop mutually agreed upon intervention goals and objectives.

Negotiate, mediate and advocate for clients.

Facilitate, transition and endings.

Evaluation—Critically analyse, monitored evaluate interventions

Qualities of Good Social Worker

1. *Values:* What are good and desirables (Beckett, 2005).
2. *Knowledge:* Information, facts, theories, data and research findings (evidence based) as well as laws, policies and procedures (Beckett, 2005).
3. *Skills:* Ability to do something, listen, gather data, organic information, write clearly and concisely, follow through, convey empathy, avoid panic, motivate others and organise a process (Beckett, 2005).

Use of Self

- Relationship enhancement skills.
- Values and ethics (Accountable).
- Knowledge of Human Behaviour therapy.
- Knowledge/skills: Problem solving process, motivation, resistance.
- Self-disclosure.
- Confidentiality.
- Cultural competence.

Skills Required for Professional Social Worker

Skill is explained as the capacity of worker to apply knowledge and understanding of a given situation. Skills are acquired through teaching and training. Skill of programming arrives at satisfactory and fruitful relationships. Analyzing skill is useful in understanding the social situation, feeling of individual and group, utilizing the resources of agency and community, serving the client for self-dependent, diagnosing and treatment. While making professional relationship with clients, it must have objectivity and confidentiality on the one hand, sensitivity and warmth on the other. Social worker has to be confident of the techniques of individual and group conscientisation; organisation and planning; building and maintaining counter system and administrative techniques.

Community Sanction, Professional Authority and Professional Culture

In order to discuss the growth of social work as a professional discipline in lucid manner, author has converged the different attributes under one heading. Social work as a professional discipline is yet to evolve fully in India. It has been conceived as a professional discipline in terms of pedagogy and curriculum, however, it lacks the governmental recognition of its professional bodies. Meaning thereby, as there is lack of acceptable and umbrella organisation, which will control and regulate social workers at the national level. However, there has been unsuccessful attempt to put bodies at the national level by the leaders and visionary people of the profession from time to time.

As there is absence of recognized professional body at the national level, hence there is lack of community sanction. The professional culture of the discipline is yet to evolve in Indian context. The history of the social work profession in India from its formative days to till date encompasses trajectory of development of profession.

Clifford Manshardt, an American missionary in Mumbai was the first person to bring professional social work in India. He later became the Founder-Director of the Sir Dorabji Tata Graduate School of Social Work (later renamed as Tata Institute of Social Sciences). He succinctly perceived social environment in India is vastly different from the West and therefore emphasized a context specific social work in India (Desai, 1985). But when the social work education programmes developed in India, the cultural, economic and social differences were not adequately taken into consideration (Thomas, 1976). The curative model of social work based on the West was overemphasized, resulting in the limitation of social sciences content necessary for understanding the Indian socio-economic structures (Mandal, 1989). This ultimately led to the neglect of numerous local pressing concerns (Pathak, 1975). Nanavatty (1985: 315) gives a clear picture of the fact in the following manner:

Social work education in India began as an adaptation of the educational programme of USA, where social work services were meant to assist the people in their adjustment to an industrial, urban and metropolis dominated social milieu. In contrast, India has millions of people whose basic needs are unmet, rights infringed and mobility restricted. Hence, social work had to primarily relate to social justice rather than promoting adjustments.

In concurrence of the above mentioned argument Desai (1985: 44) also reflects the same point and opined: In a country where the majority of people are rural, where exploitation and injustice leave the majority in a state of poverty, social work has remained to a large extent peripheral to the root causes of the problems of a non-industrial and rural society. That resulted into the absence of indigenous literature in social work. The social work educators have tried quite a number of times to promote social work and gain recognition akin to other practiced professions like law, medicine and nursing.

The first effort for professionalization of social work in India came in 1947 with the Indian Conference of Social Work (ICSW), which acted as a forum for the development of public opinion on social work and welfare. Later in the 1960s, two important associations came to the forefront, namely the Association of Schools of Social Work in India (ASSWI) in 1960 and the Indian Association of Trained Social Workers (IATSW) in 1964. Since 1970s, arrays of regional level associations such as Bombay Association of Trained Social Workers (BATSW), Maharashtra Association of Social Work Educators (MASWE), Karnataka Association of Professional Social Workers (KAPSW), and Professional Social Workers Forum, Chennai (PSWFC) have emerged. At the national level, the Indian Society of Professional Social Work (ISPSW), Associations of Schools of Social Work in India (ASSWI) and the National Association of Professional Social Workers in India (NAPSWI) and Bharatiya Samaj Karya Parishad (BSKP) emerged as the major players. Various legislative attempts have been made through the efforts of these professional associations at the regional and national level. The National Council of Professional Social Work in India Bill (1993), the National Council of Professional Social Work in India Bill (2007), and the Maharashtra Social Work Council Bill are examples of some of the efforts taken by these associations at the legislative front. However, due to the infighting between clinical social workers and social action/developmental social workers, a united face has never been shown by the social work associations. This has left the entire profession in deep slumber and inactivity. Therefore, for the future efforts to be successful, as witnessed elsewhere, it is important for the both camps to come together. In this context, the proposal by Mizra Ahmad provided new directions in social work education (Laavanya, 2013). The five-point proposal is as follows:

- Shifting from welfare to developmental and social rights orientation.
- Shifting focus from pathology to addressing the needs of development and promoting the empowerment of the vulnerable.
- Reducing the emphasis on micro level intervention strategies and more attention to be given to issues at the macro level.

- Reducing dependence on Western models and evolving indigenous models of social work.
- Keeping constant watch on the changing social, economic and political realities at the local, national and international level so that professionals can respond to the changing needs of the clientele and the society in general.

Long time has passed since Mizra Ahmad gave these suggestions. But the social work practitioners and social work educators are not keen in implementing the five-point proposal (Laavanya, 2013). One major reason for this was the lack of consensus among social work educators to the proposal. Most of the social workers from the clinical stream find the proposal of Mizra Ahmad to be biased towards macro practice. This is a compelling contention as the third point was for reducing the emphasis of micro interventions and the clinicians find it as a biased proposal, which undermines the mental health challenges in the country. To set the differences right, the National Level associations of the schools of social work should have taken a lead. In 2012, the School of Social Work in the Tata Institute of Social Sciences along with many other schools and departments of social work in India came together and floated the National Network of Schools of Social Work (NNSSW) for quality enhancement of social work education in India. The key objectives of the network were to suggest strategies for developing minimum standards in social work education, developing modalities for supporting new departments of social work, and formulation of the National Council on professional social work bill. The social work educators who attended the national network consultation resolved to make social work emancipatory, participatory and liberating (Nadkarni & Desai, 2012).

Code of Ethics in the Profession of Social Work

A social worker operates in terms of certain basic assumptions:

(1) respect for human personality,
(2) dignity of each human being,
(3) matching resources with needs,
(4) stimulating change calculated to enhance democratic values,

(5) accomplishing change through co-operation on both intellectual and emotional levels, and
(6) serving as a change agent.

The code of ethics includes giving respect to the privacy of people and reposing precedence to professional responsibility over personal interests. It also includes primary obligation for welfare of individuals including action for improving social conditions. Besides, social worker is also responsible for quality and extent of service rendered to the client.

Social Work as a Profession

The development of social work as a *practiced based discipline* was influenced by social, political and economical pressure. The change in economic system, urbanization and industrialization, leads to change in social system and have played a major role in the emergence of social work as profession. Social Work Profession believes on the equality, equity, human rights and social justice and these are very close to the heart of Profession. Social work is a professional service based on scientific knowledge and skills in human relations. It meets all the criterion of a profession, particularly with regard to promoting the well-being of individuals and society as a whole.

Professional Social workers assist individuals, groups or communities to restore or enhance their capacity for social functioning, while creating societal conditions favourable to their goals. Social worker helps people rise above some of most difficult challenges, i.e. poverty, ill health, discrimination, unemployment, disability and mental illness, and abuse. They help to prevent crises and counsel individuals, families and communities to cope with everyday life stresses.

Person in the Environment Perspective

Social worker viewed the world through a unique conceptual lens. This involved viewing the simultaneous and multiple interactions that occur between a person and their environment.

Social workers are interested in the pragmatic applications of principles drawn from psychology, social psychology and sociology.

Social Work and Social Justice

The profession of Social Work has always been a supporter of the poor, the oppressed, the marginalized and the untouchables in society. While it may be difficult, Social workers are admonished to advocate for the rights of other and to work against social injustice.

Social Work and Human Diversity

Social Workers are required to respect human diversity. To fulfil this they work to develop a liking for everyone. This would be achieved through the people you help and the people you help will transform your life as much if not more than you transform theirs.

Generalist Social Work

This is evidence based professional practice engaged in without discrimination. It entails working directly with client systems (Individuals, couples, families, groups, organisations, agencies, communities and larger human systems) to enhance human well-being and alleviate social and economic injustice.

This is based on the professional knowledge, skills, values and ethics of the social work profession to provide integrated multilevel approaches. The emphasis on importance of relationships and interactions of client systems, their environment, the issues that make them diverse and the larger context of social and historic events.

The foundation of professional Social Work practice grounded in the core values of service, social justice, the dignity and worth of every person, the importance of human relationships integrity and competence.

The professional relationship between Social worker and client means:

- It is a contract; it starts with providing help, support and ends when the problem be solved.
- It is confined according to the nature of problem and for a specific purpose.

- Its focus is on clients' needs and problems.

Social Work Profession believes in certain generic principles, these are:

- Conviction of the inherent worth, the integrity and the dignity of the individual. This is the first principle in making professional relationships.
- Right to determine the client's needs and the way to fulfil those needs. This refers to principles of choice and self-determination.
- The firm belief in equal opportunities for all, limited only by the individual innate capacity.
- Social worker offers warmth, acceptance and understanding about individuals. Social worker believes in the principles of acceptance, it means he accepts the individual as he/she is and with all his/her limitations.
- It is essential for the diagnosis and treatment of client's problems that social worker abide by the principles of confidentiality.

Challenges before Social Work as a Profession

- In many social work schools, which follow the American model of social work, has very weak footprint to support the development of Indian Social Work Profession in local context.
- Social work educators are devoid of field realities. In the designing of course curriculum, the changing need of time has not been considered and often curriculum not revised for many years.
- Social work in many schools often taught theoretically and not by practicing. Hence, there is dire need of practice-based teaching method. Thus lack of explicit ideology affects institutions imparting social work education, students, teaching and learning.
- Social workers can represent the voices of community at the policy and at the level of programme planning. However, due to lack of coordination with government

machinery the contribution of social work as profession has not been acknowledged.

- The area of specialized knowledge in social work is still somewhat limited. Little attempts have been made to develop systematic empirical knowledge related to typical problems, situation and ways of handling them.

Conclusion and Recommendations

In order to establish the social work as a full-fledged profession, two fundamental attributes are required. Firstly, there should be distinguished need of the society which provides foundation to the social legitimacy and secondly, wider recognition by the state which gives legal legitimacy to the profession. The recognition by the state involves adoption of regulatory and ethical mechanism of the profession. Where state recognition comes on the cost of independence of the profession in terms of rules and regulation; absence of state recognition impedes the holistic and contextual growth of profession in India. The prerequisites for the social work to be considered, as profession has always been there principally however, it has not been translated into the reality. The essence of profession has been missed and has not been translated into the reality in practicing the profession. It has also been witnessed that social work as a profession has not been able to make headway in India also because of absence of clarity on focus of the profession in terms of curative and developmental. In a country of billion plus population, the curative methods of social work intervention have not been able to make dent in social condition of the people in the country, hence it has not been able to transcend from classroom discourse to field-based discipline. As common people find it of lesser useful resultantly scope and scale of the discipline has reduced by the passage of time.

Social workers should responsibly use the knowledge gained from professional practice to benefit the community, this would be an integral part of their professional practice. In order to establish the credibility as a profession, there must be national level regulatory body. It will not only streamline the work of social work as a practice-based discipline but will also ensure the development of profession in coming days.

References

Bogo, M. (2007). *Social Work Practice: Concept, Processes and Interviewing,* Jaipur: Rawat Publications.

Garrow, E.E. and Yeheskel, H. (2015). "The Epistemological Challenges of Social Work Intervention Research." Research on Social Work Practice (Sage), 1-9.

Laavanya, P.V. (2013). "Social Work Associations and Professional Growth." In Y. Ronald; S. Malar and P.V. Laavanya (Eds.) *Social Work: An Introductory Text Book.* New Delhi: Regal Publications, 145-152.

Lawrence, R.J. (2016). *Professional Social Work in Australia,* ANU Press, Australia.

Pawar, M. (1999). "Professional Social Work in India: Some Issues and Strategies", *Indian Journal of Social Work,* 60(4), 583-586.

Philip, R.P. (1985). "The Social Work Profession: A Reconceptualisation", *Social Service Review,* 59(4), 560-577.

Ronald, Y. (2013). "Introduction to Social Work", In Y. Ronald; S. Malar and P.V. Laavanya (Eds.). *Social Work: An Introductory Text Book,* New Delhi: Regal Publications, pp. 3-11.

Ronald Y. (2014). "Professional Social Work: Revisiting the Past and Envisioning the Future in India", *Rajagiri Journal of Social Development,* 6(2).

11

Prerequisites of Social Work Profession

Contextualizing India

Binod Kumar

Introduction

The idea of professional social work emanates from philosophies of justice and dignity of individuals. Like any other profession across the world, social work also developed in the certain socio-political reality of the time. The oriental roots of social work dates back to the ancient period, however, the social work discipline in the current form came in the year 1936 with the establishment of Sri Dorabji Tata Graduate School of Social Work in Mumbai. The advent of professional social work in India has seen tremendous change after that. Initially, it was more focused towards the problems of workers, rural development and upliftment of the marginalized, it tends to renew its focus to the corporate social responsibility by the corporates in recent times. However, core Western principles and philosophies of the social work remain unchallenged. In the changing face of society and economy, it needs to revamp the core values, principles and philosophies to make more relevant and effective intervention to alleviate the sufferings of the marginalized.

The sheer range of social and personal problems has led to the development of a discipline. It has always borrowed heavily from the contemporary socio-political field practices. In addition to courses on social work methods and client groups, it borrows partially from psychology, law, sociology, political science, philosophy, social history, gender studies, social administration, social policy, research methodology, and so forth. Looking at the galaxy of subjects to be taught in social work course, students struggle to find books in the library that do not plausibly relate to their future tasks.

The praxis of Professional Social work relates to the poor, troubled, abused or discriminated against, neglected, frail and elderly, mentally ill, learning-disabled, addicted, delinquent, or otherwise socially marginalized. With the retreat of state and withering away of welfare state, scope and scale of social work has become ever increasing. The realm in which social work profession functions is so large that unless problems fall exclusively under the duties of the army or the fire service, then social workers are expected to do something — whatever that might be. In the wake of restructuring state apparatus and withdrawal of state, we need informed social workers; who abide and follow the basic premise of profession. Uniqueness of social work profession lies in the fact of *sui generis* client-social worker relationship, which defines ethical relationship *would-be-helpers* and *might-be-helped*. Therefore, respectively, it confers more rights and requires more obligations than 'customer' or 'service user' which exists in normal transactions.

As the world is getting transformed in numerous senses so is the case with professional social work. The way any political system or economy has been structured in any nation, it has great impact in scope and scale of profession of social work. In the time of retreat of state, scope and scale of social work has increased globally. However, Western conception of profession of social work has gone under severe transformation and has been adapted locally as per socio-ecological requirement. Western conception of social work came up with certain values, principles and ethics and the same has been adapted as per local needs in global south. In this backdrop, social work profession in India follows the global footprint. Notwithstanding, it has also adapted the globally accepted fundamentals of profession, however, social work profession is still in the crisis and struggling for its recognition at national level. In the absence of national level social work council, professionals are not regulated/abide by certain framework; hence they are working in vacuum. Without codification of ethics and rules, professionals are able to take up galaxy of work but to get recognition, acknowledgement and development of national social work council is need of hour. The need for social work council has been realized and felt in India and consultation for the same is under process. Like any other established profession social work also has basic ingredient, which requires to be adhered to. Through this chapter, author tries to enumerate essentials in social work profession.

Knowledge

Knowledge formation and knowledge enhancement through rich field practices has been intricate part of social work knowledge process apart from theoretical contracts. Knowledge in social work is integrated aspect of theories and field practices. From the very beginning of social work education, two competing conception of social work knowledge can be identified. Which are often been portrayed in the juxtaposition of the two pioneers of social work—Mary Richmond (1861–1928) and Jane Addams (1860–1935) (Trevithick, 2008).

In an ongoing debate about social work knowledge, they might be pictured in the juxtaposition of 'evidence based practice' (EBP) and 'the reflexive practitioner'. This debate is characterized by strong and often inflexible positions on how to achieve knowledge for social work practice. There are commonalities and differences between these two paradigms of knowledge (Righard & Montesino). First of all, they share a common view that it is feasible to achieve knowledge about the social and to use the same knowledge to manage social deviance. Both schools of thought agree on necessity of knowledge production in a way to attain professionalism and successful social intervention through social work profession. These premises constitute a taken-for-granted starting point for knowledge production and might be viewed as a common ground for both conceptions. However, there is multitude of differences as they rely on different epistemological understandings. Within these two conceptions of knowledge, knowledge is different 'things' achieved in different ways. In the tradition of Mary Richmond (1917), knowledge is objective, universal and accumulative and might be ascribed to a Cartesian notion of knowledge (Henkel, 1995). In contrast, in the tradition of Jane Addams (1902), knowledge is reflexive, contextual and diversified and has been ascribed to critical pragmatism (Trevithick, 2008).

The first conception of knowledge relies on a dualism of theory and practice. This division denotes that theory is considered as something created by scientists and practice as the place where the theory is to be applied. Hence, knowledge production and the application in practice are two separate procedures (Trevithick, 2008).

In the second conception of knowledge, knowledge production and application is, by contrast, conceived as one unified process, which cannot be separated from the practice context, but is generated in and through the practice. These two competing conceptions of knowledge are to be regarded as two ideal types in a Weberian sense (Trevithick, 2008).

It is clear that knowledge is divided into theoretical and practical knowledge but it also starts with theoretical knowledge as foundation. Finally, the dualistic conception of knowledge can be understood against the backdrop of the hierarchical order of knowledge. When it came to the question of integration between theory and practice, theory and practice must support each other. During the field studies, theoretical knowledge must be applied and in discussing theoretical knowledge field experiences must be followed up. Despite the dualistic approach to knowledge having assumed a dominant paradigm within social work education, of late reflexive approach has gained the momentum.

Social Work Principles

Miley *et al.* (2009) identify principles in social work as acceptance, individualization, a non-judgmental approach, objectivity, self-determination and access to resources, confidentiality and accountability. Hepworth and Larsen (1986) in Allen-Meares (2007) articulate that all people should have access to resources; that every person is unique and has inherent worth; that people have a right to freedom and that individual citizens and society as a whole should realize these principles (Prinsloo, 2014). Principles are cardinal to practice in social work profession. Whenever, social work practitioner feels dilemma of ethics and values he need to revisit the principle so as to maintain the sanctity and decorum of profession.

Values and Ethics in Social Work

Any profession dealing with human being needs to observe extra care and sensitivity. So is the case with social work profession. Ethics in social work has been basic premise on which profession of social is based upon. To ensure well-being of the client, ethics needs to be monitored and gauged specifically in the profession of social work. In the process of ensuring well-being of the client, social workers always face challenges on daily basis, as they are not always clear what action is most appropriate for their client.

Social work students are trained with specific knowledge of professional values. By the passage of time and with their immersion in the field, they face conflict of professional values and ethical dilemma. In pursuance of responsible treatment of client social workers need to raise issues of ethical dilemma and values conflict rather than ignoring it. Professionals in social believe that they know requisite values and ethics in social work but social landscape has become such a vibrant platform that it requires frequent remolding and refinement to fit in the context. As interest of client is supreme in the profession of social work, we must agree that best suitable decision for the client's life cannot be taken arbitrarily. It has been observed that specific knowledge and facts about value and ethic does not necessarily lead to appropriate practice. Many of them are better in argumentation of values and ethics rather in application, which represents imbalance in theory and practice in social work discipline.

Social work is a humanitarian science, as well as applied science; hence social workers need to arrive value-based decisions rather than decisions solely based on knowledge. Constant tension between knowledge and values in social work field practice creates dilemma for practitioner. Where values are the implicit and explicit ideas about which we cherish as ideal and preferable; knowledge on the other hand refers to empirically supported findings documented by previous research (Kreitzer, 2006).

Social work is value-based profession and from its inception, it has special focus on values with which social worker engage with client. Reamer (2006), one of the most prominent social work ethics scholars, argued that since the profession's inception "social workers' attention was focused primarily on cultivating a set of values upon which the mission of social work could be based." By the passage of time, social profession has nurtured and refined values which has given meaning and purpose to host of practitioners. Of late, enduring commitment to vulnerable and oppressed people, individual well-being, and social justice. However, by the passage of time, practice has germinated host of ethical issues which challenge its nature of value based profession. Constant tension between social workers' commitment to individual and welfare of the society at large, their own personal values and professional values are few examples of this conflict. Changing practice context of social work profession with emergence of medical model and entrepreneurial model has increased the complexity.

Reamer 1998 identified four distinct periods of ethical practice even within the brief history of social work as profession. Each period represents a unique socio-political milieu necessitated social workers to emphasize new and changing values and priorities to guide their practice.

The first period called as "Morality Period" is characterized by a paternalistic preoccupation with the poor. Later part of this period witnessed Great Depression and profession realigned the priorities to face the newer challenges of housing, health care, poverty, unemployment and education (Reamer, 2006).

Reamer (1998) mentions second wave of values in social work profession as "Value Period" in which social workers focused more on profession and its area of expertise rather than client morality. Significant efforts during this period were made to develop core professional values. During this period, Social workers were trained to uphold a "prominent set of values focused on social equity, welfare rights, human rights, discrimination, and oppression" which propelled the discussion of social work ethics into the third world. Around 1970s social work profession underwent significant transformation in its concern and values and started devoting sustained attention to values and ethics. Fourth and last period is Risk Management period, which started in the wake of changing landscape of health care technologies, unethical behaviour by professionals. This stage is characterized by significant expansion of ethical standard to guide practitioners' conduct by increased knowledge concerning professional negligence and liability.

Social work as a practice-based discipline has always

maintained a distinction because of its roots in social justice, equality, and fairness. In practice these values permeates numerous dilemma for social work practitioners. One of such dilemma more common today than never before is whether to provide a particular service despite financial constraints. In addition to upholding confidentiality, person-centred practice, professional accountability social workers need to apply ethical reasoning in their practice to resolve the problem of ethical dilemma.

These values are service to others, promoting social justice, respecting the dignity and worth of the person, recognizing the importance of human relationships and maintaining integrity and competence. An inability to conform to these basic principles, as defined through professional rather than worldview-based interpretations, is indicative of an unresolved value-practice conflict or perhaps professional unsuitability.

Social workers have inherent responsibility to put effort in meeting basic human needs. However, with difficult economic situation, limited resources, complex political choices and limited legal framework create ethical dilemma for social workers across the globe. Sometimes, social workers feel that they lack resources and legal frame is not supportive, while ethics are still bounding them.

Skills and Competencies

Competence is both a professional and pedestrian term. According to Drisko (2014), competence refers to "the ability of an individual to perform a task," further adding that "the task must be performed fully and properly" (p. 416). McKnight (2013) proposes that competence is an "ongoing ability" to "integrate knowledge, skills, judgement, and professional attributes in order to practice safely and ethically" within one's professional scope (Poulin & Matis, 2015). Simply, *competence* refers to the ability of the individual to complete tasks related to real-life situations within his or her profession (Blomeke, Gustafsson & Shavelson, 2015). Competence in social work is the ability to integrate and apply social work knowledge, values and skills in purposeful and professional manner to facilitate human and community well-being. In furtherance of bridging the gap between theory and practice, discipline of social work has a special emphasis on competency based education; which refers to outcome approach to education. The emphasis is on what comes out of social work education rather than what goes into the curriculum of social work.

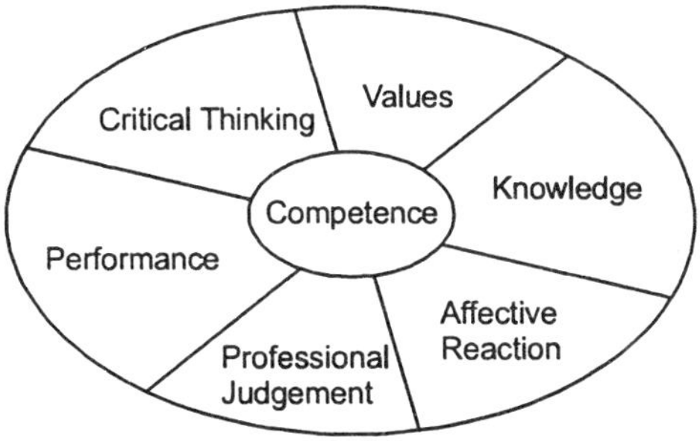

Fig. 11.1: Dimensions of Social Work Competencies (Poulin & Matis, 2015)

Competency based approach has a focus on identifying competency and practice behaviours rather than preparing the content and readings. This model of competency emphasizes on behavioural operationalization rather than having knowledge without action. Competence approach needs to calibrate itself as it has inadequate emphasis on development of the profession. As social work education and profession in India has not been able to integrate indigenous practices and responsive to global changes, it needs to focus more on training and evaluation *vis-à-vis* competence development. UGC Review Committee on social work education has voiced concern about standardization of social work education in India, however, little attention has been given to it (UGC, 1980). Academicians across the regions and institutions recognize the challenges of Indian Social Work Education even after 75 years of educational history. Without standardization and mainstreaming of educational curricula, competence and skills in social work discipline eludes more instead of giving clarity to professionals (Alexander, 2015).

Without infusing the local concern, Indian social work education has been more inspired by American model of social work education with postgraduate courses with specializations (Gore, 2002). Many social workers have voiced their concerns and have declared the American model as unsuited and redundant to Indian scenario as it has more focus on urban oriented interventions and has inadequate emphasis on broader developmental issues. Due to this model, skills and competency to intervene in the field proves insufficient for Indian social workers. Choice of specialization focused two years postgraduate course in Indian social work education has been result of American influence. Where by the passage of time American social work profession underwent tremendous changes Indian social work is still carrying the same old pattern. It is important to discuss in the backdrop of changing socio-political realities and inculcating general competence among social workers. The modes of core competence training have taken various forms in different parts of the world. In many developed countries like US, the UK, Canada, Australia and New Zealand, a generalist bachelor degree in social work (BSW) is the qualifying degree for social work practice whereas specialized practice is pursued through Masters in Social Work (MSW) (Alexander, 2015). In contrast to that MSW in India is entry-level course for practicing social work with elective specialization in second year of the course. Apart from that Western countries have also stressed about competence based social work education. The structure and modes of teaching and curricula has affected the competency of Indian social workers in large scale. Consequently, there has been emergence of many threads within social work profession in India, which is hampering the formation, and constitution of National Social Work Council. In absence of National Social Work Council, the educational space has been highly contested and unregulated (Alexander, 2015).

The importance of competence-based education has been underlined by UGC too through its various reports. In India, the UGC Model Curriculum Report 2001 recognized that the organizing elements of the educational programmes for the profession irrespective of the curriculum frame chosen were: (1) the values of the profession, (2) the skills and the methods developed for professional tasks, and (3) the major theories and concepts (UGC, 2001). These elements are similar to the competence components of knowledge, values and skills. However, the curriculum frame adopted by the UGC Model Curriculum placed the instructional content in four sets: the core domain, the supportive domain, interdisciplinary domain and elective content, without directly linking these to the organizing elements (Alexander, 2015).

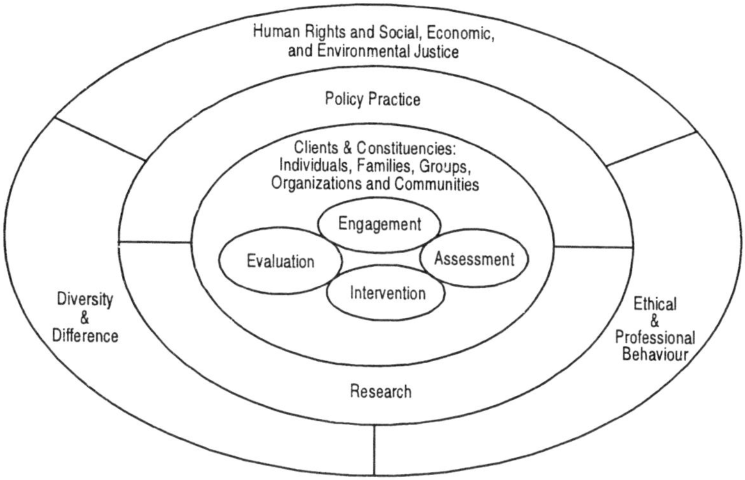

Fig. 11.2: Social Work Competencies (Poulin & Matis, 2015)

US Model

The Council on Social Work Education (CSWE) of US began the process of reviewing and revising the Educational Policy and Accreditation Standards (EPAS). It identified several principles to guide its work, one of which was to enhance programme flexibility by using a competency-based outcome approach to curriculum design; finally the competency-based education approach was adopted for the 2008 EPAS (CSWE, 2008). The 2015 EPAS identify nine social work competencies: (1) demonstrate ethical and professional behaviour; (2) engage diversity and difference in practice; (3) advance human rights and social, economic, and environmental justice; (4) engage in practice-informed research and research-informed practice; (5) engage in policy practice; (6) engage with individuals, families, groups, organisations, and communities; (7) assess individuals, families, groups, organisations, and communities; (8) intervene with individuals, families, groups, organisations, and communities; and (9) evaluate practice with individuals, families, groups, organisations, and communities. The 2015 EPAS provide a description of each that defines the competency (Poulin & Matis, 2015).

UK Model

Social work training in Europe started with a process of training for an occupation, which then developed through specialization and degree level education to professionalisation and a scientific status (Hamburger *et al.*, 2008). The Central Council for Education and Training in Social Work (CCETSW) was the earliest regulator of Social Work Education and Training in the UK, which comprises England, Wales, Northern Ireland and Scotland. The functions of CCETSW were taken over by the General Social Care Council (GSCC) in 2001, which was replaced by the Health and Care Professions Council (HCPC) in England in 2012. Before the dissolution of the GSCC in England, all the social workers in UK were guided by the National Occupational Standards (NOS) which was framed and revised by the GSCC in 2003 and 2011 respectively (CCW, 2015). CCETSW had defined the requirements for qualifying in social work in terms of knowledge, skills and values and recommended a single professional qualification with students achieving a general knowledge of all care settings and client groups. CCETSW laid down six core competencies, which were translated by the GSCC National Occupational Standards (NOS) as the six key roles of social workers: (1) Prepare for, and work with individuals, families, careers, groups and communities to assess their needs and circumstances; (2) Plan, carry out, review and evaluate social work practice, with individuals, families, careers, groups, communities and other professionals; (3) Support individuals to represent their needs, views and circumstances; (4) Manage risk to individuals, families, careers, groups, communities, self and colleagues; (5) Manage and be accountable, with supervision and support, for your own social work practice within your organisation; (6) Demonstrate professional competence in social work practice (WofScon, 2001; GSCC, 2011).

In addition to that International Social Work competency involves cross-cultural knowledge, inter-governmental work, professional exchange and a general worldview according to Healy. To ensure better practices at international level, social workers should know international and intercultural knowledge for the purpose of developing cultural sensitivity. In the wake of globalization, social work profession needs to establish inter-linkages so as to resolve interconnected issues. Post Washington consensus world has become internationalized in numerous senses. In a changed global scenario, Social work profession needs to prepare itself in such a way so that it can resolve the international interconnected issues. In this backdrop, the International Federation of Social Workers (IFSW) has laid standards for social workers, students and professionals across the globe (IFSW, 2012). A study from Hong Kong identifies five elements which contribute to international competency in Social Work: values, skills, knowledge, personal qualities and culture (Mok, 2013).

Conclusion

Being a humanitarian science, social work profession needs to engage local socio-political realities. The way core competence has been inculcated among Indian social worker has led it to be an urban centric profession. Academician across the region needs to think about making it more relevant in true sense in Indian context. The way we have imitated the American model has become irrelevant and redundant in current context. Even US has seen tremendous transformation of discipline by the passage and molded the curricula to make it more relevant. It has led to a different competence paradigm from specialized to generalist core competence. With the change in macro-economic scenario in India, there has been change at grassroots level which social work profession needs to attend. Besides, withdrawal of state has changed the landscape on which social work has been engaging traditionally. If social work needs to be relevant, it has to reinvent itself to suit the current milieu and develop the competence accordingly.

References

Alexander, J.S. (2015). "Indian Social Work Education: A Generalist Core Competence Approach", *Rajagiri Journal of Social Development, 7*(2): 91-103.

Beresford, P. and Boxall, K. (2012). "Service Users, Social Work Education and Knowledge for Social Work Practice", *Social Work Education, 31*(2): 155-167.

Chechak, D. (2015). "Social Work as a Value-Based Profession: Value Conflicts and Implications for Practitioners' Self-Concepts", *Journal of Social Work Values and Ethics, 12* (2), 41-48.

Dimitrijoska, S. and Ilievski, V. (2016). "Ethics and Value Dilemmas in Social Work", *Ethics and Value Dilemmas in Social Work, 15*(1): 49-58.

Heinsch, M.; Gray, M. and Sharland, E. (2016). "Re-conceptualising the link between research and practice in social work: A literature review on knowledge utilisation", *International Journal of Social Welfare, 25.*

Poulin, J. and Matis, S. (2015). "Perspectives Social Work Competencies and Multidimensional Assessment", *The Journal of Baccalaureate Social Work, 20,* 117-135.

Prinsloo, R.C. (2014). *Social Work Values and Principles: Students' Experiences in Intervention with Children and Youths in Detention. 28,* 545-560.

Trevithick, P. (2008). "Revisiting the Knowledge Base of Social Work: A Framework for Practice", *British Journal of Social Work,* 38*(6),* 1212-1237.

Tsang, N.M. (2014). "Knowledge, Professional and Practice Integration in Social Work Education", *British Journal of Social Work,* 44*(6),* 1384-1401.

Valutis, S. and Rubin, D. (2016). "Social Work Values and Principles: Students' Experiences in Intervention with Children and Youths in Detention", *Journal of Social Work Values and Ethics,* 13(1): 11-24.

12
Integrated Method in Social Work Practice

Swati Bist

Introduction

The societies across nations are facing problems, ranging from conflict between groups leading to political unrest in various parts of the world, displacement, social exclusion, poverty, poor health and hygiene, disability and women facing oppression in the private and public domain. Social work profession works towards eradication of poverty, inequality, and promote social justice, human rights and peace among all sections of the society. The social work profession also helps individuals to enhance their social functioning and maintain a dignified standard of living. The IASS & IFSW defines social work profession as "The social work profession promotes social change, problem solving in human relationships and the empowerment and liberation of people to enhance well-being. Utilising theories of human behaviour and social systems, social work intervenes at the points where people interact with their environments. Principles of human rights and social justice are fundamental to social work" (2004: 2). Roy and Dash defines "Social work education is value based, ethical and spiritual practice based profession aims at addressing the overall problems of individuals, families, groups and communities to attain a peaceful life" (2016: 4). The present chapter begins with shedding light on the history of development of social work profession and development of integrated approach in the contemporary times. The other section of the chapter covers the problem of domestic violence, requiring multipronged action. The chapter evaluates services being offered to women facing domestic violence by Special Cells for Women (Crime Against Women Cells, CAW cells; Special Cell for Women and Children, SPUWAC), set up by Delhi Police in NCT of Delhi in light of integrated approach in social work profession.

Social Work Practice: An Integrated Approach

The roots of Social Work Profession can be traced back to the charity organisation and settlement house movements in the West. The charity organisation could largely be credited for development of case work tradition as they worked closely with individual and provided welfare services to the families. Mary Richmond was one of the pioneer Social work professional who contributed significantly to the case work tradition and wrote a book named "*Social Diagnosis*". The case worker emphasised on working with people through individual's social relationship to address the problem lying with individual or environment. Later on, they further diversified their services to correctional, psychiatric, hospital and school setting (Larkin, 2006; Kadushin & Harkness, 2002).

Unlike Charity Organisation who emphasised on working with individual and families, the approach of settlement house movement was quiet different. They emphasised on social reform as they believed that individual's development takes place in the given environmental context. They worked with people through the formation of education and recreational groups to channelize the energies of children and youth in the socially desirable direction. In the beginning, the social work profession was largely dominated by case work tradition. Till last many decades, the group worker didn't identify themselves with social work professional and they did have separate professional bodies. During 1950s, group work practitioner joined hand with the National Association of Social Workers in USA. This led to further expansion of group work practice in providing treatment to the individuals through various group therapies in the mental health setting as they started appreciating various psychological theories (Larkin, 2006).

It is difficult to trace the history of community work as it existed times immemorial but it was recognised as a method of social work during 1960 by Council on Social Work Education in

USA. Community organisation owes it origin to charity organisation and settlement house. The Charity organisations expanded their work and they started working in the neighbourhood through the formation of "community chest" and "united fund." Settlement house movement too expanded their work during the beginning of twentieth century. They believed in environmental factors determining the prevailing conditions of the individuals and the community. They started demanding structural changes and modification in various existing legislations pertaining to children and housing rents. They believed in participation and mutual aid to develop capabilities and potentialities of the community to deal effectively with the problems. This led to the development of community work and neighbourhood intervention with the people, to identify needs and to work towards fulfilling the inadequacy in the community (Agnimitra, 2013; Siddiqui, 1997).

In India, social work profession started with the community work in the slums of the city of Mumbai, which further led to the establishment of Sir Dorabjee Tata Graduate School of Social Work. But Case work approach dominated the social work profession until 1950 with launch of massive government programme of community development (Agnimitra, 2013; Siddiqui, 1997).

At present, Social work profession draws its knowledge from diverse discipline such as psychology, sociology, philosophy and laws etc. There is no unifying theory in these disciplines which adequately gives explanation to the problem, though enhancing understanding of the phenomena partially. Ecological perspective provides conceptual guiding framework to social work profession, promoting integrated practice to deal diverse complex social situations.

According to the ecological perspective, social environment (values, norms and culture) influences individual by various levels of organisations of human relation network. Socialization of a child occurs in the context of immediate environment comprising family members and the community, which in turn gets influenced by the cultural belief of the given society. This is a dynamic transaction, where the individual and the environment both influences each other (Bronfenbrenner, 1979). Social work practitioner believes in working with person-environment interaction to deal effectively with social functioning of the individual and society. Social work practice believes in integrating diverse approaches to work with the people and address the problem in more comprehensive manner (Larkin, 2006).

Drawing inspiration from ecological perspective, the social work profession appreciates importance of interventions at various levels of social system. In social work discipline, besides teaching diverse field of social sciences such as, sociology, economics, psychology and law to name a few, it has developed its own body of knowledge, recognising six methods of working with people. These methods can be clubbed in two categories, namely, primary and secondary methods of interventions. *Primary methods* includes social case work[1], group work[2] and community organisation.[3] These methods provide opportunity to work directly with clients and groups to enhance their adjustment in the society. *Secondary method* of social work includes social action and community development[4], welfare administration[5] and research.[6] These methods are directed toward bringing changes at macro level through policies and legislations, affecting a larger section of the society or supplement in drawing out direct intervention strategies. Thus, social work profession promotes integrated practice to deal multiple aspects of the problem. It highly appreciates simultaneous working with various interrelated social system through collaboration, networking and referral services.

Addressing Problem of Domestic Violence: A Multipronged Integrated Approach

All societies across the world have witnessed a secondary status of woman as compared to man. Since ages women are being systematically subordinated by her male counterpart. Engles (1942) in his book titled *"The origin of the family, private property and the state"* made an attempt to explain subjugation of women across the globe. He wrote that earlier human societies were heading a life of nomadic. Later on, they started settling down in one place and simultaneously, started agriculture in more organised manner, giving rise to the concept of private property and further, subjugation of women to ensure control over production, that is, means of sustenance of human life and human life itself through control over reproduction.

The National Crime Record Bureau (NCRB) compiles data on crime against women which ranges from cruelty by husband and relatives to dowry death, rape, and sexual harassment, cases of immoral trafficking, kidnapping and molestation. The report brings out the fact that domestic violence constitutes half of crime committed against women during, 2016 (NCRB, 2017). These data clearly narrate that women are facing extreme atrocities and violence where they should be safe indeed. In this section, problem of domestic violence will be discussed in detail, focusing initiatives taken by Delhi Police in NCT of Delhi through setting up of special cells for women and critical evaluation of these services.

Gender based violence is so pervasive at home that women face various forms of discrimination and violence during their different phases of life. During initial years of growing up, she is vulnerable to various forms of discrimination and violence which may include lack of access to education, health facilities, malnutrition, female foeticide, female infanticide and female genital mutilation. During adulthood, she may be subjected to other forms of violence, such as, honour killing, battering and atrocities by her husband and other family members. A study conducted by OFAM (2004) brought startling facts on violence directed towards women at home in South Asia. It reported that approximately half of the women in Bangladesh and 60 per cent in Sri Lanka were subjected to physical violence by their intimate partner. The report also highlighted situation in India where every six hour, a woman is brutally beaten to death or driven to commit suicide. It is estimated that quite a significant number (15,000 per year) of women suffer from dowry related violence. According to *UNICEF Digest* (2000), about 30 per cent to 50 per cent of the women have faced physical violence during their lifetime across various countries. The report also highlights situation in India with regard to domestic violence towards women. The report says that up to 45 per cent of married men acknowledged resorting to physical abuse in their marital relationship in a survey of 6,902 men in the state of Uttar Pradesh. Of the one in four women experiencing domestic violence, majority (57%) have encountered several episodes of such assaults (WHO, 2002). Carlson (1984) elaborated the ecological framework to explain Domestic violence. Violence is a complex problem rooted in the interaction of multi-factors, i.e. Individual's attribute and his socio-cultural context. So, the problem could be approached holistically only working at both levels, micro and macro levels as it exist across all societies cutting boundaries of Nations.

Over the years, the state took many legislative measures to curb the problem of violence as the problem existed in every section of the society requiring structural and institutional changes in the society through macro processes. In the last few decades, the women's movements were instrumental in bringing new laws safeguarding women's right. During 1980s, in the wake of women's movement and various civil society organisations, Sections 498A and 304B were introduced in the Indian Penal Code (IPC). The section 498A of IPC defines '*cruelty*' against wife as "any wilful conduct which is of such a nature as is likely to drive the woman to commit suicide or to cause grave injury or danger to life, limb or health (whether mental or physical) of the woman; or harassment of the woman where such harassment is with a view to coercing her or any person related to her to meet any unlawful demand for any property or valuable security or is on account of failure by her or any person related to her to meet such demand." Simultaneously, Dowry death was defined in the section 304B of IPC as "where the death of a woman is caused by any burns or bodily injury or occurs otherwise than under normal circumstances within seven years of her marriage and it is shown that soon before her death she was subjected to cruelty or harassment by her husband or any relative of her husband for, or in connection with, any demand for dowry." Prior to these amendments in IPC, Dowry Prohibition Act was already in place to address the problem of violence at home, particularly dowry related violence. In the year 2006, for the first time domestic violence was defined with the enactment of Protection of Women from Domestic Violence Act (2005), though there existed *many legislations relating to women's rights* but none of them ever attempted to define the same. The Act gives lucid and comprehensive definition of 'domestic violence' as "any act, omission or commission or conduct of the respondent shall constitute domestic violence in case it harms or injures or endangers the health, safety, life, limb or well-being, whether mental or physical, of the aggrieved person or tends to do so and includes causing physical abuse, sexual abuse, verbal and emotional abuse and economic abuse; or harasses, harms, injures or endangers the aggrieved person with a view to coerce her or any other person related to her to meet any unlawful demand for any dowry or other property or valuable security; or has the effect of threatening the aggrieved person or any person related to her by any conduct mentioned in the above mentioned clauses; or otherwise injures or causes harm, whether physical or mental, to the aggrieved person." It recognises four forms of violence, namely Physical abuse, Verbal and Emotional abuse, Economic abuse and Sexual abuse with wide illustrations along with defining domestic violence. This helps in identifying various acts of oppression directed towards women amounting to domestic violence. Moreover, prior to implementation of Domestic Violence Act (2005), as to what acts constitute domestic violence, was left to the subjective interpretation of the individual service provider as per his cultural understanding as indicated in the study conducted by Vimochan, a non-governmental organisation. The study brings out the fact that the police personnel and lawyer widely propagate that only issues relating to dowry and certain heinous acts of violence amount to domestic violence and rest of the issues are too trivial to act and come out of the purview of domestic violence (Geethadevi, Meghana & Raghunandan, 1999). This Act recognises the role of service providers and civil society organisations in addressing the concerns of women through counselling and other support services.

Towards this end, in NCT of Delhi, Delhi Police has set up Crime Against Women Cells (CAW cells) under the supervision of DCP in each district (11 in all), and one Special Cell for Women and Children (SPUWAC) at Nanakpura, headed by Joint Commissioner of Police. The aim of these special cells is "to giving visibility to violence against women and legitimizing the violated woman's concerns and need within a pro-woman perspectives". (ERU consultant, 2016: 7). Over the years since its inception in the year 1983, it has expanded its services to meet the varying needs of women victims of violence, especially women facing domestic violence. Earlier, only in two cells (one in North-west & SPUWAC) social workers were engaged in counselling units and in rest other districts, the police personnel provided counselling to the women. Recently, the services of social workers are being expanded to other cells in each district (Dassi, 2016; ERU Consultant, 2016). Besides that, mediators appointed by Delhi Legal Service Authority (DLSA) carry out mediation services. These services help women in understanding litigation and post-litigation processes and consequences. It facilitate negotiation for *streedhan* and alimony towards mutual divorce/separation (ERU Consultant, 2016). The study conducted by Dassi (2016), reported that these services are limited to three cells only (2 CAW cells & 1 SPUWAC). There is need for expansion of these services to other cells as these are crucial in out of court settlement and meeting immediate financial concerns of the women, avoiding long years of struggle in the court battle. In regular intervals, these cells also conduct gender sensitisation programme for development of its staff, particularly police personnel placed in these special cells, in collaboration with Tata Institute of Social Sciences and Jamia Millia Islamia University. Though, these special cells are doing commendable work to address the grievances of the women facing violence at home, particularly focusing socio-legal aspect of the problem, still much more needs to be done with the individuals and the larger system simultaneously to address multiple aspects of the problem.

The police being the first point of contact for women facing violence in the criminal justice system makes these special cells (CAW cells & SUPWAC) more visible and easily accessible for women. So, keeping this in view, the need of the hour is to devise more coordinated and coherent response, requiring integrated welfare services for a violated woman within the system. One such area requiring attention could be mental health services as several research studies reported that long years of violence affects overall well-being of the women, many a times leading to severe mental health disorders, such as, sleeplessness, irritability, fear and anxiety, depression, post-traumatic syndromes and repeated suicidal thoughts/attempts etc. (Chang, 1996; Dassi, 2016; Dassi & Bist, 2014; Gells, 1979; Pagelow, 1981). As researcher and counsellor, I too got opportunity to interact with many women victims of domestic violence very often. I clearly remember, a woman narrating her share of misfortune in which she lost her mental balance due to long years of violence by her husband. At one point in her life, she started neglecting herself and failed to take care of her bodily needs, such as, failed to take bath in most occasion or avoid taking bath; failed to put cloth and sanitary pads and her mother would help her. She was on psychiatric help for more than six months and in this process the parents of the woman were helping her to get treatment as she was left to her parental home. But unfortunately, neither the police personnel nor the social worker are equipped to deal such clients as reported by ERU Consultants (2016). Mental health experts could be invited to render these services as a sound mind is prerequisite to participate in various events of life and take crucial decisions of life.

Besides covering mental health services in the system, there are few more aspects of the problem which require attention, such as, shelter, economic needs of the women etc. Many a times, a woman needs shelter, but these special cells have very poor linkage with shelter homes across Delhi (ERU Consultant, 2016; Dassi, 2016). Generally, in such situation, the woman is directed to contact local police station on her own and seek shelter home services. Similarly, in many instances woman requires financial assistance and employment as most often women are economically dependant but they hardly pay much attention to address these concerns (ERU Consultants 2016; Dassi, 2016). These special cells for women have weak linkage with other stakeholders which is crucial to combat such crisis. Towards this end, the services of the social workers could be further expanded, as presently their role is limited to providing counselling. The social worker can play an active role in Liaisoning and networking with other agencies, such as, shelter homes, protection officers which is lacking most often and other civil society organisations. They can provide employment related guidance, share information on various welfare schemes for women. The worker can also help in identifying and linking the clients with the institutions imparting skill based training in their locality through regular contacts with such organisations.

Conclusion

Human beings live in groups and individuals are interdependant on each other in a social group and social groups are also interdependant for their survival and well-being. Thus, simultaneous intervention at various levels is needed to address various social problems in totality and to meet the multiple needs of the individual and community. The problems can be addressed holistically with curative, rehabilitative and preventive approaches which demands integrated practice approach to ameliorate the problem given at hand. Age old problem of domestic violence can be addressed through giving attention to various aspects of the problem. Special Cells for Women (CAW Cells & SPUWAC), set up by Delhi Police, need to expand its services to address the complex problem of domestic violence directed towards women to meet the varying needs of women through integrated services. There is a dire need to introduce mental health services as most often multiple episodes of violence during long period affects mental health of the women. Moreover, there is a strong need to strengthen networking with other stakeholders to meet immediate needs of shelter and economic concerns of the women. Towards this end, the role of the social workers in these cells could be expanded further to provide these services.

Notes

1. *Social Case Work:* The purpose of case work is to help individual and families towards more satisfying human relation "Social case work aim to facilitate the individual's social adaptation, to restore, reshape or reinforce his functioning as social being" (Perlman, 1957, p. 7).
2. *Group Work:* Group work is basically meant to bring about changes in the social functioning of the individual or the community for which the group provides the medium. The group work can be defined as method of working with people aiming to reduce roadblocks in social functioning and accomplishment of individual's greatest capacity through group experience (Skidmore, Thackeray & Farley, 1974).
3. *Community Organisation:* Dunham (1970) defines community organisation as "a conscious process of social interaction aiming at helping people to deal more effectively with their problem by participation and strengthening cooperation of people in the community. It also endeavour to bring about adjustment between the needs of people and resources in the community" p. 4.
4. *Social Action and Community Development:* Basically, community organisation, community development and social action are interrelated activities and these activities have been placed under community work by Siddiqui, 1997. However, in recent times, Social action and community development have been recognised as distinct methods of intervention in social work literature, finding its place in secondary methods of working with people for larger social goals.

   Social action can be defined as a political process of organising people to bring change in the existing social system and institution, limiting social functioning of marginalised and weaker section of the society (Shodhaganga, n.d). Community development can be defined "as a goal of bringing about social and economic development in areas which are underdeveloped" (Siddiqui, 1997: 23). Community development is considered as process, method, a programme and a movement for planned change.

5. *Welfare Administration:* Skidmore *et al.*, 1974 define welfare administration as "the process of implementation of translating policies into action programme. The basic process involves, planning, organising, staffing and directing", p. 112. Basically, Social welfare administration is arranging and directing resources for social service programme.
6. *Research:* Though research has been recognised as one of the secondary method of social work, but it provides substantial and systematic information of the worker to enhance his practice. Research helps in understanding the magnitude of the problem & geographical areas, identifying social groups facing problems, possible social conditions (variables) and their relationship with the given problem. The research findings give basis for meticulous formulation of comprehensive programme of social development at national level, identifying the local and specific need of the communities.

References

Agnimitra, N. (2013). "Community Organisation as a method of Social work practice" In K.K. Jacob (Ed.) *Community organisation management for community Development (Community Organisation for community development-Block* 2, pp. 32-47). New Delhi: Indira Gandhi National Open University (IGNOU).

Bare Act, 2005, Prevention and Protection of Women from Domestic Violence Act, 2005.

Bare Act, 1860. The Indian Penal Code Act No. 45 of 1860.

Bronfenbrenner, U. (1979). *The ecology of human development: Experiments by nature and design.* Cambridge, MA: Harvard University Press.

Carlson, B.E. (1984). "Causes and Maintenance of Domestic Violence: An Ecological Analysis", *Social Service Review*, 569-587.

Chang, V.N. (1996). *I just lost myself: Psychological abuse of women in marriage*, Westport: Praeger.

Dash, B.M. & Roy, S. (2016). *Field work in social work education: Contemporary practices and perspectives, Atlantic,* New Delhi.

Dassi, A. (2016). *Wife-battering: A challenge to policing and social work practice (A study of domestic violence in NCT of Delhi)*, Unpublished UGC Research Award Study.

Dassi, A. and Bist, S. (2014). "Spousal Violence and health Implication: A study of lived Experience", In Bhavana Mehta (ed.), *Research for Social Work in India: Trends and Challenges* (pp. 71-85), Baroda: Shri Samarth Publication.

Dunham, A. (1970). *The new community organisation,* New York: Thomas Y. Crowell.

Engels, F. (1942). *The origin of the family, private property and the state,* 4th edition, New York: International Publishers.

ERU Consultant (2016). Evaluation Research Study of the Counselling Units at Special Police Units for Women and Children (Special Cells), New Delhi, ERU Consultant Private Limited.

Geethadevi, Meghana and Raghunandan, T. (1999). *Getting away with murder—how law, courts and police fail victims of domestic violence.* Manushi No. 117.

Gelles, R.J. (1979). *Family Violence,* Sage. Beverly Hills.

IASS & IFSW (2004). "Global Standards for the Social Work Education and Training", *Social Work Education,* 23(5): 493-513.

Kaudshin, A. and Harkness, D. (2002). *Supervision in Social Work,* New York: Columbia University Press.

Larkin, H. (2006). "Social Work as an Integral Profession", *A Journal of Integral Theory and Practice, AQAL,* Summer 2006, Vol. 1, No. 2, p. 339.

NCRB (2017), *Crime in India 2016.* retrieved from http://ncrb.gov.in/StatPublications/CII/CII2016/pdfs/NEWPDFs/Crime%20in%20India%20-%202016%20Complete%20PDF% 20291117.pdf.

OXFAM (2004), Towards Ending Violence against Women in South Asia, OXFAM Briefing Paper, August 2004. Retrieved from https://www.oxfam.org/sites/www.oxfam.org/files/violence.pdf.

Pagelow, M.D. (1981). *Wife-battering: Victims and their Experiences,* CA: Sage Beverly Hills.

Perlman, H. (1957). *Social Case Work: A Problem Solving Process,* Chicago: University of Chicago.

Roy, S. and Dash, B.M. (2016). "Field work practice in Social work education: Major components, issues and challenges", In B.M. Dash and Sanjoy Roy (eds.) *Field Work in Social Work Education: Contemporary Practices and Perspective* (pp. 3-34). Delhi: Atlantic.

Shodhganga (date not mentioned). Social work education in India: An introduction. Shodhganga is a portal hosted by the University Grants Commission (UGC), GOI, retrieved from, shodhganga.inflibnet.ac.in/bitstream/10603/23970/9/09_chapter%201.pdf.

Siddiqui, H.Y. (1997). *Working with Communities: An Introduction to Community Work,* New Delhi: Hira Publications.

Skidmore, R.A.; Thackeray, M.G. and Farley (1974). *Introduction to Social Work,* Eaglewood Cliffs: NJ Prentice Hall.

UNICEF (2000). "Domestic Violence against Women and Girls", *Innocent Digest,* No. 6.

World Health Organisation (2002), *World Report on Violence and Health. Geneva.*

Web Source

Internet (2018), http://spuwac.com/

13

Generalist *versus* Specialist Social Work

Pankaj Gupta and *Shresthi Sharma*

Introduction

In ancient period, the problems of poor, weaker, handicapped and older people were addressed by the family, community, caste groups and religious institutions. These needy people could be an individual or any group of individuals. Society was a collective unit of individuals and it had a robust mechanism to address the problems faced by its members. It was also bound to respond to the needs of its members. Informal groups as well as formal mechanisms were available, wherein the smallest issues to bigger ones were sorted out through channels available within the family or community or caste groups etc. Majority of the problems were addressed within the family whereas big problems required the intervention of caste groups or community or panchayat. As the system of joint family was in vogue, wherein the elders and other family members would be there to guide and support the family members, many problems used to get resolved within the family. On a larger level, the community or the caste groups were available to provide right kind of succour and deal with the situation that had not been resolved by the family. State had a minimum or no role to play in catering to many of the needs of the society because most of the impending issues were resolved locally, without recoursing to the cumbersome and costly mechanism that people generally resort today. Apart from this, the social norms worked more effectively and deviation from the societal norms was considered bad. It was common that society had its own internal mechanisms and strict compliance of the rules was expected from each and every member of the society. Even the requirements of the weak members of the family were taken care of by the family or community members. Therefore, State did not have to intervene in many of the matters pertaining to the needs of the weaker sections of the society.

With the passage of time, the joint family system started weaning away and nuclear families were cropping up. Rapid urbanisation and industrialisation compelled the people to migrate in urban centres for a better life and job opportunities. People started losing interest in farming and wanted to move forward in life. They migrated to the cities to have umpteen numbers of opportunities, which were available in the cities only. In the process of migration, people with wealth and good job improved their life style and enjoyed the modern amenities, which a city can offer to them. There were only a few numbers of people. But a large chunk of people were not as lucky as their other counterparts and landed up in slums, where they were bound to face a whole lot of new problems. In these places, they faced the paucity of even basic resources to keep their body and soul together. Apart from shrinking spaces in slums, these people faced other problems like health, livelihood etc. Migration to the cities and disintegration of families not only affected the poor but even the better offs, who were staying away from their families. They got entrapped into the vicious entangles of urban problems. Problems like depression, asthma etc. propped up and affected the large sections of the society. Loneliness in big and crowded city became commonplace and people were required to seek help from someone who could get them out of their psycho-social problems.

There were number of other problems being faced by the society that required some specialised agencies, which can help the society to cope with them. Therefore, the social work institutions came up to address these needs of the society. They were churning out the professional social workers with knowledge and skills to address the societal problems. Since, the numbers of problems were huge; a good number of organisations (NGOs) also came into picture. These organisations were working on different issues to cater to the myriad needs of the various sections of the society. The social worker appointed in the NGO play various vital roles in the society. One of the major roles of the social workers was to empower their client, rather than overpowering them, through their knowledge and skills.

The National Association of Social Workers (1973) defines social work as "The activity of helping individuals, families, groups, or communities enhance or restore their capacity for social functioning or creating societal conditions favourable to that goal." This definition underlines that social workers deal with individuals, families, groups, or communities and even larger units of society. At the same time, social workers help people enhance or restore their capacity for social functioning. This restoration of capacity is linked with change in person and his or her environment. Therefore, social work is professional activity which has a particular body of knowledge, values, and skills. One can find that the requirement of a trained social worker is omnipresent, where there is a need to address the social problems and developing the capacity of individuals. These problems are dealt by generalist as well as specialist social workers. Though many of the skills and knowledge commonly shared by the generalist and specialist in their area of practice yet specialised knowledge is required for addressing those problems, which requires unique intervention that can be provided by people having in-depth understanding of it.

Ashman & Hull (2012) state that social workers are generalist as they have wide range of skills to resolve the problem of the client. They address the individual issues as well as the issues confronted by the community. Yanca & Johnson (2008) focuses on the diversity competent practice skills of social worker that will help him in serving the diverse client according to their different cultural diversity. The varied sections of society are catered by the generalists as well as specialist social workers; therefore, it is essential to understand the perspective of both.

Development of Social Work as a Profession

Social work perhaps has been initiated when the humans started living a settled life. During this time an individual was taken care of by his/her group or family members. As the population grew some people became rich and some poor. Therefore, donating money to beggars or sponsoring some charity event was considered social work. Later, it became scientific and the services were focused on long term perspective. Carlton and LaNay (1999) traced the evolution of social work practice from social services but they emphasised that presently the practitioners are engaged in other set-ups like industry, health care, political etc. They also said the services are extended to prisoners, HIV & AIDS patients and homeless (as cited in Hall, 2008). They said the twenty first century witnesses the emergence of evidence based practice. But they emphatically stated that community sanction to social work profession gives legitimacy to its survival. Healy (2001) stated that it is difficult to have an exact date of the beginning of the professional social work. She highlights the fact that the social work education in America and Europe was developed in response to indigenous situation but in developing countries it was started as an influence of Western countries. She further said that the first institute of social work was started in Amsterdam in 1899. Jongh (1972), on the other hand, stated that around 1900, most of the schools of social work were started in London, Amsterdam, Berlin and New York city simultaneously (as cited in Healy, 2001: 20).

The seeds of scientific approach to social work can be traced from the establishment of Charity Organisation Society (COS) in America and England in nineteenth century that gave greater push to the concept of scientific help. In US, the first COS was established in Buffalo in 1877, which later spread to other parts of the country. These COS made the charity more organised, systematic and plugged the wastage of resources. Many of the welfare programmes and practices now reflect the element of COS strategy. On the other hand, the London Charity Organisation Society (COS) was founded in 1869. The COS was the result of humanitarian awakening and the efforts of Scottish Minister Mr. Thomas Chalmers, who advocated for engaging the non-governmental agencies in the humanitarian work. Womer (1997) states that Mary Steward, a trained COS worker, was the first recorded social worker hired by the Royal Free Hospital, London (as cited in Healy, 2001: 19). The COS made the help scientific and it ensured that assistance to the poor shall be given by assessing their need. Community organisation and case work methods were extensively used for this purpose. Investigation of the condition of the poor was the mainstay of COS and only after its completion any type of help would be extended to the poor.

In India, many social reformers like Raja Rammohan Roy, Ishwar Chandra Vidya Sagar, Vivekananda etc. have advocated for many reforms but the modern social work was initiated by the

Christian Missionaries in nineteenth century. Healy (2001) states that "Indian social work education was heavily influenced by US models for many years." The first school of social work in India was opened in 1936 at Bombay. The social work school was named as Sir Dorabji Tata Graduate School of Social Work, which is now known as Tata Institute of Social Sciences. Following it, many schools of social work started in India to promote and practice scientific help in the country.

Though social work was considered largely to extend of doling out charity but it was gradually realised that one time help was not beneficial for the individual in long run. Therefore, social work changed the strategy and now it is focusing on scientific giving. Social work has made many strides, since then, that have helped in the growth of social work as a profession. The global recognition of the profession is the testimony that the present dynamic upheavals required the well qualified and trained social workers.

Genesis of Generalist and Specialist Debate

Social work profession has become more organised and mere donation of money for one time event is done away with. The long term planning for the upliftment of the poorer and weaker sections is more acceptable now. Therefore, the social work profession becoming more focused and endeavour has been made to make sound planning so that instead of doing charity we should empower them. Though the generic social work is still used but the expert knowledge on the issue is also sought to ensure that the best is being done. This continuous systematization and development has compelled the professional social workers to gain knowledge and experience on the particular issues.

Trevithick (2011) stated that generalist *versus* specialist debate in social work profession, in England, dates back to the recommendation put by Seebohm Commission. The report prepared by the commission used the term generic to describe the whole gamut of principles and methods taught and practiced in various areas. The areas may be correctional one or mentally disturbed person or in a hospital etc. but the methods and principle used remain the same. The report also mentioned that though the social workers were employed in different departments to render services to the people in various social service departments yet the gaps, fragmentation and duplication of services created confusion among people about, which department they could approach for help. Therefore, the Commission recommended to have 'a unified provision of personal social services'. This recommendation was accepted and new Local Authority Social Services Act, 1970 was enacted which was ensued in the establishment of unified services department in England and Wales. The report emphasised that specialisation is required for enhancement of knowledge. The Commission was largely focusing on the organisational character rather than on educational aspect. Barclay report was the next major significant point in the discussion on generalist versus specialist social work. The report used the term generalist in place of generic, as used by its predecessor Seebohm Commission. The report primarily recommended for using the community based approach, which is generalist in nature. But it also recognised the need of having specialised knowledge in case of certain groups of people. The Victoria Climbe Inquiry (Laming, 2003) report emphasised the importance of having specialist services for children and their families. Following it the white paper was presented on *Every Child Matters* (DES, 2003), which has separated the child and adult services into two separate departments. The main emphasis of the report was on the physical location of the services rather than in the theoretical orientation. Next report of Lord Laming titled as *The Protection of Children in England: A Progress Report* questioned the generic nature of social work degree programmes, especially in reference to the preparedness of the social work professionals in the area of child protection. It laid emphasis that the social workers specialised in children issues shall be allowed to work in child protection area. But his report did not get the required support. The Social Work Task Force (SWTF) was set up in 2008. This task force in its two reports *Facing up to the Task* (SWTF, 2009a) and *Building a Safe, Confident Future* (SWTF, 2009b), promoted the generic degree in social work rather than a specialised one, as it equips the students to gain knowledge, skills and attitude to help their clients in holistic manner.

In India, one can find a number of NGOs working for the different groups of individuals and on different issues. These organisations get experience and skill to deal with a particular issue. The individuals working in these organisations get the exposure on the issues, in which the organisations are working. This long term exposure makes them more knowledgeable on the issue, which brings them into the category of experts. Apart from practical experience, many schools of social work have started courses in some particular area and the students are being trained into a particular issue so that they could take up the challenges in the domain where their expertise would be required.

Social Work Practice Approaches

Social work has three primary and two secondary practice methods. The first practice method of social work, 'social casework', was described in the book of Mary Richmond, *Social Diagnosis* (1917). This book worked as a bridge in social work by introducing a literature describing social work practice. In this book, Mary Richmond focused on social work practice with individuals and families and identified social work principles to work with the target group. The second method of social work is group work which has been rooted in "social reform; social responsibility, democratic ideals, and social action as well as social relatedness and human attachment" (Lee, 1991: 3). This method involves a particular process for purposeful activity with individual in the group as well as group as a whole. The third practice method is community organisation. This is concerned with coordination and distribution of resources and building linkages among existing services to meet the needs of the people. Administration and research are secondary methods of social work practice.

Generalist Social Work

The generalist approach in social work began to emerge in the late 1960s. As Balinsky stated, "The complexity of human problems necessitates a broadly oriented practitioner with a versatile repertoire of methods and skills capable of interacting in any one of a number of systems" (Balinsky, 1982). This model gave a flexible approach to social work practice for the complexity and interrelatedness of human problems. This practice contains two fundamental components. First, it provides a perspective from which the social worker views the practice situation. Social systems theory draws different ways to intervene in more than one relevant system and also helps to maintain a focus on the person and the environment. Second, the social worker is required to have a broad knowledge and skills and to have the ability to choose the appropriate practice approach which meets the needs of the client.

Generalist social work is an integration of practice, policy, and research (Generalist Social Work Practice, n.d.). Doel and Shardlow (2005) stated that in 1970s the system theory was in vogue that prompted the development of integrated method of social work practice. Instead of individual therapy, social work focused on planned change; therefore, emphasis was laid on the interaction between the individual and his immediate environment. Heus and Pincus (1986) proposed creative generalist, by which they meant that bringing together the intuitive and rational thinking along with the art of practice. Further, they stated that the expertise shows professionalism and the generalist, i.e. master of none approach, is not viewed as professionalism (as cited in Doel & Shardlow, 2005: 238). But Doel *et al.* are of the view that generalist and specialist social work have their own area of expertise. Generalist practice provides a wide system in which the social workers work. They also stated that the generalist social work practice is commonly applied in all the settings. The setting might be correctional, observation home, hospital, community etc. where the social work as a designation may or may not exist, but the core knowledge and skills remain the same.

Langer and Lietz (2015) mentioned that during the initial level of the practice, a social work practitioner would be called generalist and respond to the needs of the individuals, groups, families, communities and organisations at various levels. Accordingly, it can be construed that generalist has the fair idea of the situation he even knows what sort of intervention is required. Moreover, he seems more open to approach even an expert to deal with the problem at hand. Tucker (1996) clearly mentioned that the generalist social work gives freedom to apply multiple models, theories and techniques to intervene at micro and macro levels (as cited in Hall, 2008). He laid emphasis on the fact that the generalist social work practice allows the social worker to use any of the models or techniques while trying to identify the probable solutions to the problem. Therefore, generalist approach is useful in the terms of assessing the problem in correct perspective and applying the most suitable intervention for resolving it. Hall (2008) believes that the initial posture of social work was generalist. He also opined that generalist social work helps in moving from one methodology to other with minimum difficulty. So, the generalist approach gives prominence to the subjective application as per need of the hour.

Now, it can be said that a generalist is the one who has the peripheral knowledge on the issue. He is the one who knows a lot about the issue but does not have the in-depth knowledge. He is jack of all trade but master of none. In the context of social work, he is the one having the skills to solve the problem but he does not have very deep understanding of the problem. Social workers deal with humans whose needs are changing; therefore, many a times generalist social work is useful. But in certain cases, the expert knowledge is sought.

Specialist Social Work

Specialism means expertise in something and having in-depth knowledge on the issue. The specialist social work practice is characterized by knowledge and skills required for practice setting, population served, social problems addressed, and/or practice intervention mode. This practice focuses on knowledge, competencies and skills in specialized area of social work to serve clients' need through the in-depth knowledge of the social worker. According to Doel & Shardlow (2005) social work has many territories and social workers become specialist by gaining knowledge and experience about their territory. Horwath and Shardlow (2003) had identified eight territories of specialist practice (as cited in Doel *et al.*: 243). These are:

1. **Service user group:** The social workers work with different groups and gain specialisation in that. For example, the social worker working in child protection issue get specialised in that field, on the other hand a social worker working in a hospital setting get expertise in it. Both the fields demand distinct skills and knowledge that should match to the requirement of that particular field.
2. **Community:** It is the specialisation in a particular geographical location. So, anyone working in the

community understands the community needs and aspiration and makes plans accordingly. This gives the social workers an upper hand over others who are not working in that particular area.

3. **Expertise:** Sometimes, the knowledge and experience of social workers, in some aspect of social work, is recognised by other; therefore, the advice of such expert is sought many a times. The colleagues may seek their advice formally or informally. Their in-depth knowledge is due to their experience in that particular field.
4. **Method:** Practitioners use various methods in social work to sort out the problems of their client. When any particular method is used over a time, one will learn the nitty-gritty of it. It also help in gaining the experience on the intricacies in the implementation of the method and get specialised in that particular method.
5. **Mode:** Social workers work with different mode of practice. These modes are individual, families, groups or communities. Some social workers consider themselves as generalist and engage with many distinct modes while others may engage with one and get specialised in it.
6. **Organisational form or structure:** The organisational structure defines the roles and responsibilities of its human resource. Some of them are given the responsibility for intake of the client while others provide other services. According to the placement in the organisational structure, the social workers get expertise in that particular place in the organisation.
7. **Qualification:** The practicing social workers get post qualifying award so that it will bring expertise in their work.
8. **Setting:** The setting where the social worker is placed is also one of the ways to ascertain their specialisation. For example, social worker working in day care centre, field work, residential work etc.

Doel *et al.*, state that in some of the fields like hospital, court, school etc., the services of the social workers become secondary. It also shows that the social workers are specialised in that area.

Debate on General *Versus* Specialist Social Work

Social work profession has very wide field and one can find a social worker in most of the places. They are available in the community settings, corporate office, governmental departments etc. With the developmental process gaining momentum, the new problems have started arising. These problems may be loneliness, child protection, women empowerment, community development, livelihood etc. Traditional support systems are disappearing as the people are migrating in the urban centres for better employment and educational opportunities. Therefore, in such a scenario the services of social workers are quite essential. The social workers are trained to deal with the problems faced by the people in their daily lives. Also, in their course of study, they gain certain skill sets and expose to the reality of lives and gradually they become apt to extend the most needed help to their clients. Now, the social workers are working in both generalist as well as specialist manner to cater to the growing and changing demands of the society. They have created their own territory within which they provide services to the people. This changing role of social workers has brought forth the discussion on generalist *versus* specialist.

According to Bartlett (1970) "the concept of social functioning is providing common base for social work practice." She states that earlier 'feeling and doing' thought in social work was largely developing the skills of social workers. But now the focus has been shifted to 'thinking and knowing'. The discussion on the practice of social worker and the requirements of the professional practice has been initiated (as cited in Doel & Shardlow, 2005: 241). On the other hand, Hollis and Taylor (1951) state that there is a difficulty in developing satisfactory curriculum of social work because of the ambiguity in determining the criteria about what constitute basic and the specialised social work (as cited in Doel & Shardlow, 2005: 242). Bartlett thinks that specialization in any profession is a part of the concept of a whole but social work has been developed from parts; therefore, it is premature to call it specialised. On the other side, the Milford Conference in 1929 recommended that the social work education in universities should be generic. The Conference also recommended that the social work should be specialised in the field, where the case work as a method is being applied. According to Doel *et al.*, both the terms, in the context of social work, are still ambiguous and only time and place will decide whether the social work is generalist or specialist.

Conclusion

Social workers play a vital role in the society and take numerous challenges while delivering their professional services. The wide range of areas beckons the social workers. It is being expected that social workers should be witty and think out of the box in problematic situation. They should assist the individuals in recognising their ability and think in the right earnest to solve the problem on their own. In this effort of theirs, they require general as well as expert knowledge of the issue. Apart from this, many times the social workers work in conglomeration to have a wide impact. They create networks of like minded people to create a sound support system for their clients and it is difficult to draw a line between what constitute generalist or specialist in social work. Therefore, one is required to understand the strength and weakness of both the approaches. According to Sheldon & Macdonald (2009) social work has to deal with wide range of social and personal problems that required us to borrow heavily from other fields. There is lot of conundrum on specialist and generalist social work, as there is lack of clarity in both the terms. The students are mostly getting trained in generalist social work and they gain expertise once they start working in a particular field. There is little empirical data on the merit and demerit of specialist and generalist approaches. But many of the social workers are generalist because they use the basic skills and knowledge of social work.

References

Ashman, K.K.K. and Hull, G.H. (2012). *Understanding Generalist Practice* (6th Edition). Belmont, USA: Brooks/Cole, Cengage Learning. Retrieved from https://www.cengagebrain.co.nz/content/kirstashman33826_0840033826_02.01_chapter01.pdf

Balinsky, R. (1982). "Generic Practice in Graduate Social Work Curricula: A Study of Educators Experiences and Attitudes", *Journal of Education for Social Work*, 46-54.

Doel, M. and Shardlow, S.M. (2005). *Modern Social Work Practice: Teaching and Learning in Practice Settings* (3rd edition). Hampshire, England: Ashgate Publishing Limited.

Friedlander, W.A. (1982). *Introduction to Social Welfare* (5th edition). New Delhi: Prentice Hall of India Pvt. Limited.

Generalist Social Work Practice. Retrieved August 10, 2016, from http://wwwfp.pearsonhighered.com/assets/hip/us/hip_us_pearsonhighered/samplechapter/0205789811.pdf

Hall, R. (2008). "The evolution of social work practice: Implications for the generalist approach", *International Journal of Social Welfare,* 390-395. doi:10.1111/j.1468-2397.2008.00558.x

Healy, L.M. (2001). *International Social Work: Professional Action in an Interdependent World.* New York: Oxford University Press.

Langer, C.L. and Lietz, C.A. (2015). *Applying Theory to Generalist Social Work Practice: A Case Study Approach.* New Jersey, USA: Wiley.

Lee, J. (1991). "Forward", In Weil, M., K. Chau and D. Southerland. (Eds.). *Theory and Practice in Social Group Work: Creative Connections.* New York: Haworth Press.

National Association of Social Workers. (1973). *Standards for Social Service Manpower.* Washington, D.C.: NASW.

Richmond, M.E. (1917). *Social Diagnosis.* New York: Russell Sage Foundation.

Sheldon, B. and Macdonald, G. (2009). *A Textbook of Social Work.* London and New York: Routledge.

Trevithick, P. (2011) "The generalist versus specialist debate in social work education in the UK", In J. Lishman (ed.) *Research Highlights: Volume on Social Work Education.* London: Jessica Kingsley, pp. 233-254.

Yanca, S.J. and Johnson, L.C. (2008). *Generalist Social Work Practice with families.* Retrieved from https://www.pearsonhighered.com/samplechapter/0205470106.pdf

14

Strength-based Practice

An Alternate Approach to Social Work

Kislay Kumar Singh

Introduction

A new approach has emerged in the domain of social work that has shifted the focus from deficits to strengths (Weick, 1992). Traditional approaches to social work have changed with the change in time. Professionals or those who desired change have started challenging the traditional views with a strength-based approach to human problems. This framework put emphasis on discovering, affirming, and enhancing the capabilities, knowledge, resources, and objectives of individuals (Early & GlenMaye, 2004). This involves a systematic understanding of the situation from the client's perspective. Indeed, we have to consider people's stories, narratives, and myths that are culturally embedded in order to emancipate them. Gradually, the strength-based practice has gained momentum in various social work settings such as working with elderly, youth, family, people with addictions, schools, and communities (Saleebey, 2009).

The notion of identifying, recognizing and working with the strengths of people as a meaningful starting point for the promotion of positive change in the society, is warmly embraced. However, it is rarely accepted as the starting point for change in the individual, group and community or society by the people receiving the services in the different social work settings. It has been noticed that practitioners or professionals working in different settings often undermine the set of values, principles, and philosophy of strength-based practice in the fields. Hence, the idea of promoting strength-based practice in social work often creates an unexpected dilemma.

Focus on "what is wrong" has been the central focus of the traditional perspectives in social work practice (Miley, O'Melia & DuBois, 2004). Different approaches may define problems differently, but fundamentally all traditional approaches uphold the belief that people who have a problem may require assistance (Canda & Furman, 2010). The term, 'having a problem' indicates that problems have its place in people themselves or are inherent in people and in some way it reflects the kind of person they are (Laursen, 2003). The presence of the problems prompts professionals to highlight the areas of concern across various settings that attract the pool of experts to resolve 'what is wrong' with an individual or the existing problems in the societies. However, it has been observed that when a person acts as the expert to resolve the problems of others, he/she deny the opportunity of his/her client to participate, take control and learn in the process of solving problems that further leads to the denial of their right to self-determination.

However, looking critically at the traditional deficit-based approach to social work practice it becomes equally important to recognize that the strength-based approach does not completely negate the traditional approach. Rather it takes away some important things from the deficit-based approach. It also believes that people do experience certain problems and these problems need to be rectified, and also people need help in getting over these problems (McMillen, Morris & Sherraden, 2004). But the strength-based approach goes ahead and also looks at the drawbacks in the existing approach such as its tendency of labelling of the client, not recognizing client's capabilities and strengths, focusing too much on the deficits of the clients than his/her strengths that disable the practitioners to be integral in the process of change.

Why Strength-Based Approach to Social Work Practice?

The period of the late 1980s was marked as the rising phase of strengths-based approach, which is now considered to be an alternate to the dominant models in the field of both social work theories and practice (Saleebey, 1996). It is an attempt in response to the demand for ending the long standing conflict between social work values and practice caused by the traditional deficit-focused approach and search for the essence of social work rooted in humanistic philosophy. This approach revived the core concept of 'how people and their environment fit together' (Miley *et al.*, 2004) and promotes not only the well-being of the clients but also increase the dimensions of social work profession.

A strength-based approach offers a positive and hopeful basis for addressing the issues of individual, group and community. It enables people to take control of their own lives in significant and sustainable ways such as:

- Helping them to focus on long-term and trusting relationships,
- Enabling them to take lead in the problem-solving process of their problems,
- Working mutually towards problem-solving,
- Creating sustainable change through learning and experience, and
- By tapping the positive energy and traits of the client.

To put it simply, a strength-based approach is a detailed method of working with individual, group, and community and resolves the problems faced by them. It avoids to overlook the problems of a person and foster aspiration, hope, and acceptance within the person (Pulla, 2006). It strives to recognize the available person's resources and his/her strengths that will lay the basis to address the problems faced by them and provide the sustainable solutions.

Beliefs of Strength-Based Approach

Clients are trustworthy is the core belief of the strength-based approach (Early & GlenMaye, 2004). This approach urges social work practitioners/professionals to re-examine their approach towards the client. They need to change their mindset and old beliefs about the clients. This requires a huge courage and persistence to suspend the initial beliefs and recognize the social work profession through this alternate approach (Saleebey, 2009).

In order to practice social work from the strength-based approach, one must abide by the following beliefs:

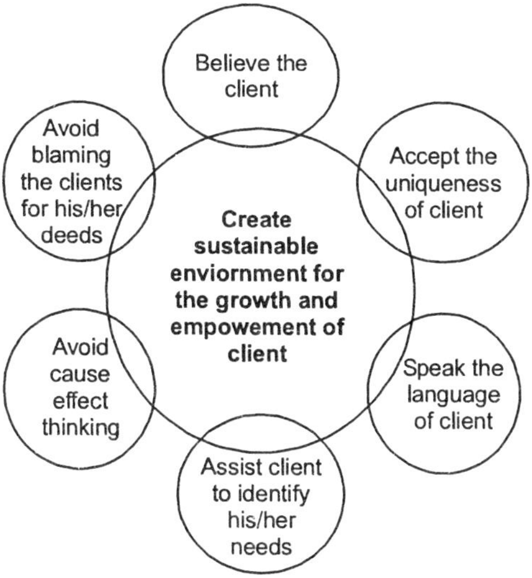

Fig. 14.1: Beliefs of Strength-Based Approach
Source: Adapted from "Strengths-Based Approach in Social Work: A distinct ethical advantage" by V. Pulla, 2017, *International Journal of Innovation, Creativity, and Change*, 3(2): 106.

Defining Strength-Based Practice

Strength-based practice helps the individual, group and community to identify the fences that allow the persistence of oppression in the society as well as reinforce such actions that promote change, development and empowerment of human-being (Robbins, Chatterjee & Canda, 2006). The empowerment of the client recognizes the uniqueness of an individual and it is similar to the right to self-determination. Therefore, the client's growth and empowerment is central to the strength-based approach (Cowger, 1994). It is a collaborative process that permits both service providers as well as clients to come together in order to provide the solution based on the client's strengths and resources. Working in a collaborative fashion offers an opportunity for the client to be a part of the process of service producers rather than solely at receiving ends.

Following are some definitions of the strength-based approach from the writings of various scholars:

- The core elements of strength-based philosophy uphold the belief that all clients have strengths and resources that may help them to come out from the problems (Laursen, 2003). It also believes in the creativity, knowledge, and courage of both clients and the practitioners.
- The strength-based approach helps to identify the factors that assist individuals, groups or community to lead happy and prospective lives and support them (Barwick, 2004).
- The strength-based approach is considered as the organizing principle for combining the theories and practice strategies that often focus on the positive attributes and underdeveloped capabilities of clients or even communities who are in some way undervalued their abilities and/or looking for help in the crisis (Nissen, 2006). The strength-based approach was urgently developed to counterbalance the effects of negative labeling of problems and subsequent practitioner-driven interventions that altogether led to poor results (*ibid.*).
- The strength-based practice strategies are developed on the principle that even the most troubled client has unique talents, skills, and other resources that can be rationalized in the process of his/her recovery and development (Cox, 2006).
- The strength-based practice allows practitioners/ professionals to explore and realize clients' strengths and resources in the process of assisting them to achieve their goals, recognize their dreams and shed the irons of their own inhibitions and misgivings (Saleebey, 2001).

For Comparison of Traditional Deficit-focused Approach and Strength-based Approach see Table 14.1.

Common Myths about Strength-Based Approach

In order to avoid confusion about the strength-based approach, we need to consider following some common myths:

Table 14.1: Comparison of Traditional Deficit-focused Approach and Strength-based Approach

Traditional deficit-focused Approach	*Strength-based Approach*
A person is defined as a 'case' and symptoms add up to a diagnosis.	Person is defined as unique; traits, talents, resources add up to strengths.
Therapy is problem focused.	Therapy is possibility focused.
Personal accounts aid in the evocation of a diagnosis through reinterpretation by an expert.	Personal accounts are the essential route to knowing and appreciating the person.
The practitioner is skeptical of personal stories, rationalizations.	The practitioner knows the person from the inside out.
The centerpiece of therapeutic work is the treatment plan devised by practitioners.	The centrepiece of work is the aspirations of family, individual, or community.
The practitioner is the expert on the client's lives.	Individuals, family, or community are the experts.
Possibilities for choice, control, commitment, and personal development are limited.	Possibilities for choice, control, commitment, and personal development are open.
Resources for work are the knowledge and skills of the professional.	Resources for work are the strengths, capacities, and adaptive skills of the individual, family, or community.
Help is centred on reducing the effects of symptoms and the negative personal and social consequences of actions, emotions, thoughts, or relationship.	Help is centred on getting on with one's life, affirming and developing values and commitments, and making and finding membership in or as a community.

- It is another glorified version of positive thinking,
- It basically 're-frame' the people's perception to look for good even in the worst conditions,
- It mainly re-marks weakness as strength,
- It avoids the reality of the existence of serious symptoms and problems that continue to persist, and
- It assesses the inherent strength of the client's family or relatives and provide a solution based on them.

Standards for Strength-Based Approach

Critics of strength-based approach argues that neither this model actually different or new from earlier traditional approaches

(McMillen *et al.,* 2004) nor it is based on the evidence of efficacy (Staudt, Howard & Drake, 2001). Indeed, practitioners of different settings are using more positive and different words to describe it. For example, in community development, the term 'asset-based' is used to label communities as a place of potential rather than areas of deficiency (Kretzmann & McKnight, 1993). However, the strength-based approach not only entails of positive reframing of problems, but it also refers to a constant focus on identifying of client's strength and resources that directly or indirectly enhance their situation (Early and GlenMaye, 2004).

The different uses of terminology may lead to confusion and misunderstanding for the practitioners or professionals. Though people may understand this approach, it does not mean that they will be confident enough to apply it in practice. In order to clarify what constitutes of strength-based approach, Rapp, Saleebey & Sullivan (2005) offer six standards as follows that illustrate a strengths-based practice:

- **Goal oriented**: Strength-based practice is a goal oriented. It allows individuals, groups or community to set their goals in their lives to an extent and select the means to achieve it.
- **Systematic assessment of strengths**: This model emphasizes the set of systematic principle for assessing the strength of individuals, groups or community with an emphasis on the present. Though, the past resources may also be used.
- **Resources from the environment**: Strengths proponents advocate to recognize the inherent resources that may be used to attain the goals and objectives of clients. It also believes that the community is the main source of opportunities, supports, institutions, and resources that have something to contribute which may be useful for others (Pulla, 2017). It is the role of the practitioner to link these resources to create a healthy environment for clients.
- **Explicit methods are used for identifying the client and environmental strengths for goal attainment**: Explicit methods that have adopted for each client will be different in the strengths-based approaches. For instance, in strengths-based case management, individuals will go

through a specific 'strength assessment' that help them to set the goals and tasks (Saleebey, 2009).

- **The relationship is hope-inducing**: The main objective of the strength-based approach is to strengthen the hope/ confidence of the client. Further, the proponents assert that hope can be realized with the help of strong relationships with people, community, and environment (Rapp *et al.*, 2005).
- **Meaningful choice**: This method emphasizes on the provision of meaningful choices and clients have the freedom to choose. The role of professionals is to aware and explain choices to clients and encourage them to make their own decisions based on their informed choices (Pulla, 2017).

The strength-based approach does not overlook the difficulty that client face. However, it allows practitioners to see options rather than constraints, possibilities rather than problems and, wellness rather than sickness (Kretzmann & McKnight, 1993). The proponents of the strength-based approach consider everything as a strength that assists a client in dealing with the problems of life. Strengths may vary from person to person and encourage a holistic assessment of the strengths of the client in a specific situation. Therefore, it is difficult to draft an exhaustive list of strengths for professionals, practitioners, and researchers.

Principles of Strength-based Approach

The strength-based approach as a philosophy of practice propels that individuals, groups, family or community hold the key to their own transformation and meaningful changes. It stops social work practitioners or researchers from considering procedures, techniques, and knowledge as the keys to change. It recommends to ask various questions that invite a curious exploration based on a set of values and attitudes (Early & GlenMaye, 2004). It helps practitioners to define the clients' situation and evaluate their problems in order to give meaning to those aspects that affect their surroundings. The strength-based approach also integrates the principles of social justice, self-determination, transparency, sharing of resources, and human rights.

Scholars and professionals have developed the following principles that serve as the basis for guiding and implementing the strength-based practice:

- Every person has the unique strengths. The situation/story of a client will be determined by their potential and capabilities, not by their limitations (Saleebey, 2009).
- Rather labelling the problems, the focus should be on the strengths of a client.
- One should look at the challenges as capacity fostering that helps to create hope in the clients.
- The professionals should use the language of clients that helps to assess the problems properly.
- The professionals must uphold the belief that change is inevitable.
- Positive change occurs in the context of authentic relationships. It helps clients to realize that they are important and useful to others and their communities (Pulla, 2017).
- Client's perspective of reality or their story is primary. Therefore, professionals need to value and start the change process with what is important to the person, not act as the expert (Weick, Rapp, Sullivan & Kisthardt, 1989).
- Capacity building is a process and a goal — a lifelong journey that is dynamic as opposed to static (Robbins *et al.*, 2006).

Significance of the Strength-based Approach

The strength-based approach is a model for practice that is based on a philosophy of values and attitudes. It is the strength-based values and attitudes that are the primary drivers of the intervention process and outcomes, not skills and knowledge. Skills and knowledge are drawn upon as resources to serve the principles that enable individuals to better understand their strengths and capacities to determine their own potential and path towards success (Kretzmann & McKnight, 1993). In this approach, the types of resources are as important as they are offered and mobilized to complement the intended client's strengths and goals. Although the strength-based approach offers an appealing alternative to traditional expert, deficit-based models and the significance of its effectiveness of these practices is still undermined (Saleebey, 1996).

Research highlights that strength-based interventions have a positive psychological impact, particularly in enhancing individual well-being through the development of hope. One of the aims of strength-based practice is to enable people to look beyond their immediate and real problems and encourage to imagine a future that inspires them, providing hope that things can improve (Rapp *et al.*, 2005). Strength-based approaches are shown to be effective in developing and maintaining hope in individuals. The strength-based practice is therapeutic in nature that helps to locate, articulate, and build the individual's assets or capabilities (Park & Peterson, 2006). It also assists in finding solutions for current problems based on the available resources. This practice is based on the recognition that networks often have more influence over an individual reaching a goal than any external person, including the practitioners (Weick *et al.*, 1989). On an individual level, strengths-based practitioners often identify family and community as a source of social networks. Proponents of this model assert that people within social networks can provide unparalleled insight into the strengths, talents, and challenges of a loved one.

With the help of the knowledge of local people, the power of local associations and the supportive functions of local institutions and services, strength-based community development approaches draw upon existing strengths to build stronger and more sustainable communities (Saleebey, 2009). It has been observed that by encouraging pride in achievements and a realization of what people have to contribute communities generate increased confidence in their ability to be producers not recipients of development (Foot & Hopkins, 2010).

Role of Social Work Practitioner

The notion of working with the beliefs of the strength-based approach may seem difficult to many practitioners. As they need to re-examine the way they work. They need to be more focused on the future than on the past and to focus on strengths instead of weaknesses in order to resolve the problem. In this context, the core elements of a Gandhian model of development looks appropriate and respectful to all (Pulla, 2006). It advocates to focus on strengths, assist a self-directed transformation in order to bring forward change that is empowering to people and reflect on how they want to change their situations.

The role of the practitioners becomes less about being a fixer of problems and more about being a co-facilitator of solutions (Brun & Rapp, 2001). Such type of involvement emphasizes that being a professional does not always mean having all the solutions. Professionals or facilitators must help the individual to recognize their strength even in the adverse situations. The emphasis should be on promoting client's need and create an opportunity for their growth and development (Pulla, 2017). Along with individuals, practitioners also learn and reflect on the process of practice in order to have a positive and lasting effect on the development of service.

Conclusion

This approach demands a different way of looking at individuals, families, and communities. Broadly, a client must be seen in the light of their capacities, talents, competencies, possibilities, and hopes in order to help him/her from any form of circumstance, oppression or trauma that creates a crisis in their everyday life. The strength-based approach requires an accounting of what people know and what they can do. It constitutes of resources existing within and around the individual, family, or community. It requires courage and diligence on the part of social work fraternity to recognize this noble profession through this alternate lens. Such a re-vision demands the suspension of initial disbelief in clients. Practitioners often do not engage in hearing and believing what their clients tell them, what their particular stories might be, especially if they (clients) are engaged in the abusive, destructive, addictive, or immoral behaviour.

The strength-based approach values two things—(a) the power of the self to heal, and (b) strategies to recognize the helping environment. Practitioners or those desiring change must hear the individual, family, or community stories and look for an alliance with the hope that problems of the client must be resolved that benefit their recovery and empowerment. The job of facilitators is to help individuals and groups to develop the language, summon the resources and manage the subjectivity of life in their world.

In the strength-based approach, how social worker encounters their fellow human beings is critical. They must respect individuals and treat them equally. They should enthusiastically meet them and engage in dialogue for sharing mutual knowledge in order to understand the problems clearly. The process of coming to know each other should be a mutual and collaborative one. The individuals and groups to whom the professionals assist also must be able to recognize their circumstances, their struggles and their experiences themselves. The notion of identifying oneself, one's situation and the condition is the beginning of real empowerment.

References

Barwick, H. (2004). *Young Males: Strength-based and Male-focused Approaches: A Review of the Research and Best Evidence*. New Zealand: Ministry of Youth Development.

Brun, C. and Rapp, R.C. (2001). "Strengths-based case management: Individuals' perspectives on strengths and the case manager relationship", *Social Work, 46*(3): 278-288.

Canda, E.R. and Furman, L.D. (2010). *Spiritual Diversity in Social Work Practice: The Heart of Helping*. New York: Oxford University Press.

Cowger, C.D. (1994). "Assessing client strengths: Clinical assessment for client empowerment", *Social Work, 39*(3): 262–268.

Cox, K.F. (2006). "Investigating the impact of strength-based assessment on youth with emotional or behavioural disorders", *Journal of Child and Family Studies, 15*(3): 287-301.

Early, T.J. and GlenMaye, L.F. (2004). "Valuing families: Social work practice with families from a strengths perspective", *Social Work, 45*(2): 118–130.

Foot, J. and Hopkins, T. (2010). *A Glass Half Full: How an Asset Approach can Improve Community Health and Well-being*. London, UK: Improvement and Development Agency.

Kretzmann, J.P. and McKnight, J.L. (1993). *Building Communities from the Inside Out: A Path Toward Finding and Mobilizing a Community's Assets*. Evanston, Illinois: Kretzmann and McKnight.

Laursen, E.K. (2003). "Frontiers in strength-based treatment", *Reclaiming Children and Youth, 12*(1): 12-17.

McMillen, J.C.; Morris, L. and Sherraden, M. (2004). "Ending social work's grudge match: Problems versus strengths", *Families in Society: The Journal of Contemporary Social Services, 85*(3): 317-325.

Miley, K.; O'Melia, M. and DuBois, B. (2004). *Generalist Social Work Practice*. New York: Pearson.

Nissen, L. (2006). "Bringing strength-based philosophy to life in juvenile justice." *Reclaiming Children and Youth, 15*(1): 40-46.

Park, N. and Peterson, C. (2006). "Moral competence and character strengths among adolescents: The development and validation of the Values in Action Inventory of Strengths for Youth", *Journal of Adolescence, 29*: 891-910.

Pulla, V. (2006). "Strengths Based Strategies." In V. Pulla and C. Montgomery (Eds.), *Strengths based Strategies, Resilience as opposed to Deficits: Working with Strengths*. Australia: Brisbane Institute of Strengths Based Practice.

Pulla, V. (2017). "Strengths-Based Approach in Social Work: A distinct ethical advantage." *International Journal of Innovation, Creativity and Change, 3*(2): 97-114.

Rapp, C.A.; Saleebey, D. and Sullivan, W.P. (2005). "The future of the strengths perspective", *Advances in Social Work, 6*(1): 79–90.

Robbins, S.P.; Chatterjee, P. and Canda, E.R. (2006). *Contemporary Human Behaviour Theory*. Boston: Allyn and Bacon.

Saleebey, D. (1996). "The Strengths Perspective in Social Work Practice: Extensions and Cautions", *Social Work, 41*(3): 296-305.

Saleebey, D. (2001). "The diagnostic strengths manual?", *Social Work, 46*(2): 183-187.

Saleebey, D. (Ed.). (2009). *The Strengths Perspective in Social Work Practice.* Boston: Allyn and Bacon.

Staudt, M.; Howard, M.O. and Drake, B. (2001). "The operationalization, implementation and effectiveness of the strengths perspective: A review of empirical studies", *Journal of Social Service Research, 27*(3): 1-21.

Weick, A. (1992). "Building a strengths perspective for social work", In D. Saleebey (Ed.), *The strengths perspective in social work practice,* pp. 27–38. White Plains, NY: Longman.

Weick, A.; Rapp, C.; Sullivan, W.P. and Kisthardt, W. (1989). "A strengths perspective for Social Work practice", *Social Work, 34*(4): 350-354.

15

Social Work Education and Review Committees in Social Work

An Indian Perspective

Dimple Mishra

Introduction

Social Work as a discipline began to be taught in Indian Higher Education system way back in 1936 with the establishment of the Sir Dorabji Tata Graduate School of Social Work under the leadership of Sir Clifford Manshardt which is now known as Tata Institute of Social Sciences (TISS), Mumbai. TISS has got its acknowledgment as one of the important pioneer institutes promoting social work education and practice in India as well as in Asia. In India, professional social work owes its origin to a short-term training course on social service organised by the social service league at Bombay for men and women who were willing to volunteer for social service.

The first curriculum introduced by TISS included methods of social case work, administration and research. Subjects related to sociology, economics, psychology and human development were also offered. Subject matter on target groups included the child, the family, juvenile delinquents and medical and psychiatric information. All these courses were compulsory, and no provision for specialization was available. For ten years, the curriculum did not change and the subjects continued to be pretty much the same (Desai, 1985). Thomas and Varghese (2012) in their paper argue, the initial syllabus was based on the curricula of American schools of Social Work with British pattern. In fact, several pioneers in

Social Work education in India had their orientation to the profession in American establishments. Therefore, there was little initiative to develop an Indian based curriculum for both theory and practice. The whole effort was directed towards trying and fitting the Western content by adapting the curricula to suit the Indian social conditions.

After attaining independence, TISS introduced specializations in Medical and Psychiatric Social Work, criminology and correctional administration, labour welfare and personnel management. However, many schools of Social Work followed the generic pattern of Social Work education programme. Right from the very beginning of Professional Social Work education in the country, the functions and duties of Professional Social Worker has been debated on various forums.

"Social work is a practice-based profession and an academic discipline that promotes social change and development, social cohesion, and the empowerment and liberation of people. Principles of social justice, human rights, collective responsibility and respect for diversities are central to social work. Underpinned by theories of social work, social sciences, humanities and indigenous knowledge, social work engages people and structures to address life challenges and enhance well-being" (IFSW, 2014). The above definition may be amplified at national and/or regional levels.

In the scholarly world Social Work is viewed as a practice-oriented profession as well as an academic discipline which recognizes that interconnected historical, socio-economic, cultural, spatial, political and personal factors provide opportunities and/or barriers to human well-being and development. Structural barriers lead to the perpetuation of inequalities, discrimination, exploitation and oppression. The development of critical consciousness through reflecting on structural sources of oppression and/or privilege, on the basis of criteria such as religion, class, language, gender, race, disability, culture and sexual orientation, and developing action strategies towards addressing structural and personal barriers are central to emancipatory practice where the goals are the empowerment and liberation of people. In solidarity with those who are disadvantaged, the profession seeks to alleviate poverty, liberate the vulnerable and oppressed, and promote social inclusion and social cohesion (IFSW).

In India, professional social work owes its origin to a short-term training course on social service organised by the social service league at Bombay. The training course included those men and women who were willing to volunteer them for social service. Till that time social workers did not get any salary or remuneration for their work. It was simply a social service to the needy people guided by the principle of humanity. Later on, the Tata Institute of Social Sciences was established in the year of 1936 in Bombay. The institute started a course of professional training in social work (Bhattacharya, 2011).

The University Grants Commission (UGC) appointed the First Review Committee for Social Work Education in 1960 and the Second Review Committee in 1975 aimed at compiling status report and for the promotion, maintenance of the standards of education, co-ordination of Social Work education, training, research and practice.

First Review Committee on Social Work Education in India, 1960

The First Review Committee on Social Work education in India, 1960 appointed by the UGC, was of the view that Social Work should concern itself with promoting welfare of the people from weaker and vulnerable sections of the society. The Committee recommended that the teaching of Social Work should be done at both under graduate and post-graduate levels. While field-work was recommended for both under-graduate and post-graduate levels, project report based on field research was made an integral part of the post-graduate teaching in Social Work. The Committee identified various fields, such as labour welfare, rural development and community organisation, tribal welfare, medical and psychiatric Social Work, correctional work, family and child welfare, work with elderly, welfare of the handicapped etc. wherein Social Workers should intervene mainly by using the methods of social case work, social group work, community organisation, social welfare administration and social research and statistics. The Committee conceived of formal training of Social Work as an endeavour to develop trained manpower to provide social and welfare services scientifically and effectively (UGC, 1965).

Whereas, the growing model of "*Bharatiyakaran*" in social work specific context is in much prevalence and even in debates. The

Bharatiyakaran of social work curriculum is holistic, integrated, and anti-discriminatory in nature. The concept of 'Bharatiyakaran of Social Work' is based on three major premises — Indianisation, Indigenization and Decolonization (Dash, 2018). It also aims to Integrate perspectives of Indian scriptures, culture and rituals, indic experiences, as well as Indo-centric fieldwork practicum in social work education. The rich social service traditions, role of religion and impact of spirituality has been given due place in the curriculum. Besides that, the Indic approaches of social welfare, Buddhism, Hinduism, Jainism, Sikhism, Vedic approaches has been added. The Indian concepts of social welfare like *dharma, danam, yagna, punya; purushartha, bhakti* etc. has been incorporated in the curriculum (Dash, 2018). The indigenous experiments conducted by Nanaji Deshmukh, Anna Hazare, Baba Amte, Vandana Shiva, Bindeswar Pathak etc. has been included in the social work curricula. The senior social work academicians and professionals from different central and state universities across the country gathered in this workshop and drafted a new curriculum of Master of Social Work (MSW) programmes for Universities in India (Dash, 2018).

Second Review Committee on Social Work Education in India, 1975

The First Review Committee for Social Work Education got published in 1965. Since no subsequent review of Social Work Education had been undertaken, a Second Review Committee was appointed by the panel on Social Work Education of the UGC, at its meeting on 28th April, 1975. The Second Review Committee on Social Work Education, identified two types of tasks of professional Social Workers: (1) developmental and (2) remedial or rehabilitative (UGC, 1980). It categorically observed that the major goal of Social Work is to enhance the well-being of people to develop their capacities to become participating and contributing citizen. Developmental tasks of the profession are related to work with specific target groups where social functioning is of crucial concern to social welfare, ensuring interdisciplinary delivery of service, providing opportunities for the involvement of communities in problem solving and bringing about change in institutional structure and processes which retard, block or deflect development. However, Social Work cannot, in the process, ignore the tasks which are remedial and rehabilitative for those whose functioning is already impaired. What is sought to be achieved is to rearrange our priorities so that the primary problems affecting the larger segment of our population receive greater emphasis than the residual problems. Therefore, while our major tasks would be developmental, we would also continue to perform the remedial tasks. In order to undertake these tasks effectively the Committee suggested four functions: (a) delivery of services/change function, (b) planning, policy, development, programming and administration related to the delivery of services, (c) monitoring, evaluation and research concerning delivery of services, and (d) supervision, training and evaluation of man power required for the delivery of services.

The Review Committee on Social Work Education in India (1978) has evolved specific objectives of fieldwork training in social work education. The major objectives of fieldwork practicum in social work education are as under:

1. To develop professional skills through practical learning, apply acquired knowledge for the study of relevant facts, analysis of the problems and selection of appropriate means towards the solution of those problems.
2. To develop the skills for solving the problems in work at the micro level (individual, family and groups) and change at the macro level (community, social system including social institutions and wide range processes).
3. To provide concurrent opportunities for the integration of classroom learning, fieldwork practice and *vice versa* (feedback mechanism for both fieldwork practice and classroom learning).
4. To develop the skills required for professional practice at a particular level of training.
5. To objectively develop professional attitude involving impartiality and non-judgemental attitude.
6. To develop professional values and commitments, such as respect for human dignity and worth, right to participation and self-determination compatible with a better society.
7. To develop an awareness of self and one's professional ideas.

Third Review Committee on Social Work Education, 2001

The Third Review Committee in 2001 spoke the need of relating social work education to the social realities. It recommended the curriculum to be divided in three sets. These are: (1) Core set includes the philosophy, ideology, values, ethics, theory and concepts. (2) The supportive set deals with knowledge and skills to assist the core set. (3) The interdisciplinary set includes theories, concepts from other disciplines which relates with social work according the students choice (Thomas, 2010). But the Third Review Committee of social work education has not been published yet.

Prof. Sanjay Bhatt clearly categorized development of social work education into various stages such as:

1. Initiation/Inception (1936-46)

It is denoted by establishment of Sir Dorabji Tata Graduate School of Social Work established in 1936 and now called as Tata Institute of Social Science (TISS).

2. Experimentation (1947-56)

In this phase, Delhi School of Social Work, Kashi Vidyapith, Gujarat Vidyapith and similar other institutions were established.

3. Expansion (1957-76)

In this phase, many social work educational institutions in Maharasthra, Gujarat, Uttar Pradesh, Tamil Nadu and other states were established and there was expansion in terms of number of institutions across the length and breadth of the country.

4. Moderation/Stagnation (1977-86)

Unlike expansion phase, in this period we do not see many new social work education institutions in the country.

5. Explosion (1987)

This phase crossed the 200 mark in terms of social work institutions in India (Thomas, 2010).

The UGC Model Curriculum, 2001

The UGC in its Model Curriculum developed in 2001 divided the curriculum of social work programmes into four broad domains, which include: the Core Domain, the Supportive Domain and the Interdisciplinary Domain and fourth cluster is titled as Elective Content.

The Model Curriculum of UGC, 2001 states that the nature of instructional time frame, practice learning, opportunity provisions, instructions for practice learning, along with the nature of assessment for social work are different. The Curriculum classification categories and the nature of educational experiences necessary for this profession. Three different norms as requirements accepted in the Second Review Committee (1975) and reiterated in the Curriculum Development Centre's Report (1990) are stated here:

1. Practice teaching-learning is like learning in a laboratory. The difference is that, this learning is carried out in the real life situations among the communities, groups, families/individuals and in organisations providing services. Every learner is required to spend a minimum of fifteen hours a week in a setting/organisation to learn practice. Each learner should get about forty-five to sixty minutes of individual instruction. Hence, the teacher-learner ratio suggested is 1:8 to 10. practice learning calls for individual guidance and small group guidance.
2. Core domain instruction-calls for small group teaching methods and the class-room practice. These methods are best employed when the numbers making up the class is small, necessitating break up of large groups into those around twenty. The number of teachers required for the same content is naturally larger.
3. The third concern emerges from the need of minimum norms/requirements for starting a programme of social work profession. The UGC Panel of Social Work Education has worked out 'basic minimum' requirements, and the Commission has in its 'in house' meeting accepted these norms. Therefore, universities providing affiliation, and those setting up programmes must consider the basic

minimum requirements if 'a standard' is to be established, retained and propagated, to march towards excellence. The minimum norms/requirements including academic faculty, well-ventilated classrooms and office space to function, teacher development programmes, in service training and growth opportunities etc.

National Assessment and Accreditation Council (NAAC)

The National Assessment and Accreditation Council (NAAC) is an autonomous body established by the UGC to assess and accredit institutions of higher education in the country. It is an outcome of the recommendations of the National Policy on Education (1986) which laid special emphasis on upholding the quality of higher education in India. To address the issues of quality, the National Policy on Education (1986) and the Plan of Action (POA-1992) advocated the establishment of an independent national accreditation body. Consequently, the NAAC was established in 1994 with its headquarters at Bangalore. The Primary objectives of NAAC are promoting, evaluating and maintaining the quality of higher education in India. It provides guidelines for preparing, 'self-study report' by the institutions applying for accreditation.

NAAC has developed a manual for self-study of Social Work institutions which is the outcome of the proceedings of the national seminar on standards for assessment of quality in Social Work education organised by Tata Institute of Social Sciences and sponsored by the National Assessment and Accreditation Council on November 11-13, 2003.

The manual gives an overall curriculum structure and allocates credits, hours and marks for each component of Social Work education. It has the set standards for teaching-learning and education, curricular aspects; research and consultancy and extension; infrastructure and learning resources; student support and progression; and organisation and management of the Social Work institutions.

Limitations in Developing Indigenous Literature in India

Over the eight decades of professional Social Work in India has been marked by few triumphs and too many travails that warrant a serious discussion on what the future holds for a 'profession' beleaguered by several internal and external constraints and considerations including lack of indigenous literature, weightage for field work, and the fact that most social work educators are not practitioners unlike the counterparts in several developed countries. Hardly any genuine effort made for Continuous Professional Development (CPD), development of field (service) action projects, non-professionals at education and training, lack of standards in education and training and for establishing a 'National Council for Social Work Education and Training in India'.

The major shortcoming of social work education in India is its inability to sufficiently indigenize its knowledge-base. The basic teaching material with respect to interventionist methods (the holy trinity of social case work, social group work and community organisation) is still primarily American. The challenge, as mentioned before, has not been met and there is often a lingering doubt in the mind of many social work educators and trained social workers whether social work in India can afford to be only concerned with specific individuals, groups and communities when the problems are really the problems of large masses of people (Gore, 1985:151). Many of the problems that are identified as problems of the socially oppressed and economically deprived sections cannot be called mental problems (to use the American phraseology). The social and cultural context of these problems is well beyond the reach of moral-ethical and/or psycho-social paradigm of intervention (Srivatsava, 1999).

The Limitations can be seen through some of the following review of the literature:

The literature resource on Social Work in India, however, is very limited as Social Work schools depend to a larger extent on Western literature. Chowdhary (1992) in his reflections on Social Work education remarked that one of the major complaints about professional Social Work education is the inadequacy of indigenous literature in Social Work without which it is very difficult to maintain the standard of Social Work education. The contributions of Social Workers through research are more to social science disciplines than to Social Work.

The existence and triumph of Social Work profession rest with the standard of Social Work education. The more standardized the training, the more is the value additions to his profession

(Desai, 1994). Indian Social Work literature is also limited in its research and writing, exploring the field situation in India particularly referring to the strength and limitations of the existing pattern. Much of the available literature is based on Western culture from where even the theoretical perception has been borrowed.

Singh (2010) conducted a study on 'status of field work and research in Social Work education: with special reference to Hindi speaking areas in India' with specific objectives to reveal the nature and content of field work training in different schools of Social Work especially in Hindi speaking areas in India. The objectives of the study were: (1) to find out the background and perception of the Social Work students and educators regarding the objectives, content of field work, supervision and research undertaken at schools of Social Work; (2) to find out the new process and mechanisms of field work and (3) to explore and evaluate the emerging trends of field work and research today with new requirements of the present scenario.

The major focus of the study was to know the qualification, additional qualifications, teaching experience in Social Work, research experience, involvement in organisation/projects before joining teaching, association with professional organisation, teacher agency meeting and its frequency, satisfaction with field work, change in field work process, extent of field work training in job profile, regarding complexity of Social Work problems and need for new mechanism or theory etc. Singh had found in his study that around 80 per cent students are satisfied with their field work dealing with social issues and problems because they get help from the department as well as agency supervisors.

It was observed that their study was basically focused with a two dimensional approach (two way) with students and teachers to know the nature, content and involvement of main components of field work in Social Work training. In fact, Thomas (2010) described that there are three important components of field work training, namely the social agency, the student, and the supervisor (both teacher and agency supervisors). The student is a learner and operates between the client and the agency and between the agency and the field supervisor. The agency and the field supervisor primarily aim at training the student. It is the agency which provides an opportunity to the learner to translate the theory and principles of Social Work from class room into action.

Bhanti (1996) has provided some insights into the existing pattern of field work training and supervision in schools of Social Work in India. In his book *"Field Work in Social Work Perspective"*, the author has shown concern over the status of the profession and the irrelevance of the field work education in existing social system in India. The book provides a detailed description of the different components of Social Work field education. The author has pointed out the lack of fixed field work curriculum for Social Work students and has given suggestions for designing field work curriculum.

Subedar (2001) has discussed field work supervision in his book *"Field Work Training in Social Work"*. The author has elaborated upon all the aspects of prevailing trend in field education in Social Work in Indian Universities. The book has highlighted the lack of literature on concurrent field work training and pointed out the lacuna existing in the field education in some universities and has attempted to devise modalities for field practicum for Social Work students. Methods of practice such as community work, group work and case work has been elaborately discussed. The need, importance and functions of supervision of field practicum constitute an important part of the book. The author has described the problems in field practicum and its supervision faced by students, teachers, agencies as well as the institutes and has given suggestions to improve the situation and overcome the challenges faced in the process of field work and supervision.

The Education Policy and Accreditation Standards of the Council on Social Work Education (CSWE), states that "the purposes of social work education are to prepare competent and effective professionals; to develop social work knowledge and to provide leadership in the development of service delivery systems." (CSWE, 2001: 5). It means that social workers are not only expected to be informed about relevant theories, but they must apply these theories to practice so that unfavourable conditions in the society can be ameliorated. This calls for the application of knowledge and theory learned from the classroom to practical situations and effecting their integration.

Tsui and Ho (1998) have also outlined the numerous existing models for Social Work supervision and have built upon a comprehensive model for Social Work supervision in which they emphasized culture as a major context for supervision. Hensley

(2003) studied the value of supervision in training the Social Workers and gave some suggestions for improving the same. He emphasized that the qualification to become a supervisor must be clearly defined by the agencies and training for them should be made compulsory. He further suggests for group supervision in addition to individual supervision and establishment of guidelines and professional ethics for supervision. He also points out some aspects of supervision like cross-cultural supervision, cross-gender supervision, burn out and stress as areas for future studies.

Giddings *et al.* (2007) have expressed their concern over the emergence of a trend of inadequate supervision in Social Work. They contend that educationally monitored practice is essential for teaching students to integrate theory and practice in order to develop a professional concept of self. They have developed a four staged model—integrative supervision model—to train post MSW students to integrate theory with practice for developing professional competency. This model is supposed to fill the gap occurring due to inadequate supervision.

Abram *et al.* (2000) conducted a qualitative study to explore the dynamics of the relationship between the practicum student, the offsite MSW field instructor and on site non-MSW field supervisor. The authors conducted a focused group discussion with nine professionals who had the experience of supervising MSW students for their practicum. They found that an effective practicum outcome is the result of the active involvement of all the three parties in this triad model. However, this study was done with a very small sample with a qualitative aspect.

Rafat Aara (2013) conducted a comparative study on 'Supervision in Social Work Practicum in Conventional and ODL system', which covered several aspects pertaining to supervision. The prime rationale for choosing this study was to explore the much underresearched aspect of social work profession in India, that is, supervision of field practicum. It was observed by the researcher that in the conventional system there was the lack of uniformity with regard to the curriculum for field practice among the institutes. In the conventional system, the students were evaluated for their practicum based on the written reports, presentations and orally during *viva voce*. The concerned supervisor assigned the internal marks and the external examiner marked the students based on their performance in the *viva voce*. Failure in the practicum meant failure in theory and practical both and the students had to repeat the year. Assigning of credits to the theory courses was also not followed uniformly throughout the sample institutes.

In ODL, the evaluation of field practicum was done based on the student's performance in the field and the written reports in the field work journal by the field work supervisor and by the faculty exclusively based on written reports in the field work journal. Oral examination of field practicum was not conducted in the ODL. The learners were evaluated internally by the concerned field work supervisor and externally by the faculty at the School of Social Work, IGNOU. The field work supervisor assigned fifty per cent of the marks and the faculty assigned fifty per cent marks. Failure in the practicum in the ODL meant repeating the practicum only and not theory. Credit system was found to be followed in the ODL in which credits were assigned to theory as well as practicum.

Saju (2016) in his study of 'Strengths and Limitations of Field Work Practicum in Social Work Education in Kerala' states that classroom teaching and field practicum are two integral and indispensable parts of Social Work Education. Social work practice itself is a type of situated knowledge that is shaped and contextualized in the complexity of the social world. Social work educators are expected to play the central role of assisting the students in making smooth transfer of social work education and concepts to practice setting. However, there is documented proof on the lack of congruence between what is being taught in education and what actually occurs in the field (Penna, 2004). Many social researchers have reported that while practitioners can identify different techniques they use in practice, they cannot attribute it to a specific theory (Gould & Harris, 1996). The pursuit of knowledge building continues to dominate Social work even though research and discourse literature consistently demonstrate the rift between practicum and education.

The UGC Model Curriculum, 2001 highlighted the need of relating Social Work education to social realities. UGC and NAAC tried to bring the profession to a single platform by introducing and designing model curricula, developing a manual to maintain minimum standard of quality at several levels. It was a big challenge to these national bodies to implement a uniform syllabus across all universities in the country (Thomas, 2010: 57).

Nevertheless, the professional education discipline is pervaded by several perils. In the words of Second UGC Review Committee on Social Work Education, "even after several decades of purposeful existence of the profession of social work practice, it is yet to make its presence strongly felt among the general people in the country. Poor visibility of the profession, inadequate public recognition, identity crisis, lack of indigenous knowledge base, inappropriate response to the changing needs of the field, poor research base, lack of linkage between classroom theories and reality of the field and many other related problems are the leading obstacles in the path."

Incorporation, Development and Findings of Indigenous Knowledge-Based Literature in India

India is so diversified in culture, tradition, custom, beliefs etc. So the one model would not suit the entire gamut of social work. Therefore, it is a high need to incorporate and develop indigenous knowledge based literature. As a moving trend many scholarly articles are coming out in the form of indigenous knowledge-based literature. Earlier the curriculum of social work was heavily relied on Western model. But now more weightage is being given to indigenous practice based literature. Despite of limitations, the IGNOU has come in front to develop and incorporate indigenous knowledge-based literature.

Philomena D'Souza (1978) stated that education for social work is directed towards professional competence, to enable to function effectively as social workers. Thus, it aims to impart to students knowledge, skills, attitudes and values which will contribute to this functioning. Seven goals of Social Work Education have been stated by Philomena D'Souza in her study on field instruction. These are:

1. Helping students to recognize the intrinsic dignity of person and the values of family life, and developing attitudes and practices consistent with these values.
2. Helping students to evolve a positive philosophy of life that is based on the understanding of the social, economic and cultural faces of the people with whom they work.

3. Providing opportunities for individual growth and development so that the student may learn to think critically of himself/herself in relation to other people.
4. Teaching principles and techniques of social work and helping students to apply these successfully to practice situation.
5. Preparing students for leadership through consciously integrated use of scientific knowledge.
6. Stimulating public interest in the furtherance of social welfare activities on scientific lines.
7. Attainment of these goals requires a core programme including both classroom instruction and field work. It is with the latter that this study is concerned with.

Development of Indigenous Literature in India

This section highlights that School of Social Work (SOSW) at Indira Gandhi National Open University (IGNOU) contributed a lot for the social work education by developing social work materials ingeniously under the dynamic leadership of Professor Gracious Thomas, with the support of several eminent social work educators, from different central and state level universities of India as well as from several foreign universities.

In the area of contribution to knowledge base for learners of Social Work, IGNOU, has developed various indigenous materials as part of curriculum for both BSW and MSW students. These include on origin and development of Social Work in India, social science concepts for Social Work; Social Work and social development; women and child development; international Social Work; Social Work in African context; disaster management; HIV/AIDS; stigma and discrimination; review of studies in Social Work; introduction to philanthropic Social Work; Social Work and tribal development; Social Work and counselling; Social Work and criminal justice system; Social Work practicum and supervision; Social Work research; case and counselling, working with individuals; social group work; working with groups, community organisation; management for community development and social action; various courses on philanthropy mainly constitute the core areas of Social Work and related subjects offered by Indira Gandhi National Open University.

Prof. Gracious Thomas the founding director of School of Social Work in IGNOU has developed various indigenous methods, namely, advocacy, networking; awareness campaign; public interest litigation; resource mobilization; which has been recently included in MSW curriculum. The Schools of Social Work of IGNOU has also developed course materials on Religions and Social Work as it believes the role of religion in ushering a vibrant Social Work education and practice. Accordingly, the impact of religions, viz., Hinduism, Islam; Sikhism; Jainism; Buddhism and Christianity on Social Work education and practice has been included in the course materials of BSW/MSW of Indira Gandhi National Open University.

Besides these theoretical contents, IGNOU has also developed a separate full paper titled 'Social Work Practicum and Supervision' that gives detailed theoretical perspectives on Social Work practicum: concept, meaning, nature, importance and scope; history of Social Work practicum; development of field education; Social Work practicum in global and national scenario; Social Work practicum in open and distance learning; orientation for Social Work practicum; roles and expectations in Social Work practicum, role and expectations in Social Work training institutes; principles and skills for Social Work and agency practice; models and modes of Social Work supervision; administrative and environmental aspects of Social Work supervision; supportive functions in supervision; field practicum supervision in distance learning mode; individuals, family, and community; medical, psychiatry, and child care; education and research; correctional services; corporate sector; donor agencies; and NGOs. The course material on Social Work practicum and supervision is organised around the basic information on Social Work practicum, i.e. the concepts, importance, models, national as well as international scenario and its applicability in the open and distance learning system. It also focuses on roles and expectations of various stakeholders involved in Social Work practicum.

Apart from this, a practitioners guide for Social Work practicum has also been developed that capacitates the learners in the area of field work practice in Social Work, principles of Social Work practice; Social Work practice skills; guidelines for agency practice; recording; role and task of field work supervisor; guidelines for academic contents; evaluation in ODL; all with an orientation in distance education and Social Work.

The practitioners guide for Social Work practicum is the first attempt in India to develop a comprehensive field work guide for educators and supervisors of the programme of study in Social Work through distance learning. This guide has been prepared keeping in view distance learners in Social Work for the first, second and third year of BSW, the PGDSW, and first and final year of MSW. It also includes the illustrations of case work, group work and community organisation and the secondary methods of Social Work.

The pre-end and term-end self-assessment forms are being developed to ensure that learners duly fill the pre-assessment form during the induction programme during the beginning of the session/year and similarly at the conclusion of the session/year, the learners should fill term end assessment form which is a repetition of pre-term assessment form. The objective is to facilitate the teachers as well as the students to know the extent of knowledge and skills gained and attitudinal changes that have occurred among the learners as a result of the training programme during year.

Findings of Social Work Education through Open and Distance Learning (ODL), IGNOU

- Establishment of first School of Social Work under ODL (IGNOU).
- About 7,000 students have graduated in both BSW and MSW respectively, i.e. employment for 14,000 families.
- About two dozen M.Phil/Ph.D. candidates successfully completed their pre-doctoral/Doctoral degree programmes.
- Published around 400 books (blocks) with ISBN No. in English and Hindi.
- About 100 audio/video programmes are there.
- Revised materials would be available from July 2018.
- PDF to a Delhi University faculty by ICSSR on Social Work through ODL.
- Has a 150 million projects, namely the CBCI Chair-Mega Project.
- Reaching out to 12 countries.
- Catering to over 50,000 students.
- Facilitated about 3000 social workers with travel grants.

- Organised over 30 National and State level seminars.
- Facilitated hundreds of social work academicians to improve their research abilities, writing skills, editorials skills etc.

Learning Support System for Learner

- Academic Counsellor/Field Work Supervisor.
- Print Material.
- E-Resources.
- Gyanvani, Gyandarshan.
- Audio/Video Conferencing.

Recommendations

Since social work literature, modes of practice, approaches, theories, have been heavily borrowed from Western countries, so we need to develop the indigenous approaches too. This requires that the academicians and practitioners must document their experiences so as to facilitate the process of developing indigenous approaches (Thomas : 2010).

Social Work Education is being shaped by University Departments; the quality of University Departments would define the quality of Social Work Education. If the university departments of central and state level have a collective Vision and Mission from three different angles or dimensions then it can lead to a better articulation of the Social Work Education. The three dimensional approach is:

The first dimension is the legacy of the schools/departments in terms of:

- Its Vision and Mission.
- Its conviction for value based Social Work Education.
- Its conviction to train students as compassionate and competent change agents in the society.
- Its ability to provide learning opportunities through class room interaction library and internet resources.
- Provision of positive learning experience through field action projects.

- The departments' contribution to the advancement of the profession.
- Its contribution for interdepartmental cooperation.
- Its contribution for generation of knowledge in the form of publications.
- Its contribution for organizing events of Continuous Professional Development (CPD).
- Its contribution in research—both theoretical and applied.
- Its interface with Governmental Organisations (GOs), Non-Governmental Organisations (NGOs), Corporate Organisations (COs) and the larger civil society.
- Its efforts to promote scholastic performance among staff and students.
- Its strength of Alumni and Alma matter relationships should be improved and streamlined.

The second dimension is Social Work Educators need to maintain:

- Conviction and competency in teaching.
- Track record in practice in the form of field action projects or direct practice.
- Contribution in the area of research both theoretical and applied.
- Educators' contribution to the advancement of professional organisation.
- Educators' interface with Governmental Organisations (GOs), Non-Governmental Organisations (NGOs), Corporate Organisations (COs) and the larger civil society.
- Educators' contribution in the mentoring the young Social Work Learners.

The third dimension is to focus on Community action by Schools of Social Work:

- The national and state level professional bodies.
- The national and state level regular events for Continuous Professional Development (CPD).
- The national and state level advocacy initiatives.
- The national and state level lobbying efforts.

Conclusion

Professions based on human relationship such as social work must have its knowledge base truly reflecting values, culture, problems of society in which it has to be taught and practiced. About social work education in India, it will be inappropriate to say that social work educators have not responded to the need of indigenizing social work knowledge. It, however, is seen in the writings of the professionals that there is need of Indigenous Knowledge Base and its dissemination. Through the incorporation of Indigenous Knowledge Base of classroom teaching to practice learning and *vice versa,* the quality and standard of social work education can be improved. In fact, the time is apt that factors inhibiting growth of Indigenous Knowledge Base are systematically studied, documented and addressed so that development of Indigenous Knowledge Base can get momentum for its visibility.

More effective social services can be developed when social workers understand and are committed to developing methods that support Indigenous communities (academicians, practitioners, local people etc.) in their cultural recovery and self-determination efforts. For social workers, these insights can increase when Indigenous worldviews, knowledge, and dialogues are accurately and sufficiently represented in Social Work practice and educational curriculum. Teachers, practitioners and learners should come together with collective vision and mission to overcome the problems and challenges to strengthen the social work education and training in India.

References

Aara, R. (2013). *A Comparative Study on Supervision in Social Work Practicum in Conventional and ODL System,* An Unpublished Ph.D. Dissertation, Indira Gandhi National Open University, New Delhi.

Abram, F.Y., Hartung, M.R. and Wernet, S.P. (2000). "The Non MSW Task supervisor, MSW fields instructor, and the practicum student", *Journal of Teaching in Social Work,* 20(1), 171-185.

Bhanti, R. (1996). *Field work in Social Work perspective.* Udaipur: Himanshu Publications.

Bhatt, S. and Phukan, D. (2015). *Social Work Education in India: A Resource Book.* Jamia Nagar, New Delhi: Alter Notes Press Publisher.

Botcha, R. (2012). "Problems and challenges for social work education in India: Some recommendations", *International Journal of Multidisciplinary Educational Research,* Vol. (1), Issue-3.

Botcha, R. (2016). *Retrospect and Prospects of Professional Social Work Education in India.* An Unpublished Ph.D. Thesis, New Delhi: Indira Gandhi National Open University.

Chandrapa, S. and Saxena, A. (2017). "Social Work: A Practice-Based Profession, *Research on Humanities and Social Sciences,* Vol. (7), No. 17. Retrieved from http://. www.iiste.org.

Chowdhary, D.P. (1992). *Introduction to Social Work: History, Concepts, Methods and Field.* New Delhi: Atma Ram and Sons.

Council on Social Work Education (2001). *Education Policy and Accreditation Standards.* Alexandria, VA: CSWE.

D'Souza, P. (1978). *Field Instruction in Social Work Education,* An Unpublished Doctoral Dissertation, Tata Institute of Social Science, Mumbai.

Dash, B.M. (2018). Bhartiyakaran of Social Work: Understanding the Meaning and Concept, *New Delhi Times,* 7 December, 2018.

Desai, A.S. (1985). "The foundations of social work education in India and some issues." *The Indian Journal of Social Work,* 46(1), 41-57.

Desai, A.S. (1994). *A Study of Social Work Education in India: Students, Educators and the Educational Process,* TISS, Bombay.

Giddings, M.M., Vodde, R. and Cleveland, P. (2007). "Examining student field instructor problem in practicum beyond student satisfaction measures." *The Clinical Supervisor,* 22(2), 191-214.

Gould, N. and Harris, A. (1996). "Student imagery of practice in social work and teacher education: A comparative research approach." *British Journal of Social Work, 26,* 223-237.

Hensley, P.H. (2003). "The value of supervision." *The Clinical Supervisor, 21(1),* 97-110.

IASSW and IFSW (2014). "Global Definition of Social Work." Retrieved from ifsw.org/get-involved/global-definition-of-social-work/.

Kathiresan, L. (2014). "Theorizing from Practice: Critical Reflection as a Tool for Social Workers." *Social Work Journal (Bi-Annual),* Volume-4, Number 2, pp. 1-7. Retrieved from www.aus.ac.in.

"Made in India: Social Work Journey." *Social Work Education Through Open and Distance Learning: Opportunities for Change.* Two-days (22nd and 23rd February, 2018) National-Level Workshop conducted by IGNOU.

Manshardt, C. (1985). "Education for Social Work." *The Indian Journal of Social Work,* Vol. XLVI No. 1.

NAAC (2004), A Manual for Assessment and Accreditation of Social Work Education Programme, New Delhi.

Penna, S. (2004). "Perils of applying theory to practice." *Critical Social Work. 1*(1), 1-13.

Saju, P.P. (2016). *Strengths and Limitations of Field Work Practicum in Social Work Education in Kerala.* A Published Thesis. New Delhi: Indira Gandhi National Open University.

Singh, A.N. (2010). "Status of Field Work in research in social work education with special reference to Hindi speaking areas in India", *Social Work Journal.* Vol. (1), pp. 1-11.

Srivastava, S.P. (1999), "Addressing the Future of Professional Social Work in India", *The Indian Journal of Social Work, 60* (1), pp. 118-139.

Subedar, I.S. (2001). *Field Work Training in Social Work,* Jaipur: Rawat Publications.

Thomas, G. (2010). *Origin and Development of Social Work,* Indira Gandhi National Open University, New Delhi.

Thomas, G. and Varghese, J. (2012). "Social Work Education around the world", *Encyclopedia of Social Work,* Vol. 4, pp. 1385-1396. Lucknow: New Royal Book Company.

Tsui, M.S. and Ho, W.S. (1998). "In search of a comprehensive model of supervision." *The Clinical Supervisor, 16*(20), 181-205.

University Grants Commission (1965). *Social Work Education in Indian Universities,* University Grants Commission: New Delhi.

University Grants Commission (1980). *Review of Social Work Education in India: Retrospect and Prospect Universities,* Report of the Second Review Committee, University Grants Commission, New Delhi.

University Grants Commission (2001). *UGC Model Curriculum,* University Grants Commission, New Delhi.

Websites

https://www.duexpress.in/masters-in-social-work-gets-bharatiya

https://www.newdelhitimes.com/social-work-curriculum-in-india-moving-towards-bharatiyakaran/

https://www.newdelhitimes.com/social-work-fraternity-to-get-new-curriculum-and-indian-social-work-day/

16

Impact of Globalization on Social Work Education and Practice

Avtar Singh

Introduction

Globalization is not a new phenomenon. It began in the late nineteenth century, but its spread slowed during the period from the start of the First World War until the third quarter of the twentieth century. This slowdown can be attributed to the inward looking policies pursued by a number of countries in order to protect their respective industries. The process of globalization accelerated during the 1980s and it is growing and developing ever since. Globalization in its contemporary form has emerged after the collapse of the Soviet Union in the early 1990s, and the apparent triumph of Western Capitalism. Since then, the G7 and international funding agencies have made this the dominant economic credo constantly promoting it as the panacea for poverty and economic backwards. Globalization as an interchange of various attributes among different societies is not a new phenomenon, but an ongoing process. What makes the present day process of globalization different and distinct from the earlier ones is the rapid increase in the frequency and the density of these interchanges. It is important to learn more about the current pace of the process of globalization and related aspects.

Globalization is expected to be a process through which an increasingly free flow of ideas, people, goods, services and capital would lead to the integration of economies and societies. It is characterized by an accelerated flow of trade, capital, and information, as well as mobility of individuals, across geographical borders. It reflects comprehensive level of interaction than that has occurred in the past, suggesting something beyond the word "international." It implies a diminishing importance of national borders and strengthening of Identities, that stretch beyond those rooted in a limited locale in terms of particular country. It can also be defined as the intensification of worldwide social relations which link distant localities in such a way that local happenings are shaped by events occurring at any distant place and *vice versa*. It is this construction of time-space compression that has given rise to popular notion of "One-World", "Global Village", etc. (Singh, 2012).

Globalization is repeatedly propagated to common people as a womb of 'progress'. People and nations who own resources and political power create conditions for others to follow this model of progress. Globalization is an economic system that does not talk of globalization of humanity, ethics or religion. Instead, it assures that benefits will flow to rich nations and the rich classes more than what they have and wants others to believe that they too will receive some of the benefits in the process. The rich nations and people in the world have welcomed the process of globalization. It is only those poor nations and poor people discriminated on the basis of caste, gender, minority status and colour, which resist globalization. They resist globalization because of their past experience and history, which has proved time and time again that no amount of progress, wealth or power in a nation has ever been equally distributed amongst all its citizens.

What have been the effects of India's globalization? Faced with an acute foreign exchange crisis in 1991, the Narasimha Rao Government had little option but to make 'virtue out necessity' and to liberalize and globalize. However, it went ahead long into the reform and liberalization process. Trade and investment policies, and most economic sectors, were opened up within a short time frame without adequate safeguards. Import duties were substantially brought down and numerous non-tariff barriers eliminated. Even import of second hand capital goods was permitted. All this caused much damage to domestic industry. The liberalization, and "Reform", launched in 1991 did, of course, bring some notable benefits to India. It released the enormous entrepreneurial talents of its people as also the considerable brain power capabilities of its educated youth particularly in the computer software and information technology fields in which India is now an acknowledged global leader. Unfortunately, GOI policies during the 1998-2008 periods have been heavily in favour of the urban and corporate sectors and the foreign investor. Because of this the rich-poor and urban-rural divides have greatly widened.

Accordingly, the review of literature is based on discussion of the impact of globalization on social work profession in general and its effects on Indian social work in particular. This chapter provides insights into the professional status of social workers in India mainly on the lines with affiliation of professional status by public, social work subject's own knowledge base and regulation of this knowledge. Regulation of knowledge include formal training of social work, role of association of social work, code of ethics to follow and professional status.

History of Globalization

Socialization of people for improving business and financial activities across the globe can be referred as globalization. It is not a new phenomenon as people kept searching new places and avenues to increase their business activities as evident by explorations of Vasco da Gama, Columbus and East India Company. Bitter experiences from East India Company and British rule makes Indian little bit cautious for adventures of globalization. This has been the root cause for delay in liberalization in India. They had committed previously by opting for isolation.

Globalization has been a historical process. During the Pre-World War I period of 1870 to 1914, there was rapid integration of the economies in terms of trade flows, movement of capital and migration of people. The growth of globalization was mainly led by the technological forces in the fields of transport and communication. Indeed there were no passports and visa requirements and very few non-tariff barriers and restrictions on fund flows. Globalization process was slow between the First and the Second World War. After World War II, all the leading countries resolved not to repeat the mistakes they had committed previously by opting for isolation.

India is also following the global phenomenon. As part of globalisation, the economic reform packages were introduced in

India in the beginning of 1991. These reform packages imposed a heavy compression on the public budgets on education sector, more specifically on higher education. This has trickled down to public expenditure on education in general, and higher education in particular.

Concept and Definition of Globalization

Globalization refers to the spread of new forms of non-territorial social activity (Ruggie, 1993; Scholte, 2000). To make term more clearly, Globalization has been defined as the process of rapid integration of countries and happening through greater foreign trade and foreign investment. In essence, it refers to increased possibilities for action between and among people in situations irrespective of geographical considerations as per the definition of social theorists.

In very simple terms globalization can be depicted as increasing global interconnectedness. It is primarily an interchange of economic, social, cultural, political, technological attributes that takes place between societies when different societies come into contact with each other. Though this interchange is going on for times immemorial, this process was termed as "globalization" for the first time around the second half of twentieth century while much of the literature on this has appeared since the late 1970s and 1980s (Beyer, 2003).

Globalization is defined as "the diminution or elimination of state-enforced restrictions on exchanges across borders and the increasingly integrated and complex global system of production and exchange that has emerged as a result. Globalization is ....a widening, deepening and speeding up of interconnectedness in all aspects of contemporary social life from the cultural to the criminal, the financial to the spiritual.

In terms of globalization, it is described as an economic, social, cultural, political and environmental issue of central importance to their practice of social work. *Globalization is a process of converting producers in Third World countries into consumers through a capitalist economic process (Sri Lanka). Globalization is the process of 'worldwide unification' of economic, social, political and cultural orientation through a borderless society thereby losing the country's indigenous cultural orientation (Philippines).*

Last but not the least, in the social field, the tidal wave of global culture is seeping the indigenous cultures all over the world. Mahbub and Manfred define: Globalization involves economic integration, the transfer of policies across the border, cultural stability transmission of knowledge, industrialization and urbanization in a global order. It is a process of world shrinkage of distance getting shorter, things moving closer. It pertains to the increasing ease with which somebody on one side of the world can interact, to mutual benefit, with somebody on the other side of the world (Manfred, 2013).

For example, the development of the internet and of social media has made it possible for individual around the world (extensity) to communicate with each other frequently and copiously (intensity) and almost instantly (velocity). From the above account, it can be concluded that globalization is a multifaceted, multidimensional and comprehensive phenomenon having its potential impact on a whole range of contemporary social, political, cultural and economic relationship.

Professional Status of Social Work

Under the impact of international social work, there has been a great demand for social work to be given a professional status. This is largely because of its increased role in the global context and its constant struggle for identity at a time when there is recognition for it in several countries. According to the International Association of Schools of Social Work and International Federation of Social Workers (2002), now social work is being practiced in varied settings and in many different countries. It is now been practiced in 144 countries. This has sometimes led to cross-border comparisons of its various features (Weiss-gal and Welbourne, 2008).

A Global definition of social work and global minimum standards for the profession were agreed by the IASSW and the IFSW in 2001. The process of arriving at a definition presented significant challenges due to different worldviews (Hare, 2004; Sewpaul, 2006). Some standards or values put forward were challenged as ethnocentric and/or colonial, while conversely there was concern that an uncritical acceptance of all normative cultural customs might condone harmful or abusive practice (Trygged,

2010). The most recent global definition of social work adopted by the IASSW and IFSW in July 2014 states:

> Social work is a practice-based profession and an academic discipline that promotes social change and developing, social cohesion, and the empowerment and liberation of people, principles of social justice, human rights, collective responsibilities and respect for diversities are central to social work. Underpinned by theories of social work, social science, humanities and indigenous knowledge, social work engages people and structure to address life challenges and enhance well-being.

Although some people have argued that human rights discourse is an unwelcome Western imposition, it complements a social justice and needs model because it is entitlement based (Skegg, 2005).

In some poorer countries, access to money, books, computers and the internet may be difficult, making it hard for social workers to read relevant literature and attend international conferences to exchanges ideas. The IFSW and IASSW have subsidized conference fees and travel costs for poorer countries (Hugman, 2010), but this is not the first barrier. Both organisations are English-speaking. In countries where English is not the first language, exchange is difficult, and even in European countries there may be language and cultural difficulties, despite similar social and political systems and reasonable widespread fluency in English as a second language (Green, 1999).

The International commitment in social work to human rights, social justice and working with the individual at the interface with their environment sets it apart from these other profession. These are valuable principles which social work needs to reclaim actively and defend vigorously in order to be a profession worth fighting for. The years ahead look likely to be challenging ones for social work, requiring a good critical understanding of the role of the profession within the broader welfare state, as a basis for standing up for its professional principle (Green & Clarke, 2016).

Dimensions of Globalization

As the *Human Development Report of 1999* notes, the present day globalization is characterized by (1) new markets, (2) new technology tool like internet, cellular phones etc., and (3) new actors like the World Trade Organisation (WTO) with authority over national governments, the multinational corporations with more economic power than many states, the global networks of non-governmental organisations (NGOs) and other groups.

Globalization, as such encompasses many dimensions (See Table 16.1).

Among these various dimensions economic integration is considered to be a dominant feature. In the economic sense we can define globalization as integration of rational economics into the international economy through trade, foreign direct investment, capital flows, migration, and the spread of technology.

Social Problems of Globalization

Globalization has given birth of unaccountable social problems along with plethora of opportunities. Although international events have always impinged on the lives of ordinary people, the process of globalization is now having a major impact around the world. Globalization has been appreciated by some; it has been condemned by others. Although some welcome the growing interdependence of economy, nations, and cultures, others reject the view that increased internationalization has positive implications for humanity. The trends towards globalization have been accompanied by new social problems that social work profession needs to address. The globalization has also opened up many avenues of opportunities for social work professions to expand its knowledge base, improve its practice skills, and enhance its development as a profession. Let us first deal with the problems and later to talk about the opportunities.

- As the global economy has expanded; the incidence of poverty and deprivation in many parts of the world has increased (World Bank, 2001). Whereas some nations, particularly in Eastern Asia, have benefited from the expansion of the global economy, many people in the world's poorest nations have been left behind, and the incidence of absolute poverty in many African, Asian and Central and South American countries has increased.

Table 16.1: Form of Globalization

Forms of Globalization	*Description*
Competitive	In order to survive on the new vast global market arena companies must adopt new strategies in every field of their business. Many Competitors are forced to leave the market or look for the new niches.
Cultural	The developing of cross-cultural spread of multiculturalism and the birth of new phenomenon called "world culture".
Ecological	The main issues of ecological globalization are global warming and pollution.
Economic	A greater global connectedness of economic activities, through transnational trade, capital flows and migration.
English language	English is the most popular language in the world. About 75 per cent of the world's radio programmes are in English. About 90 per cent of all Internet traffic uses English. Using one common language increase communication, and at the same time stimulates the process of globalization.
Financial	The creation of global financial markets and diminished barriers for external financing.
Industrial	Development of worldwide production markets, diminishing of limits (time, distance and others) between manufacturers and consumers. Accelerating free movement of goods, materials, labour.
Informational	The use and rapid development of satellites, telephone and Internet and other means of communication and data transmission connect geographically remote locations.
Legal/Ethical	The creation of the International criminal court, The Hague Tribunal, and other international justice organizations.
Political	The creation of such global organization as World Trade Organization, World Bank, and International Monetary Fund, "which regulate the relationships among governments and guarantees the right arising from social and economic globalization".
Social	The creation and development of the system of non-governmental organizations as main agents of global public policy, including humanitarian aid and developmental efforts.
Technical	The creation and development of a global telecommunications infrastructure and technologies as the Internets, communication satellites, submarine fiber optic cable, and wireless telephones make the distances fade.

- The expansion of global economy has been substantiated with the problem of structural adjustment (Watkins, 2005). It refers to the policies adopted at the prompting of the International Monetary Fund and World Bank by developing countries with seeking international credit to stabilize their economics.
- The concomitant effects of structural adjustment are trade liberalization, increased deregulation, and retrenchments in public expenditures. In addition, many middle and low income families in the industrial countries have also suffered as a result of economic globalization.
- Unemployment has been another issue accompanied by family disintegration, poverty, despair, violence, and drug abuse. Whereas multinational firms and investor in the centres of global economic power have enjoyed unprecedented prosperity, incomes for many ordinary people have stagnated.
- Globalization has also fostered increased ethnic conflict and violence in many parts of the world. This problem is related to the growth of migration, but it is also a function of the tensions accompanying economic, political, and social integration. Entire nations are now experiencing massive suffering, and large numbers of families and even whole communities have been dislocated.
- Globalization has also created massive new population movements, which have resulted in dislocation and problems of cultural adaptation and acceptance. Problems such as the exploitation of women migrants (particularly in domestic service), the harsh treatment of illegal migrants, and the growing attachment of racist sentiments to social policy issues affecting migrants are also areas of concern (United Nations, 2001).
- The global refugee problem may not be a new one, but it now exists on a huge scale as an outcome of enormous globalization process (United Nations, 2001).

Globalization and Social Work Practice and Education

While 'globalization' generally is a burgeoning topic, only three studies specifically on social workers' practice perceptions of globalization were found, and only one of these specifically addressed education for practice in a comprehensive manner. One study surveyed social workers (n=25) affiliated with the International Federation of Social Work (IFSW) (Rowe, Hanley, Moreno & Mould, 2000). This qualitative study primarily explored what globalization meant to social workers and how they saw it affecting their practice. The sample, however, was derived from an international social work organisation database, and therefore, respondents were likely to be more familiar with international issues. The results were predominantly substantive descriptions of day-to-day practice with high-risk groups such as asylum seekers and dislocated low income and HIV clients, often from developing economies, and the practitioners were effusive in their analysis of the link between global changes and their clients' problems (Rowe *et al.*, 2000). The respondents were adamant that the globalized experiences for their clients were mostly negative, and that globalization failed to address the consequences of the resultant imbalance in power and resources. They suggested social work needs to look beyond the traditional micro/macro dichotomy and work to address the negative impacts of globalization (Findlay & McCormack, 2007).

After eight decades of establishment of social work education in India, social work education has grown according to the changing trends and needs of the Indian society. Since 1990, the curriculum, teacher-learning aspect, research consultancy and training, infrastructure and learning resources, student support and progression, organisation and management and healthy practices have changed significantly due to the impact of globalization on Social Work education. However, the objectives of social work education according to the first survey on Social Work education by the United Nations (1950) is to produce social workers who are: (i) Intellectually and technically qualified, and (ii) Personally qualified to perform social work functions in such social welfare programmes as the country concerned has established to promote social and economic well-being. On the whole, Social Work education should emerge as a non-partisan, non-sectarian, technical or professional activity, having as its primary purpose, the effective implementation of social welfare measures on behalf of members of the community who may be in need of expert assistance in respect of their socio-economic problems. So this research is an attempt to understand the pre-globalized era and the impact of globalization era on the Social Work education in India.

Globalization affects each country in a different way due to each nation's individual history, traditions, cultures, resources and priorities. A social work-based definition of globalization describes the concept as—a process of global integration in which diverse people, economies, cultures and political processes are increasingly subjected to international influences (Midgley, 1997: xi). Additionally, Midgley suggested that globalization indicates ¯the emergence of an inclusive worldwide culture, a global economy, and above all, a shared awareness of the world as a single place (1997: 10). In the 21st century, globalization leads to changes that challenge social work practice and education, and the idea of postmodernism challenges the validity of a universal knowledge base. This is because where societies are built on different cultural and social assumptions globalization raises questions about the dominance of any particular set of ideas, both generally and in social work. The influence of globalization on Social Work educator's knowledge, attitude and practice of Social Work education has raised questions about whether Western models of social work education and organisation are universal in their application.

Professional social work practice involves logical application of its principles, values and skills so as to bring transformation in challenging situations of society and of individuals. Due to privatization and globalization, there is an emergence of new forms of repression in India (Narayan, 2008). Rapid economic socio-cultural changes negatively affect the lives of women, minority groups, underprivileged children and poor (Nadkarni, 2011). Further, a large gap between technological advances and conventional approaches of Indian society makes the situation more complex (Narayan, 2008).

Current social work practice in India needs to take into account the challenges put on its economy and culture catalyzed by liberalization and privatization. The professional social work practice should be focused on strong description of profession while the aims of social work both at national and international forums. There is a need to redefine the social work practice in order to make it responsive to contextual needs and to be tolerant to the impact of globalization. This requires to be done with a clear vision of Indian context and experiences (Alphonse *et al.*, 2008; Narayan, 2008). Contextual social work practice needs to constantly appraise its functioning in order to accommodate the needs of the ever changing society (Narayan, 2008).

Impact of Globalization on Social Work Education

Globalization is not only associated with finance and business in the world, but it has its connection and effects on individuals and their families, their various aspects of life and their various roles. As an effect of globalization, the public sector has been replaced with private sector resulting in deterioration/changes of individuals roles, discrimination against vulnerable groups etc. this changing scenario has created immense difficulties for social workers who were expected not only to respond to the deleterious effects of globalization on local communities but also to make a critical analysis of the dialectics of local and global factors (Alphonse, George and Moffatt, 2008).

Similarly, Narayan (2008) argued the need to 'indigenize' and to 'internationalize' social work practice simultaneously to meet the demands of globalization. Further, globalization highlights the need to attend global standards in social work training and practice. Considering that, the International Association of Schools of Social Work and International Federation of Social Work drafted criteria for social work training and practice (Alphonse *et al.*, 2008). The international social work embraced and set new guidelines for social work practice as a response to globalization which supports the UN declaration of human rights and integrated human right perspective to their definition (Caragata and Sanchez, 2002; Cox, 2000, both as cited in Alphonse *et al.*, 2008; Nadkarni, 2011).

Reading this, it is clear that social work needs re-organisation and re-construction of its practice and education throughout the world. In order to achieve flexible and open social work, which is a key in responding to globalization, a lot of changes must be made regarding social work practice and education, including preparation of social workers, social work students and service users for those changes.

Although these changes are present in everyday work, a question of social work practitioner's awareness of globalization processes still remains. In her study in 2001, Dominelli (2007) has found that social workers in Great Britain had limited insight of influences of such processes on social work practice at the local level. Even though they recognized greater cross-cultural exposure, enhanced understanding and skills to deal with international social problems, they were still quite pessimistic about the shifts in practice toward commercialization. Universities didn't succeed in producing a model of education for training the practitioner since they were unable to grasp the complexity of the shifting context in which courses operate. Hence despite their effort, social work in Britain remains a divided profession, which empowers government to impose its ideas about how social work education and practice should look.

Empowerment, social work education and practice could be the second way in responding to globalization. To have an empowered profession, Karvinen, Gould and Baldwin (in Payne & Askeland, 2008: 95) emphasize that social workers must claim expertise in redefining the issues that clients and communities face; they must develop knowledge about how to transform the situations in which clients and communities find themselves and they need to find new approaches when previous work qualifications are no longer relevant after changes in society. Non-empowered social workers are unable to support clients in their empowering processes. Social workers can empower themselves, for example, by developing the critically self-reflective practitioner, who is able to practice within the value perspective of the social work profession; by recognition of the relationship between personal life experiences and personal value systems and social work practice (IASSW & IFSW, 2003).

The impact of globalization on social work education imply to many as a modification of the curriculum taught in our universities on the line of that being followed in foreign universities. It is to be crystal clear that there is no flaw in the curriculum being taught in our universities. Frequent analysis carried out by UGC and Universities has shown that our curriculum is a global one and is on par with a highly placed university in a developed country. The flaw is then certainly in the process of delivering this social work education to the aspiring students. Globalization of social work education is to be focused on improving the mentoring capabilities and the mentoring process of imparting this global curriculum. The mentors in India seem to lack of NGOs-institute partnership which is an important aspect of globalization Policy in India. Hence local NGOs-institute partnership might be of great help to Indian social work education. Hence collaboration of Indian institutes with global or multinational companies involved in advanced research areas might provide the Indian social work students a chance to implement their knowledge in practical areas. This practical aspect of social work education might prove to be a great boost to the sloppy development process in India.

Social work has always been an international profession, although international issues have rarely assumed much significance on UK curricula or programmes (Lyons, 2006; Powell and Robinson, 2007). Early social work pioneers worked and lived across national borders and many were politically active. A concern with international social justice issues such as poverty, famine, women's rights and world peace brought these pioneers together and "through scholarship and advocacy, organisational leadership and international travel and direct cultural borrowing [they] contributed to [International] diffusion of social work knowledge" (Hegar, 2008: 722). Globalization makes such international cooperation and the exchanges of ideas and experience across national boundaries even more important for contemporary social work.

Challenges before Globalization

Globalization, as a process, has brought many of the positive improvements in fields of economy, science and technology, but it also brought some undesirable consequences like unemployment, poverty and social exclusion that directly concern social work. By causing these undesirable consequences, globalization imposes a challenge on social work, helping economically and politically excluded social groups.

The next big challenge of globalization is international competition. This necessitates rapid bridging of the technology gap between domestic and foreign production. This is no easy matter and costs billions of dollars, which most countries are unable to finance from domestic resources. They thus incur large foreign debt. In their efforts to bridge the technology gap these countries are confronted with the five monopolies the advance countries, particularly their multinational companies, possess, viz. on high technology, on financial flows, on natural resources (most "Arab oil" is in their hands); on mass media and on sophisticate (Nazareth, P.A., 2011).

Responses to Globalization

The twenty first century presents unique challenges for the technical education system. Technical education must be able to respond to rising student expectations and the demands of global competition. The quality of knowledge generated within technical education institutions, is increasing determining the nations' global competitions. This possesses a major responsibility on the institutions of technical education in countries like India. With abundance of human resources India is eminently equipped for growing itself as a global leader in the knowledge society. Development of any nation does not depend on the available resources but on effective utilization of these resources. Unless effective technical education is provided to the youth of the nation, the process of development cannot be accelerated. The globalization can prove to be an effective means of modifying the flawed education policy on the lines of those developed countries that have successfully transformed themselves to an economic power with the help of their technical education.

To respond to these effects social work education and practice should become more open and flexible, Social work educators should strive to create critical self-reflective practitioners who are able to empower both themselves and their clients in a way which seeks to find new approaches, new solutions and new outcomes. The concept of international social work is imposed by commitment of social work to science, and it relies on the assumption that it can develop universal knowledge, implying that social workers can apply this universal knowledge to anyone in the field of their work, independently of their cultural background, values, norms and behaviour patterns.

Social work on a global level emphasizes the approach to education and training that supports development and preservation of human rights, pluralism, multiculturalism, anti-racism, social justice and peace. Social workers in this respect must become globally conscientious learners who are empowered by the experience of global education and thus able to respond to effects of globalization. Social workers should also be committed to lifelong learning, and the way to that is through curriculum which must help students to develop skills of critical thinking, openness to new experiences, new paradigms and new points of view. By inspiring and learning from each other, social workers around the world are transforming the way their profession engage with the world. Social work must not avoid nor ignore the processes that globalization imposes. As a 'global profession', it has to embrace the globalization, adopt it as positive change and work along with it. There are some advantages of professional social work to responding to the globalization challenges (Sinha, 2012) enumerated below:

- Indeed, social work has benefited from international exchanges from its very beginning. The emergence of case work and settlement work as prime social work practice methods in the United States at the end of 19th century owed much to British innovations. Similarly, the writings of American social workers as well as Indian in the early 20th century were widely adopted in Britain and in other parts of the world where social work was emerging as a profession. By the 1980s, social work profession was well established internationally in both the Western industrial countries and the nations of the Third World. Following the collapse of Soviet Communism, social work spread to regions where the profession was previously unknown.
- Despite these achievements, social work is not fully prepared to respond to the challenges and opportunities of globalization. Greater efforts are needed to ensure that the profession is able to address the pressing social problems associated with globalization. Similarly, much more needs to the done to ensure that social work fully exploits the opportunities afforded by increased internationalization.
- It requires that social work enhance its efforts to inculcate an international outlook among its students and that practitioners become more aware of the way international events affect their daily practice. Steps need to be taken to

improve international exchanges and encourage social workers to become more involved in the activities and programmes of international agencies. Only in this way social work will be able to respond to the demands of an emerging global society in the new economy.

- A good example of the positive exchange of international professional experience is provided in the account by Martinez-Brawely and Deleven (2000) of project that involve the transfer of practice innovations from England to the United States. The British "Patch" model of social work practice was really helpful to the needs of rural social work in United States. It is basically decentralized of public social services to small, local, community-based teams of social work practitioners who become intimately familiar with the people and with the neighbourhoods in which they work.
- Efforts should be made to modify the social work course curriculum where international social work components are enormously emphasized. The Council of Social Work Education in United States, India and other countries are taking this initiative and recognize the importance of including appropriate content to increase students' awareness of international issues.
- A greater effort is also needed to strengthen the activities of the international professional associations. There are a few international professional associations which are continuously trying their best to uphold the profession for promoting greater international awareness and engagement in the profession. The tragic part is that all these types of associations are suffering from financial and organisational support and as a result their activities are not widely published. These associations and organisations are to encounter the process of globalization.

Opportunities of Globalization

- Globalization offers new opportunities for social work to expand its knowledge base. By engaging more actively in international activities, social work educators can enhance their understanding of pressing contemporary social problems. Problems such as AIDS, homelessness, substance abuse, and child neglect have critical; international dimensions that, if properly understood, can provide deeper insight into etiological and related issues.

- Comparative research allows hypotheses to be tested more widely and promotes a more accurate conceptual knowledge base within the profession.
- Globalization can also facilitate social work's efforts to enhance its own professional development. Greater international contacts will contribute to a greater shared identity among social workers, improved opportunities for collaboration, and a greater commitment to respond collectively to the challenges of an independent world. The instruments like International Federation of Social Workers, Association of Schools of Social Work, European Association of Social Workers need to be augmented (Healy, 1995).
- Today, when the air of social development discourse is thick with terms like 'development' and 'empowerment' much emphasis is given to the civil society obligations, roles and responsibilities, alongside the important role played by government agencies. Both have to play their role collectively with intense co-operation and collaboration. Indeed, the recognition of the civil society's contribution arises out of the realization that the requirements of 'welfare', 'development' and 'empowerment' of the marginalized sections of society are too diverse and demanding for the State apparatus to handle effectively.

Conclusion

To sum up, with the opening up of the economy and the liberalization of trade under the WTO regime, India can no longer afford to carry on with labour market rigidities. Now there is new urgency to improve the quality of Indian products and the competitive strength of the Indian industry. Special efforts are needed to upgrade skills and improve labour productivity at a much faster pace to survive and grow in the fast changing world business environment. For this, labour policy will have to move away from restrictions and regulations to facilitation and promotion of growth with increased labour participation in management.

A globalization process that is not conducive to social development and ignores the aspirations of people in terms of better employment opportunities, access to decent incomes and, a reasonable quality of life, is unlikely to be welcomed. It would certainly not be sustainable. Governments have to ensure that globalization genuinely serves the common person. If the process of globalization being benefits 'somewhere else' or for 'some others' and if it increase disparities rather than reducing them, it would certainly be counter-productive. Globalization is a process, an approach, a strategy that can be harnessed for development but its goals and direction have to be set by social policies. Economic development is, at best, 'the means', not the ultimate 'end' of development, Globalization has to serve this ultimate end.

The Government, on its part, should make all possible efforts to dispel the fears of trade unions by enlarging the scope and coverage of the social security net. It must develop labour market institutions to assist workers in upgrading skills and make available alternative job opportunities. Globalization is affecting social work practice around the world. It has increased social problems, but also increased. One thing is clear, in this context of rapid change; many practitioners agree that the traditional dichotomies of macro/micro social work or of international/domestic issues must be set aside. The various levels of social work intervention cannot but fully understood or addressed in isolation from each other. If we as social workers are to live up to our values of working in the interest of society's disadvantaged—or as is increasingly urged, working towards social development — then we must begin to cooperate in efforts to counteract the negative impacts of globalization and take full advantage of its opportunities.

As a conclusion to this, it is clear that social work needs to develop a new framework of action, in which the awareness of globalization processes will provide a foundation on which to establish new and modern social work. Overall, this framework needs to include cultural, economic, social and political features on theory and practice but also to develop openness to new experiences and paradigms, a commitment to lifelong learning and creation of a morally active and responsible profession aware of globalization forces. But what do these general guidelines really mean for social work and how can they be implemented in the already existing framework? We suggest five ways which we believe could be effective in adapting social work to global change.

Regardless of social worker's awareness of globalization, we can conclude that social work today desperately needs to find a way to respond to global processes. Globalization itself is neither positive nor negative process. Whether globalization be a positive or negative process depends on the context in which it is felt. There are various ways to respond to its effects, especially negative ones. Some of the ways could be for example, making a greater effort in protection of citizens' and workers' rights, control of global capital movements, management of transnational companies or creation of non-governmental organisations (NGOs). NGOs have the capacity to respond to problems and campaign against damaging movements in global capital and transnational companies. NGOs can also form a counterbalance to transnational companies and their globalizing tendencies (Payne & Askeland, 2008: 18).

If social workers do indeed accept the challenge, to cooperate across national boundaries and build this solidarity, then we may be able to make visible the human effects of economic globalization and effectively resist its negative effects. Kaseke (2002) urges social workers to tackle economic problems and to work to create social safety nets that feature equitable redistribution of income on the national, as well as the international level. Casework addressing individual problems remains important to people's on-going well-being but ultimately, social workers must support social development in order to reduce poverty and inequality. Economic globalization internationalizes certain elements of inter-societal exchanges without addressing the consequences of imbalances in power, resource and quality of life (Mohan, 2005). As social workers our mandate is to work to address these negative consequences and resist their imposition.

References

Agarwala, R. (2003). "Labour Institution in a Globalized Era", *Economic and Political Weekly,* 13 September, Vol. 37, 13.

Alphonse, M.; George, P. and Moffatt, K. (2008). "Redefining social work standards in the context of globalisation: Lessons from India", *International Social Work 51*(2): 145-158.

Battacharya, Purushottam and Roy, Ajitava Chaudhuri (ed.). (2000). *Globalisation and India: A Multidimensional Perspective.* New Delhi: Lancers Books.

Baxi, Upendra (1992). *Globalisation: A World Without Alternative*. New Delhi: Sare Economists.

Bodhi, S.R. (2011), "Professional social work education in India: A critical view from the periphery", *The Indian Journal of Social Work, 72*(2): 289–300.

Cable, V. (1999). *Globalisaiton and Global Governance*. The Royal Institute of International Affairs, London.

Correa, C.M. (2000). Intellectual Property Rights, the WTO and Developing Countries: The TRIPs Agreement and Policy Options. *Third World Network*.

Dhingra, N. and Dhingra, I.C. (2014). *Essays: Indian Economy*, New Delhi: Book Age Publication.

Dixon, J. and Macarov, D. (1992). *Social Welfare in a Socialist Country*, London: Routledge.

Dominelli, L. (2005). "Social Work Education under Globalisation: Trends and Developments in the United Kingdom", *Portularia*, Vol. 5, No. 1, pp. 59-75.

Dominelli, L. (2007). *Revitalising Communities in a Globalising World*, Ashgate, Hampshire and Burlington.

Estes, R. (2003). *Trends in the World Social Development: The Social Progress of Nation*, 1970-78. New York: Praeger.

Ferguson, I.; Lavalette, M. and Whitmore, E. (2005). *Globalisation, Global Justice and Social Work*, London and New York: Routledge.

Findlay, M. and McCormack J. (2007). "Globalization and Social Work Education and Practice: Exploring Australian Practitioners' Views", *Journal of Sociology and Social Welfare*, Vol. (2007), No. June, [Online] Available at: http://findarticles.com/p/articles/mi_m0CYZ/is_2_34/ai_n27265538/

Gidden, A. (1991) *Modernity and Self-Identity*, Cambridge: Polity Press.

Gidden, A. (1991). *The Consequences of Modernity*, Cambridge: Polity Press.

Goldar, B.N. (2002). *Trade Liberalization and Employment: The Case of India*, ILO, Geneva.

Gordon, Sandy (1997). "Globalization and the Economic Reforms in India". *Australian Journal of International Affairs*. Vol. 51, No. 1, pp. 73-89.

Green, L. and Clarke, K. (2016). *Social Policy for Social Work*, Delhi: Rawat Publication.

Green, L. (1999). Getting the Balance Right: A Cross Comparative Analysis of the Balance Between Legal Intervention and Therapeutic Support Systems in Relation to Response to Child Sexual Abuse in England,

The Netherland and Belgium. A report prepared for the European Commission, November 1999, under the Daphne Initiative, project 98/205s.

Hare, L. (2004). "Defining social work for 21st Century: the International Federation of Social Workers' Revised Definition of Social Work", *International Social Work* 47: 407-24.

Hazel, H. (1999). *Beyond Globalization: Shaping a Sustainable Global Economy.* West Hartford, CT: Kumarian.

Hungman, R. (2010). *Understanding International Social Work: A Critical Analysis,* Basingstoke: Palgrave Macmillan.

IASSW and IFSW-International Association of Schools of Social Work and International Federation of Social Workers (2003) *Global Qualifying Standards for Social Work Education and Training,* [Online] Available at: www.ifsw.org/p38000255.html

Kaseke, A.S. (2002). *The Work of Nations,* New York: Alfred Knopt.

Khor, Martin (2001). *Rethinking Globalization: Critical Issues and Policy Choices,* Bangalore: Books for Change.

Manfred, B., Steger (2013). *Globalization: A Very Short Introduction,* Oxford University Press.

Midgely, J. (2001). "Issues in International social work: Resolving critical debates in the profession", *Journal of Social Work,* 1(1): 21-35.

Mohan, B.S. (2005). *Social Development: The Developmental Perspective in Social Work.* Thousand Oaks, CA: Sage.

Munch, Ronaldo. (2003). *Globalization and Labour,* Delhi: Madhyam Books.

Nadkarni, V. (2011). "Editorial, social work education." *The International Journal, 29*(8): 815-17.

Nadkarni, V. (2012). National Network on School of Social work—A proposal, National network meeting with the Planning Commission, Mumbai: Tata Institute of Social Science.

Nagpaul, H. (1967), "Dilemmas of Social Work Education In India", *The Indian Journal of Social Work,* XXVIII(3): 270-284.

Nayyar, D. (1997). *Globalization; The Past in Our Future.* Third World Network: Penang, Malaysia.

Pathak, B. and Tripathi, S. (2000). *Globalization and the Poor in India.* L.B.S. Institute of Rural Management and Rural Development, Patna.

Payne, M. and Askeland, G.A. (2008). *Globalization and International Social Work—Postmodern Change and Challenge,* Hampshire and Burlington: Ashgate.

Ray, Kalyan (2004). *Globalization or Colonization,* Delhi: Deep and Deep Publication Pvt. Ltd.

Rowe, W.; Hangley, J.; Moreno, E.R. and Mould, J. (2000). "Voices of social work practice: International reflections on the effects of globalization." *Canadian Social Work.* 2.1, 65-86.

Roy Choudhury, Supriya, (2004). "Globalization and Labour", *Economic and Political Weekly,* 3 January.

SEWA (2004). *Impact of Globalization on informal Sector. A Case Study of SEWA members.* http://www.sewa.org

Sewpaul, V. (2006) "The Global-Local Dialectic: Challenges for African Scholarship and Social Work in a Post-Colonial World", *British Journal of Social Work,* 36(3): 419-34.

Siddiqui, H.Y. and Sukhramani, N. (2001). "Occupational social work in India", R. Paul. Maiden (Ed.), *Global Occupational Social Work* (pp. 43 64). New York: The Haworth Press, Inc.

Singh, N. (2012), *Industrial Sociology,* New Delhi: Tata Mcgraw Hill Education Private Limited, pp. 239-273.

Singh, Y. (2004). *Ideology and Theory in Indian Sociology,* Jaipur: Rawat Publications.

Sinha, D. (2012). *Social Welfare and Social Work,* New Delhi: Concept Publishing Company Pvt. Ltd.

Skegg, A. (2005). "Brief Note: Human Rights and Social Work: A Western Imposition or Power to the People?" *International Social Work,* 48(5): 667-72.

Stiglitz, E. Joseph (2003). *Globalization and its Discontents.* New York: Norton and Company.

Tragged, S. (2010). "Balancing the Global and Local: Some Normative Reflection on International Social Work", *International Social Work,* 53(5): 644-55.

Tsang, N.M. (2007). "Beyond theory and practice integration in social work: Lesions from the West"; *International Social Work,* 41(2): 169-180.

Websites

http://shodhganga.inflibnet.ac.in/bitstream/10603/50612/12/12_chapter%202.pdf

http://www.undp.org/governance

http://www.ifsw.org/p38000255.html

17
International Social Work

Manju Goel

Introduction

Social Work is an applied profession that uses knowledge to effect change at all levels, i.e. individual, institutional, and societal. Social work practice and policy are increasingly shaped by global phenomena, and there are many opportunities for social work to make an impact on the world level. Therefore, a dynamic, action-oriented conceptualization of international social work is required. Social workers can benefit from knowing how the issues in their state are played out in other states. There is so much to learn of innovative practices and of possible solutions to social problems that never would have been imagined without an international exchange of information. International Social Work is generally understood to encompass global and policy issues, comparative social policy, international professional organisations, social work practice focused on development of human rights, or migration, especially that in international agencies. International social work practice is also specific to the human rights of vulnerable populations such as racial, ethnic, and sexual minorities, poverty, homelessness, hunger, migration, child welfare policies, geriatric care, youth welfare, family welfare, women empowerment, HIV/ AIDS prevention, substance abuse treatment, income maintenance and support programmes, services to people with disabilities, probation and correctional social work, community organizing and development, family disintegration, juvenile delinquency, and health care provisions.

The concept of international social work was first used by George Warren in 1943 to describe social work practice in agencies that were engaged in organised international efforts. Sanders (1984) and Sanders and Pedersen (1984) defined international social work as a distinct field of practice and stressed the importance of specific skills and knowledge to enable social workers to work in international agencies such as the International Committee of the Red Cross. Over time, the term international social work also came to encompass domestic social work practice with immigrants and refugees. Healy (2001) does not view international social work practice as a field, but uses the term international action and makes the case that due to increased global interdependence, both local social workers and domestic human service agencies have greater opportunities and even a responsibility to engage in international activities. The use of the term international action as the basis of the definition of international social work has led to four practice categories:

- *Internationally related domestic practice and advocacy:* It includes working with the refugees and immigrants, international populations, international adoptions, and so forth.
- *Professional exchange:* It involves communication of knowledge and sharing of experiences.
- *International practice:* It involves direct work in international agencies, such as relief and disaster work.
- *International policy development and advocacy:* It involves the formulation of policy positions and actions to resolve global social problems.

International Social Work includes the exchanges of ideas by social workers at international meetings as well as inter-country work, intergovernmental work, and relief work. International Social Work contains four main types of activities: (a) international social case work; (b) international assistance, public and private, to disaster or war sufferers and distressed minority groups; (c) international conferences on social work; and (d) international cooperation by governments and private bodies through the medium of the league, in combatting disease and securing social and political peace and harmony throughout the world (Warren, 1939).

According to Barker (1999), international social work is a term loosely applied to (1) international organisations using social work methods or personnel, (2) social work cooperation between countries, and (3) transfer between countries of methods or knowledge about social work.

Cox and Pawar (2006) defined that International social work is the promotion of social work education and practice globally and locally, with the purpose of building a truly integrated international profession that reflects social work's capacity to respond appropriately and effectively, in education and practice terms, to the various global challenges that are having a significant impact on the well-being of large sections of the world's population. This global and local promotion of social work education and practice is based on an integrated perspectives approach that synthesizes global, human rights, ecological, and social development perspectives of international situations and responses to them.

Healy (2008) focuses on four social work practice areas: domestic policy advocacy and practice where there is a distinct global context; professional exchange of ideas; practice in relief and development situations; and global policy advocacy.

Healy and Link (2012) defined that International social work is concerned with the development, administration, implementation, research, and evaluation, in and through global social institutions and organisations, of policies and programmes that promote human rights, human diversity, the well-being and empowerment of people worldwide, and global and social and economic justice. In the postmodern era, international social work values, difference and diversity in human experience and seeks to engage with and to learn and adapt from people creating indigenous solutions to socio-economic problems around the world. International social work subscribes to ideologies, value systems, and theoretical approaches that support these directions.

International Association of Schools of Social Work and the International Federation of Social Workers (IASSW/IFSW) (2001) agreed upon in Copenhagen on international definition of social work, not a definition of international social work.

The social work profession promotes social change, problem solving in human relationships and the empowerment and liberation of people to enhance well-being. Utilising theories of human behaviour and social systems, social work intervenes at the points where people interact with their environments. Principles of human rights and social justice are fundamental to social work.

The following global definition of the Social Work Profession was approved by the IFSW General Meeting and the IASSW General Assembly in July 2014:

> "Social work is a practice-based profession and an academic discipline that promotes social change and development, social cohesion, and the empowerment and liberation of people. Principles of social justice, human rights, collective responsibility and respect for diversities are central to social work. Underpinned by theories of social work, social sciences, humanities and indigenous knowledge, social work engages people and structures to address life challenges and enhance well-being."

International Social Work: Tracing History

Social Work has its roots all over the World. In ancient times, social work is intricately linked with the idea of charity work and the practice of providing for the poor has roots in all major world religions. The modern social work profession and programme has its roots in 19th century philanthropy. The practice and profession of social work has a relatively modern and scientific origin, and is generally considered to have developed out of three strands. The first was individual casework, a strategy pioneered by the Charity Organisation Society in the mid-19th century. The second was social administration, which included various forms of poverty relief — 'relief of paupers'. Statewide poverty relief could be said to have its roots in the English Poor Laws of the 17th century, but was first systematized through the efforts of the Charity Organisation Society. The third consisted of social action — rather than engaging in the resolution of immediate individual requirements, the emphasis was placed on political action working through the community and the group to improve their social conditions and thereby alleviate poverty. This approach was developed originally by the Settlement House Movement.

Most social workers understand the term international social work to refer to social work practice with people in different countries or to the professional exchanges that take place among social workers in different countries. Originally, the term was used to refer to social work practice in international agencies such as the United Nations or the Red Cross, but today it describes all forms of social work practice involving international clients. International social work practice includes opportunities for social workers to practice in other countries and in international social service and development agencies. International social work has its beginning when the profession was developed in the late 19th century. In the late 19th century, a group of American social workers travelled to England and brought back the concept of settlement houses. As a result, settlement houses were established in numerous American cities (Lyons, 1999; Healy, 2001). The primary tasks during the early development of the profession were to forge ties within the profession and learn from practitioners in other countries. Consequently, international organisations such as the International Association of Schools of Social Work and the International Federation of Social Workers were established in the early 20th century, shortly after the birth of the profession (Hokenstad *et al.*, 1992; Ramanathan and Link, 1999; Lyons, 1999; Healy, 2001).

Developments in professional social work in the United States were also adopted by Europeans and spread to Asia, Africa, the Caribbean, and the Pacific and Australia. In some cases, missionaries played a key role. For example, in India, the Reverend Clifford Manshardt, a missionary employed by the American Board of Missions in Western India, established the country's first settlement house in 1926. It was located in a shantytown community in Bombay called Nagpada. Rev. Manshardt subsequently met Sir Dorabji Tata, the wealthy Indian industrialist, and as a result of their collaboration, the world-renowned Tata Institute of Social Sciences was created in 1936. The institute was the first professional social work school in India, and Rev. Manshardt became its first director (Kendall, 2000). It continues to be one of India's most prestigious schools of social work and an internationally recognized leader in social work education. The British imperial government in London also encouraged the introduction of social service programmes in its colonial territories (Midgley, 1981). Usually this involved creating programmes for young criminal offenders. Social workers from Britain were often recruited to establish these programmes, and in time, they were augmented to respond to other pressing social needs such as child neglect, begging, and destitution. In many cases, a separate department of social welfare was established. For example, in 1943 the position of secretary of social services in the office of the colonial governor in Ghana was created. This development resulted in the creation in 1946 of a full-fledged department of social welfare and housing, which subsequently became known as the Department of Social Welfare and Community Development. The department assumed responsibility for a vocational training centre for people with disabilities, several youth clubs, a juvenile court, and the probation service. It later expanded into rural areas by providing literacy education for farmers, village community centres, and assistance with small-scale agriculture and community road construction. In 1950, the department created its own social work training school, and in 1956, it entered into an agreement with the University of Ghana to establish a university-level social work programme (Blavo and Apt, 1997).

International Professional Associations

Social workers have a number of professional associations that provide ethical guidance and other forms of support for their members and for social work in general. These associations may be international, continental, semi-continental, national, or regional. First international professional association evolved out of a major international social work conference held in Paris in July 1928 with representatives from forty two countries (Healy, 2001). By the time a second international conference was held in Frankfurt, Germany, in 1932, three additional countries, including the United States, had joined. However, progress was severely impeded by the Second World War, and it was only in 1950 that a plan for reorganizing the group was discussed. The result of these efforts was the creation of the International Federation of Social Workers, established in 1956. Today, the federation represents national professional social work associations from eighty countries. In 1929, forty-six schools of Social Work from ten countries came together to found the International Committee of Schools of Social Work. The Committee subsequently became known as the International Association of Schools of Social Work (Kendall, 2000). Today, the Association represents schools of social work in more than one hundred countries.

Following the Second World War, Western social workers significantly expanded their practices to a global scale while focusing on humanitarian aid and social development issues. With the goal of creating more economic and social opportunities in relief and development work, social workers from Western countries became involved in the UN Relief and Rehabilitation Administration's (UNRRA) programmes, which became a hub of international social work activities. The UNRRA's programmes contributed to the spread of international social work, as well as international social work education (Healy, 2001). During this post-Second World War period, social work education in Western countries became greatly involved in training and educating social workers for developing nations (Ramanathan and Link, 1999). Subsequent commentators (Midgley, 1990) have considered this period as an example of professional imperialism, whereby Western social work theories, practice methods, and skills flowed one way from the world's richest nations to the poorer African, Asian, and South American nations. Since the 1990s, after a two-decade decline of international social work, primarily because developing countries adopted new social work paradigms and practice methods that better reflected their particular circumstances and needs (Asamoah *et al.*, 1997), international social work has taken a new path. Practitioners in both developed and developing countries have adopted a more cautious approach to international social work practice, which has built upon mutual exchange of ideas, resources, and services; collaboration; and respect for differences (Midgley, 1997).

In the years following Second World War, the rise of Communist governments in Eastern Europe, China, and elsewhere impeded the international expansion of social work. Generally, these governments did not approve of social work. Although social work had been established in several countries that subsequently came under Communist rule, the profession was not well developed in these countries, and in many cases, the few social work schools that had been established disappeared. For example, schools of social work in China, which were among the oldest in Asia, were closed down after the Communist government came to power. On the other hand, in Poland, where the country's first school of social work was founded in 1925, professionally educated social workers continued to find employment in the government's social and health services (Healy, 2001). While Communist governments in some parts of the world hampered the profession's development, social work expanded rapidly in the newly independent developing countries of the Global South in the 1950s and 1960s.

In some cases, the foundations for social work's development had been laid by the colonial governments that had introduced public social service programmes and supported the creation of social work schools. In the 1950s, the United Nations, which actively supported the international spread of social work, augmented the colonial governments' contributions. United Nations advisers who travelled to the developing countries to assist governments to expand their welfare programmes frequently proposed that professional social work schools be established. For example, in the early 1950s, a United Nations team advised the Pakistani government that professional training programmes in social work were urgently needed to meet the staffing needs of the country's social welfare services. As a result, Pakistan's first professional school of social work was established in Lahore in 1954 (Midgley, 1981).

Despite the retrenchment of government social service programmes in many parts of the world in the 1970s and 1980s, social work programmes continued to expand, particularly in Western industrial countries. In developing countries, on the other hand, serious debt problems and the imposition of structural adjustment programmes by international agencies such as the World Bank have severely curtailed opportunities for professional practice in the public social services. However, the continued flow of international aid to the developing world has resulted in the expansion of non-profit community-based organisations, many of which employ social workers.

Social work has also expanded in the former Soviet Union, the former Communist countries in Eastern Europe, and China. The first social work educational programme in the Soviet Union was established at the Moscow Academy of Pedagogical Sciences during the Gorbachev administration in the mid-1980s, and by the early 1990s, about thirty social work programmes had been created in the country (Guzetta, 1995). Social work schools have also been established in Eastern European countries such as Albania, Bulgaria, Lithuania, and Romania. There were similar developments in China in the late 1980s, when the government began to permit universities to establish social work courses. A unique feature of the development of social work in China has been a close collaboration between schools of social work in China and in Hong Kong and a determination on the part of Chinese social work educators to develop a curriculum that is uniquely suited to the country's needs (Yuen-Tsang and Sibin, 2002).

Though social work throughout the world shares common features, social work scholars and leaders in some countries often strongly advocate one practice approach or field of practice, which, they contend, should be given preference. As Hokenstad and Midgley (1997) note, social workers in India and South Africa have been encouraged to pay particular attention to economic development and to engage in forms of practice that promote development. In Latin America, emphasis has been placed on political activism, and social workers have been urged to mobilize poor people to campaign for social justice. In several African countries, social workers have been called on to help stem the AIDS pandemic, which has claimed so many lives and decimated so many families and communities. In addition, social work in some countries has acquired unique features. In European countries such as Denmark, Germany, and the Netherlands, social pedagogy has emerged as a distinctive branch of social work practice. Although social pedagogy is similar to community social work practice, it has a strong educational component and seeks to use educational techniques to promote community involvement. However, it is not limited to community settings, and it is also applied in residential care and youth work (Midgley, 1997). Another example comes from India, where social workers have historically been involved in personnel management, or labour welfare, as it is known. In many African countries, social workers have long been involved in rural community development work, using traditional community organizing techniques to mobilize local people to build feeder roads and bridges; engage in agricultural projects; construct community centres, schools, and health clinics; and promote village industries (Midgley, 1997). These innovations and diverse forms of social work practice reveal the extent to which the social work profession in different countries has adapted to different economic and cultural contexts as well as challenges.

In contemporary Society problems such as poverty, family disintegration, malnutrition, alcohol and drug abuse, inequality, HIV/AIDS, child abuse and neglect, homelessness, mental illness, and social injustice persist on a huge scale. Nevertheless, social workers have made a difference, and their contribution has been recognized. Social workers around the world are known for their commitment to addressing these problems, promoting people's well-being, and advocating social justice. Increasingly, efforts are being made to address these problems at the international level. In addition to more frequent exchanges among social workers from different countries, the emergence of social work as a global profession has been accompanied by greater collaboration and engagement with international issues by social workers everywhere (Midgley, 1990).

Historically, international social work has been viewed as a specialist field of practice undertaken by a small group of social workers with specialist skills (often including the ability to speak more than one language) or interests that equip them to work abroad. Some of the first publications about international social work defined the field in this way. When the first entry on the subject was published in the *Social Work Yearbook* in the United States in 1937, the author, George Warren, explained that international social work involved disaster relief, assistance to war victims and refugees, international public health measures, and involvement with international organisations such as the League of Nations and the International Labour Organisation (Healy, 2001).

Walter Friedlander stressed this last aspect in his best-selling 1955 textbook, *Introduction to Social Welfare,* one of the first to contain a separate chapter on international social work. Friedlander noted that international social work was the youngest branch of the profession at the time, and that its goal was to promote the welfare of the world's people through the employment of social workers in international organisations such as the United Nations, the World Health Organisation, the Red Cross, the YMCA and YWCA, and the International Child Welfare Union. At the time, many social workers still viewed international social work as a specialist field of practice that takes place in international agencies. The term has been broadened to describe a specialized field of practice involving social workers who practice abroad.

Social workers have long been involved with the major international social welfare agencies. They have found employment in international government agencies such as the United Nations, including the United Nations High Commission for Refugees and UNICEF, and in non-governmental agencies such as the Red Cross and Save the Children. In the early decades of the twentieth century, administrators of these international agencies and the founders of social work established close links. The Red Cross was one of the first international agencies to employ social workers. Social workers also contributed to the creation of new international agencies such as Save the Children, which was established at the end of First World War by the British social worker Eglantyne Jebb (Healy, 2001). Today, the fund makes a major contribution to child welfare around the world. Like the Red Cross, the fund became a major employer of professionally qualified social workers.

Social workers were also actively involved in the League of Nations, the precursor to the United Nations. Although the League did not operate its own programmes, it produced studies and reports that were used to publicize social problems such as drug abuse, prostitution, child labour, and the trafficking of women. The League also encouraged its member states to take steps to address these problems. Social workers played an important role as experts and advisers, and they helped draft these documents and disseminate the League's recommendations (Friedlander, 1955). When the United Nations was established in 1945, social work had secured widespread international recognition, and, as noted earlier, the United Nations actively promoted the profession's international development during the 1950s and 1960s. The United Nations also employed social workers, particularly in its specialized agencies, such as the United Nations Relief and Rehabilitation Agency and UNICEF (Friedlander, 1975). The United Nations Relief and Rehabilitation Agency was established by the Allied Powers in 1943 to provide emergency relief to the millions of people whose lives had been devastated by Second World War. It became a major employer of social workers, who played a particularly important role in meeting the needs of refugees, orphans, and separated families (Friedlander, 1975). Social workers employed in international agencies such as CARE, World Vision, Christian Aid, Save the Children, OXFAM, Caritas

Internationalis, and Catholic Relief Services are deeply engaged in development work.

In contemporary Society social workers find that greater engagement with international social work helps them appreciate the extent to which the problems they address are linked to global realities. This fosters a better understanding of human needs and social problems. Social workers see their professional lives enriched as a result of engaging with their colleagues in other parts of the world. International exchanges in social work have clearly helped to promote the growth of social work as a profession, and they help individual practitioners enhance their knowledge and skills. By attending international conferences, reading international journals, and travelling to meet colleagues in other countries, social workers share information and experiences and enhance their understanding of professional practice in other countries. All these factors contribute to social work's professional development and the improvement of professional practice.

Development of Global Standards for Social Work Education

The process of developing global standards for education and training in the social work profession is as important as the product or actual standards that are developed. In order to understand such an initiative it is important that the opinions, values, and beliefs across the global social work profession are considered and reflected in the development of universal standards for education. Given the centrality of the process-product dialectic, and the fact that the principles under scoring the standards come to light, out of the process, it is vital that the standards considered take in to account all global points of view in social work education. Social work education, globally speaking, must consider the need of context-specific realities in given environments, communities, and societies in conjunction with the ambiguities surrounding the education and practice of social work professionals around our world.

International Federation of Social Workers (IFSW) and International Association of Schools of Social Work (IASSW) created a document that details a set of standards with respect to different schools globally and their core purposes or mission statements, programme objectives and outcomes, programme curricula including field work, core curriculum, professional qualification of staff, social work students; structure, administration, governance and resources, cultural diversity, and social work values and ethics. As a point of departure, IFSW and IASSW created an international definition of social work as a profession. Further, IFSW and IASSW defined and detailed the core purposes and functions of social work on a global scale.

Many social work educators and practitioners in the international circuit are concerned that defining universal standards in social work education and practice will succumb to a Western-dominated point of view. Given the Western hegemony in social work education and practice, and that many Western nations, have fairly settled and well established criteria of what social work is and what it means to provide good social work education and practice in their communities and regions (Payne, 2001). Such concerns are to be taken with great solemnity and not just as a supposition by a few professionals involved in international social work.

Much of what constitutes good social work education in Western Europe and in North America is founded on ethnocentric and egocentric premises. The majority of Western Europe and North American countries have specifically defined and, detailed national standards of social work practice that may or may not fit with the definition of social work education in underdeveloped nations. Among international social work educators there is ongoing concern that context-specific realities. The resources available to individual institutions to meet the new global standards should be taken into consideration. In the development of global standards, it was noted that this should not create unintended negative consequences by disadvantaging some educational institutions. As much as global standards may be used to benchmark national norms and standards, as far as possible, regional, national, and international experiences and practices need to be incorporated into the formulation of establishing universal international social work standards for education and practice. The circular, interactive, and discursive processes in developing national and global standards should become and remain continuous, dynamic, and fluid, adapting to a rapidly changing world. The process and product dialectic in the formulation of the global standards for social work is crucial.

Social work education and practice is operationalized differently within varied global levels and even within various nations and regional boundaries with its control and *status quo* functions being dominant in some contexts. As a point in fact, this would not be disputed by most in our profession. Lorenz (2001) considered the ambiguities, tensions, and contradictions of the social work profession, which have to be constantly negotiated and re-evaluated to constitute its successes and challenges. It is, perhaps, these very dichotomies that have led to the very rich diverseness of the local, regional, national, and international dialectic of social work education and practice that provides legitimacy for the development of global standards.

Growing Challenges for Social Work

Social work practice is created within a political, social, cultural and economic matrix that shapes the assumptions of practice, the problems that practice must deal with and the preferred outcomes of practice. Over time, the base forces that create practice and create the context for practice, change. Practice created in one social order is often inappropriate for work in another social order. Since the social order changes over time, practice created at one point in time may no longer be appropriate in the future. Many social work educators and professionals have discussed the issues of "internationalization" of social work as a method to address the new and complex social problems stemming from complexities of international contexts. The ramification of a global economy for social justice is complex and is one of the most important challenges for social work in the 21st century (Polack, 2004). This is not to imply that international social work should be viewed solely on the basis of technological changes and trends that result in socio-economic interconnectedness over the recent decades. As social work practitioners and educators, it is important to recognize that we have a history of involvement in humanitarianism across the globe, as evidenced by contributions of paraprofessionals and non-social work degreed persons involved in the United Nations, the Peace Corps, international NGOs, and International Red Cross/ Red Crescent Movements.

Friedlander (1975) acknowledged social work's need for a broader, global perspective in helping with the conceptualization of the social environment. It is no surprise that for many years social workers have taken it upon themselves to work for international social development agencies and non-governmental organisations in direct services, administration, programme planning, and development. Social workers' commitment to social problems around the globe and the initiatives that cross borders and boundaries are not simply attributed to recent trends involving globalization. Social work professionals have been pursuing a long standing tradition to the principles of human rights and social justice in our world. It is important to point out that globalization is not a new concept but has been under many guises for centuries. What is new is the pace of globalization and the effects that globalization have on transforming societies and cultures (Ramos and Brair-Lawson, 2004).

The New International Social Worker

Social work has a rich history in micro and macro practice that addresses individual and community needs as well as confronts their root causes by challenging systems, institutions, and policies that keep oppression intact. Social workers have played several roles in addressing social justice issues across the globe. These include poverty, inequality, human rights, slavery, sex trade, refugees, adoption, global warming, terrorism, and labour issues. Unfortunately, the work of social workers on an international scale has not been high-profile and often marginal when compared to other professions. It is critical for social workers to take a stalwart position on the importance of international human rights.

On a global scale, human rights have eroded due to increased military might on foreign soil, unprecedented detainment of suspected terrorists without due process or legal representation, and legislation that restricts people in the name of national security. Of equal importance for social workers in the 21st century, climate change has serious implications for the future of the planet. Clearly, global warming will have a great impact on how social workers practice internationally. We can expect increasing numbers of climate refugees, changes in lifestyles globally, creation of new jobs, and elimination of others as well as a change in the way we conduct our day-to-day lives. The impact of climate change will be most evident for people in developing nations, the poor, the undereducated, the unskilled labourer, and the vulnerable.

International Social Work Curriculum

International Social Work Curriculum provides an introduction to social work practice in an international context and understanding about theoretical models to consider processes of social development in a global, cross-cultural context. Dynamics of power in global social work is a central focus in understanding the diverse roles and activities that social workers play in different countries and when practicing in another country. Since international social work practice is a relatively new field, the focus of the course is on helping each student develop her/his conceptualization of international social work practice, including the areas of policy planning, programme administration, direct practice, consultation, and research. For instance, aspects of international social work practice can include: advocate, practitioner with individuals, families, and groups, consultant, educator, and researcher. An essential aspect of the course is ongoing experience in an international partnership, either through in-country learning experiences (internships), ongoing contact with social workers or clients from other countries, or an ongoing on-line relationship with a social worker in another country. International Social Work Curriculum helps the students to acquire an analytic frame of reference for understanding central problems addressed by cross-cultural and global practice at the micro, meso, and macro levels as a base for international social work practice. After reading international social work course one is able to conceptualize dynamics of power, oppression, and justice in the context of the relationship between the social worker and clients in international practice settings.

As educators, we have a responsibility to help students grapple with the uncertainty of a rapidly changing world. The social work student should be ready to engage in contradictions, ambiguity, and discussions on the erosion of Western lifestyle as we now understand it. This should not be construed as a negative consequence but an opportunity for dialogue and seeking creative action to unique global problems. Along with, this is the need to value and promote differences of opinion, diverse ways of thinking about our planet, and unique ways of approaching social work practice. Rather than arming social work students with theories and models of practice to make them feel comfortable that there is a proscribed way of practice, we have a responsibility to help students think outside the box and accept that insecurity, uncertainty, and discomfort are characteristic of the human condition. The world is in crisis ecologically, economically, and politically. Social work education needs to help students understand the current global issues and to embrace the ideology that in times of crisis there are also times for new opportunities (Ife, 2007).

International Social Work: Fields for Practice

Table 17.1 identifies the primary processes and major outcomes associated with eight levels of international social work practice: individual empowerment, group empowerment, conflict resolution, institution-building, community-building, nation-building, region-building, and world-building.

Development-focused social work specialists can be found in every country and in virtually all sectors of practice. Development-focused international specialists function within social work as caseworkers and group workers, community organisers, administrators, social planners, researchers, consultants, educators, and members of boards of directors. They also serve in the councils of governments and are members of national parliaments and are employed by or serve as consultants to the United Nations and other quasi-governmental bodies.

International social work deals with universal problems experienced by people around the world. There are actually many employment opportunities within this important field.

Global Social Work: Global social work deals with problems that are caused between countries, that occur across national boundaries or that are issues that countries work together to collectively solve. International social workers focus on problems that affect billions of people spread throughout in over 300 countries and districts. While international social workers do not attach any special value and importance to any specific country or people, they firmly stand against xenophobia and ethnocentrism. They are concerned with bigger issues, like how to effectively intervene, ameliorate and solve local problems and life difficulties experienced by people around the world.

Table 17.1: Levels of Development-Focused Practice in International Social Work

Practice Levels	*Major Focus Area*
Individual and group empowerment	Individuals and groups learning, through self-help, mutual aid, and conscientization strategies, how to perceive and act on the contradictions that exist in the social, political, and economic structures intrinsic to all societies.
Conflict resolution and peace building	Efforts directed at reducing (1) grievances between persons or groups or (2) asymmetric power relationships between members of more powerful and less powerful groups.
Institution building	Refers both to the process of "humanizing" existing social institutions and that of establishing new institutions that respond more effectively to new or emerging social needs.
Community building	Through increased participation and social animation of the populace, the process through which communities realize the fullness of their social, political, and economic potential; the process through which communities respond more equitably to the social and material needs of their populations.
Nation building	The process of working towards the integration of a nation's social, political, economic, and cultural institutions at all levels of political organization.
Region building	The process of working towards the integration of a geopolitical region's social, political, economic, and cultural institutions at all levels of social organization.
World building	The process of working towards the establishment of a new system of international relationships guided by the quest for world peace, increased social justice, the universal satisfaction of basic human needs, and for the protection of the planet's fragile ecosystem.

Source: Richard, J.E. (2010).

Child Rights: One of the most important global issues is child rights and protection. Social workers around the world strive to uphold the fundamental human rights of children. They provide support to vulnerable populations, such as exploited, trafficked, impoverished, and HIV/AIDS affected children. They deal with abuse, child labour, gang activities and indifferent local authorities. They promote psychosocial well-being, education, family unity, separation prevention, social development and access to basic health care. Social workers usually focus on the United Nations Convention on the Rights of the Child (CRC) and they may even find employment through the UNICEF programme.

Foreign Assistance: Some international social workers focus on temporary or permanent foreign assistance programmes. They contribute their knowledge and skills to developing areas during disaster relief and development initiatives. For example, they usually help out during international disasters, such as earthquakes and hurricanes, in foreign countries. These social workers deal with civil-military issues, aid effectiveness, foreign assistance reform and local policy change. They advocate for more effective and sustainable programmes that protect human rights, safety and dignity. These social workers may work for non-profit humanitarian groups like Inter Action's Foreign Assistance Reform Programme, the Centre For Global Development Resources and the Aid Effectiveness' Modernizing Foreign Assistance Network.

Gender Equity: There are many international initiatives that promote gender equity, such as the United Nation's Third Millennium Development Goal (MDG), the promotion of gender equity and empowerment of women, and the globally ratified Convention on the Elimination of Discrimination Against Women. Social workers focus on minimizing prejudice directed against women that damages their social, emotional, and economic well-being. Many Americans are not aware that many women in developing countries around the world face extreme discrimination when it comes to simple things like owning property, starting a business and even applying for a driver's licence.

Additional Areas of Interest: International social workers focus on global health and dealing with health epidemics in poor countries. Common health issues include HIV/AIDS, family planning and reproductive health. Working for geriatric care, mental health and well-being, counselling to adolescents on their academic and personal concerns are some of the significant issues. Immigration and refugee rights are becoming a sensitive political issue in the U.S. International social workers act as both policy advocates and direct service providers to immigrant and refugee populations. They may coordinate community support programmes for refugee families, or they may carry out research that advocates for stronger refugee resettlement services.

International social work is practiced across of broad range of sectors, that is, public and private institutions and organisations that seek to promote the common good through the provision of specialized services and other activities (for example, health, education, transportation, communications, finance). Table 17.2 identifies the major sectors in which international social work is practiced.

Table 17.2: Interdisciplinary Practice Sectors in International Social Work

• Addiction	• Energy	• Poverty
• Aging	• Environment	• Religion and religious organizations
• Agriculture	• Food	• Refugees and internally displaced persons
• Child welfare	• Health	• Reproductive health
• Communications	• HIV/AIDS	• Rural development
• Consumer security	• Housing	• Social services
• Criminal and juvenile justice	• Human rights	• Sports
• Culture	• Income support	• Technology
• Defence	• Immigration and migration	• Transportation
• Disaster relief and management	• Leisure time and recreation	• Urban development
• Economic development	• Microfinance and social entrepreneurship	• War and terrorism
• Education	• Population	
• Employment		

Source: Richard, J.E. (2010).

International social work is an extremely important field of work that always needs qualified and dedicated workers. Anyone who wants to become a social worker will need to have at least an accredited and NASW approved bachelor's degree in social work.

Conclusion

Many of the most challenging domestic social problems confronting social workers in the world are rooted in transnational forces that originated in other regions of the world like global poverty, disparity, the growth of political and economic refugees in the world; war, terrorism, and human rights violations such as the growing world problem human enslavement; global warming; global pandemics; and problems of homelessness combined with increased unemployment and underemployment. In an increasingly globalized world, the relationship between local, regional, national, and international is becoming increasingly distorted. Social work practitioners often work within a localized context, yet draw on policies and practices devised across the globe. Approaches for the international profession of social work should be grounded on empirical evidence and offer constructive assistance within a broad range of social development solutions that can be applied to discrete social needs. There is a need for new approaches to the education of social workers for international practice. Globalization has the potential to transport traditional social policy analysis into an ever-widening international arena, even to the extent, through information technology, of helping people to influence their own governments to consider human rights issues in foreign relations. Modern means of communication and increased ease of travel means that traditional barriers to the exchange and development of ideas are less problematic. It is important for practitioners, policy makers, and researchers that positive dialogue, global exchanges, and research forums exist for the free exchange and mutual development of ideas.

References

Asamoah, Y.; Healy, L. and Mayadas, N. (1997). "Ending the international–domestic dichotomy: New approaches to a global curriculum for the millennium", *Journal of Social Work Education*, 33(2), 389–401.

Barker, R.L. (1999). *The Social Work Dictionary*, 4th edition. Washington, DC: NASW Press.

Blavo, E. and N. Apt (1997). "Ghana", In N.S. Mayadas, T.D. Watts and D. Elliott (eds.) *International Handbook on Social Work Theory and Practice*, pp. 320–343. Westport, CT: Greenwood Press.

Cox, D. and Pawar, M. (Eds.). (2006). *International Social Work: Issues, Strategies, and Programmes*. Thousand Oaks, CA: Sage.

Friedlander, W.A. (1955). *Introduction to Social Welfare*. New York: Prentice-Hall, Inc.

Friedlander, W.A. (1975). *International Social Welfare*. Englewood Cliffs, NJ: Prentice-Hall.

Guzzetta, C. (1995). "White Ethnic Groups", In R.L. Edwards (Ed.-in-Chief), *Encyclopedia of Social Work* (19th ed., pp. 2508-2517). Washington, DC: NASW Press.

Healy, L.M. (2001). *International Social Work: Professional Action in an Interdependent World*. New York: Oxford University Press.

Healy, L.M. (2008). *International social work: Professional action in an interdependent world*. 2nd Edition. London and New York: Oxford University Press.

Healy, L.M. and Link, R.J. (2012). *Handbook of International social work: Human Rights, Development, and the Global Profession*. New York: Oxford University Press.

Hokenstad, M.C.; S.K. Khinduka and J. Midgley (1992). *Profiles in International Social Work.* Washington DC: NASW Press.

Hokenstad, M.C. and Midgley, J. (1997). *Issues in International Social Work: Global Challenges for a New Century.* Washington DC, NASW Press.

Ife, J. (2007). *The New International Agendas: What Role for Social Work.* International Federation of Social Work. Retrieved on 2-4-2017 from http://ifsw.org/statements/the-new-international-agendaswhat-role-for-social-work/

Kendall, K.A. (2000). *Social Work Education: Its Origins in Europe.* Alexandria, VA: Council on Social Work Education.

Lorenz, W. (2001). "Social Work in Europe: Portrait of a Diverse Professional Group." In S. Hessle (Eds.). *International Standard Setting of Higher Social Work Education.* Stockholm Studies of Social Work. Stockholm Sweden: Stockholm University.

Lyons (1999). *International Social Work: Themes and Perspectives.* Aldershot: Ashgate.

Midgley, J. (1981). *Professional Imperialism: Social Work in the Third World.* London: Heinemann.

Midgley, J. (1990). "International social work: Learning from the Third World"., *Social Work, 35*(4): 295-301.

Midgley, J. (1997). *Social Welfare in Global Context.* Thousand Oaks CA: Sage.

Payne, M. (2001). "Social Work Education: International Standards." In S. Hessle (Eds.). *International Standard Setting of Higher Social Work Education.* Stockholm, Sweden: Stockholm University Studies of Social Work.

Polack, R.J. (2004). "Social Justice and the Global Economy: New Challenges for Social Work in the 21st Century." *Social Work.* 49(2), 281-290.

Ramanathan, C.S. and Link, R. (1999). *All our futures: Principles and resources for social work practice in a global era.* Melbourne: Brooks/ Cole-Wadsworth-International Thompson Publishing.

Richard, J.E. (2010). *United State-Based Conceptualization of International Social Work Education.* Retrieved on 12-05-2017 from https://www.cswe.org/getattachment/459d3db5-d4b8-413d-9ed0-a7633e306e8c/US-Based-Conceptualization-of-International-Social.aspx

Sanders, D. (1984). "Developing a Graduate Social Work Curriculum with an International Cross-cultural Perspective", *Journal of Education for Social Work, 13*(3): 76–83.

Sanders, D.S. and P. Pederson (eds.) (1984). *Education for International Social Welfare.* New York and Hawaii: Council on Social Work Education and University of Hawaii School of Social Work.

Yuen-Tsang, A.W.K. and Sibin, W. (2002). "Tensions confronting the development of social work education in China: Challenges and opportunities", *International Social Work, 45*(3): 375-388. London; Thousand Oaks: Sage Publications.

Index